The Drama of Cosmic Enlightenment

For forty years Sangharakshita has been playing an important part in the spread of Buddhism throughout the modern world. He is head of the Western Buddhist Order (Trailokya Bauddha Mahasangha), and is actively engaged in what is now an international Buddhist movement with centres in thirteen countries worldwide. When not visiting centres he is based at a community in Norfolk. His writings are available in eleven languages.

Also by Sangharakshita:
A Survey of Buddhism
Flame in Darkness
The Enchanted Heart
The Three Jewels
Crossing the Stream
The Essence of Zen
The Thousand-Petalled Lotus
Human Enlightenment
The Religion of Art
The Ten Pillars of Buddhism
The Eternal Legacy
Travel Letters
Alternative Traditions
Conquering New Worlds
Ambedkar and Buddhism
The History of My Going for Refuge
The Taste of Freedom
New Currents in Western Buddhism
A Guide to the Buddhist Path
Learning to Walk
Vision and Transformation
The Buddha's Victory
Facing Mount Kanchenjunga
The FWBO and 'Protestant Buddhism'
Buddhism and the West

The Meaning of Orthodoxy in Buddhism
Mind—Reactive and Creative
Aspects of Buddhist Morality
Buddhism and Blasphemy
Buddhism, World Peace, and Nuclear War
The Bodhisattva: Evolution and Self-Transcendence
The Glory of the Literary World
Going For Refuge
The Caves of Bhaja
My Relation to the Order
Hercules and the Birds and Other Poems

SANGHARAKSHITA

THE DRAMA OF COSMIC ENLIGHTENMENT

•

PARABLES, MYTHS, AND SYMBOLS

•

OF THE

•

WHITE LOTUS SUTRA

•

WINDHORSE PUBLICATIONS

Published by Windhorse Publications
3 Sanda Street
Glasgow G20 8PU

© Sangharakshita 1993
Cover design Dhammarati

Printed by The Cromwell Press,
Melksham, Wiltshire

The cover shows the Buddha preaching the White Lotus Sutra.
Detail from an embroidery, China, 8th century,
courtesy of the Trustees of the British Museum

British Library Cataloguing in Publication Data.
A catalogue record for this book is available from the British Library

ISBN 0 904766 59 4

Contents

EDITOR'S PREFACE

Chapter One THE UNIVERSAL PERSPECTIVE OF MAHAYANA BUDDHISM 7
QUESTIONS AND ANSWERS 23

Chapter Two THE DRAMA OF COSMIC ENLIGHTENMENT 35
QUESTIONS AND ANSWERS 53

Chapter Three TRANSCENDING THE HUMAN PREDICAMENT 69
QUESTIONS AND ANSWERS 83

Chapter Four THE MYTH OF THE RETURN JOURNEY 89
QUESTIONS AND ANSWERS 103

Chapter Five SYMBOLS OF LIFE AND GROWTH 119
QUESTIONS AND ANSWERS 133

Chapter Six FIVE ELEMENT SYMBOLISM AND THE STUPA 143
QUESTIONS AND ANSWERS 157

Chapter Seven THE JEWEL IN THE LOTUS 169
QUESTIONS AND ANSWERS 185

Chapter Eight THE ARCHETYPE OF THE DIVINE HEALER 193
QUESTIONS AND ANSWERS 207

NOTES 213
RECOMMENDED READING 221
INDEX 223

Editor's Preface

IN CULTURES THROUGHOUT THE WORLD, the figure of the story-teller, encircled by a crowd eager to know what will happen next, is central and vital. In stories and tales, myths and legends, a culture recognizes itself and identifies its needs and its ideals. On an individual level too, through these narratives we recognize the deep and inchoate stirrings within our own hearts. Our strongest memories of stories may be associated with childhood, but the hold of story-telling on our hearts did not really leave us when we grew up; it took on new guises. In our culture, scientists and the manipulators of the media may appear to be the purveyors of truth, but it is still to stories: films, novels, even computer games—that we turn for a more satisfying version of reality. Stories have the power to cut through our mental chatter and hold us spellbound, strangely attentive to the fate of imaginary or long-dead characters. And when we emerge from the compelling world of the imagination, in some mysterious way we seem able to make more sense of the ordinary world that we experience day to day.

At the beginning of the *White Lotus Sutra* we meet the Buddha as a story-teller, surrounded by a great crowd of disciples—monks and nuns, laymen and laywomen—not to mention a vast assembly of non-human beings. The Buddha chooses to start telling stories to his audience because conceptual explanation has failed to convince all of its members. Indeed, it has thrown them into utter confusion. The Buddha has simply pointed out that, despite all their spiritual attainments, they do not yet know everything. They have something more to learn. The very idea sends shock-waves through the entire assembly. Five thousand disciples, unable to believe their ears, get up and walk out—and those who stay are bewildered. What more can they have to learn, profoundly versed in the Dharma as they are? What can the Buddha mean?

The Buddha was perhaps expecting this. Remarking that 'through a parable, intelligent people reach understanding', he launches into a story that will explain matters. This one parable is quite enough to convince some people, and as more and more parables are told, more and more disciples do at last grasp what the Buddha has been talking about. They rejoice, they tell parables of their own expressing their gratitude, they shower the Buddha with double handfuls of jewel-flowers—and, most importantly, they commit themselves to his new teaching.

We ourselves are living at a time when it is hard to avoid feeling that we know it all. We may even feel that we know too much—and, at the same time, that we are not really certain of anything. Bombarded with information as we are, what we really need, we may feel, is not more teaching, but more understanding. In our over-stimulated state, it may come as quite a relief to listen to stories such as those the Buddha tells in the *White Lotus Sutra*, and take them into our hearts. Allowing ourselves just to sit and listen is by no means just a childish distraction. 'Listening'—receptivity, willingness to learn, open-heartedness—is, according to Buddhism, the first level of wisdom.

At the same time, such simple fare may not be intellectually satisfying; we may feel the need for some kind of interpretation to chew over. This need is not unique to our own time and culture. Throughout the long history of the *White Lotus Sutra*, which was first written down in the first century CE after many years of being passed on by word of mouth, responses to the text have alternated between the expositional and the devotional, according to the mood of the time. Some people, like the great Zen master Hakuin—though he did later change his mind—have found the sutra disappointing. No doctrines, no teachings, just a lot of old stories. Other people have gone to the opposite extreme and made the chanting of the praises of the sutra their sole spiritual practice.

When the *White Lotus Sutra* was flourishing in China, many of the sutra's adherents took a doctrinal approach. Monks would give series of lectures on the text—eight being the usual number—and after each lecture scholars from rival Buddhist schools would interrogate the speaker, trying to find a flaw in his arguments; a judge would decide the winner of the contest. At other times the emphasis has been on the reverential decoration and adornment of the text. It was copied in gold and silver leaf on the best dark blue paper; it was embellished with stupas and lotuses and mantras. The best-known stories became the subjects of lavish illustrations. The seeds of both the expositional and the devotional approach to the text are sown in the sutra itself, which frequently exhorts its hearers to expound it, recite it, copy it, and pay homage to it.

This book represents a drawing together of the strands of tradition associated with the *White Lotus Sutra*. It is in fact based on a series of eight lectures given not in the sutra's heyday in China, but in the heyday of the hippie culture in London, in 1970, by the venerable Sangharakshita. At that time Sangharakshita had been back in England for only a few years after twenty years spent in India. Having known that he was a Buddhist since the age of sixteen (at which time he was still living in his native London), he had taken the opportunity to remain in India at the close of the second world war, and had been ordained as a Buddhist monk in the Theravāda tradition at Kuśinagara, the place of the Buddha's death. Since then he had received teachings from Buddhist teachers of many different traditions, and had established his own vihara near the Himalayan town of Kalimpong. It was a return visit to England in 1964 which made him realize the need for authentic Buddhist teaching in the West, and this had led him to found the Western Buddhist Order in 1968.

At the time he gave these lectures Sangharakshita was thus the focus of a growing Buddhist movement. The audience which crowded into a London hall to hear him speak on the sutra was typical of its time: long-haired and brightly dressed. The atmosphere may have been redolent with exotic—and sometimes proscribed—fragrances, but it was enthusiastic and energetic. In the first lecture Sangharakshita made the point that Buddhism—Mahāyāna Buddhism at least—always speaks the language of its audience, not just literally but metaphorically. He then proceeded to expound the *White Lotus Sutra* in the language of the audience now eyeing him from behind its long hair (Sangharakshita's hair, incidentally, was just as long), dropping in occasional references to Zen, yin and yang, psychotherapy, and other popular subjects of the day. Thus was the assembly drawn into the strange atmosphere of the sutra— whose genre Sangharakshita described as 'transcendental science fiction'—and regaled with a lively retelling of its parables. Once again the drama of cosmic Enlightenment was holding its audience spellbound.

Fifteen years later, in the course of a seminar held at Padmaloka, a retreat centre in Norfolk, the ancient custom of interrogating the speaker was revived, even though the questioners may have had no idea that they were the upholders of such a lineage, and were not representatives of different Buddhist groups. On this occasion the interrogation came from a group of Sangharakshita's own students who had questions to ask both for the benefit of their own Dharma practice and in preparation for leading study on the sutra themselves.

In one of the lectures Sangharakshita refers to the kind of spiritual aspirant who demands, as a matter of good religious form, 'Tell me how I can become Enlightened, right now if possible'—but who has no intention of putting any advice proffered into practice. On the occasion of this seminar, however, the questioners meant business. Although some of the questions were doctrinal, many were of a practical nature: Is psychotherapy useful to spiritual practice? How can we overcome the fear of change? How do we encourage the urge to Enlightenment to become our dominant motivation? What is the best way of studying non-conceptual texts like the *White Lotus Sutra*? In this book these questions and answers are interwoven with the lectures, complementing them, adding perspective and depth to the pictures they paint. At times the discussion becomes quite technical, and it ranges over a broad range of topics; where appropriate, I have added footnotes giving brief explanations of technical terms, or suggesting sources of further information.

The more decorative, devotional approach is echoed in Varaprabhā's illustrations, which combine the comparatively modern lino-cut technique with the inspiration of the exquisite illustrations of the sutra produced hundreds of years ago in China and Japan. Of course, although this book may represent the inheritance of ancient traditions, it is also the product of more modern, even technological, spheres of Buddhist activity. Recordings of Sangharakshita's original lectures were provided by Dharmachakra Tapes, the charity responsible for recording and distributing lectures by Sangharakshita and other members of the Western Buddhist Order. The questions and answers were transcribed by the Transcriptions Unit which, headed by Dharmacāri Śīlabhadra, has been engaged for a number of years in publishing Sangharakshita's study seminars. Together these are the guardians of this particular oral tradition; it is the effort of those involved in both which has made available the raw material for this book—and potentially many more. *The Drama of Cosmic Enlightenment* is the first fruit of a new venture (the Spoken Word Project) dedicated to making Sangharakshita's oral teachings available in print. Many thanks to all those who have given so generously to support this work.

Thanks are also due to the many people who have worked on *The Drama of Cosmic Enlightenment*, perpetuating the tradition of 'protecting, keeping, reading, reciting, and preaching' the *White Lotus Sutra*. Thanks especially to Dharmacāri Śāntavīra for his meticulous sub-editing, Helen Argent for her help with the Index, Dharmacāri Susiddhi for compiling the Recommended Reading list, to Dharmacāriṇī Varaprabhā and to Diane Quin, the designer, for adorning the text so beautifully. My personal thanks go to Dharmacāri Jinānanda, the co-ordinator and chief editor of the Spoken Word Project, for his incisive advice and his great patience, and to Dharmacāri Nāgabodhi for all his encouragement. Of course, this is Sangharakshita's book, first and last—his are the 'merits of the preacher', as the sutra puts it—and all our thanks must go to him for his teaching and inspiration. I would like also to record my gratitude for the advice and encouragement he has so willingly given at every stage in the book's production.

Although reading is usually a solitary activity these days, perhaps we can imagine, as we begin to read, that we are part of the vast audience that has gathered to hear the *White Lotus Sutra* in many ages and many cultures. To enter the world of the *White Lotus Sutra* is, as Sangharakshita warns us in his introduction to the text, to enter a very strange and mysterious world indeed. As we do so, his advice is that we should just sit back and allow the sutra to have its effect on us. We cannot infer from this that we can afford to be 'armchair Buddhists', but we can have confidence that the starting point of spiritual practice is receptivity. The sutra is the *White Lotus Sutra of the Real Truth*, and if we allow it to unfold before us untold miracles will occur. Of course the best miracle—the only real miracle—is, as the Buddha once said, the commitment of an individual to the path of spiritual transformation.

Karen Stout
Spoken Word Project editor
Arunachala Community
Norwich
March 1993

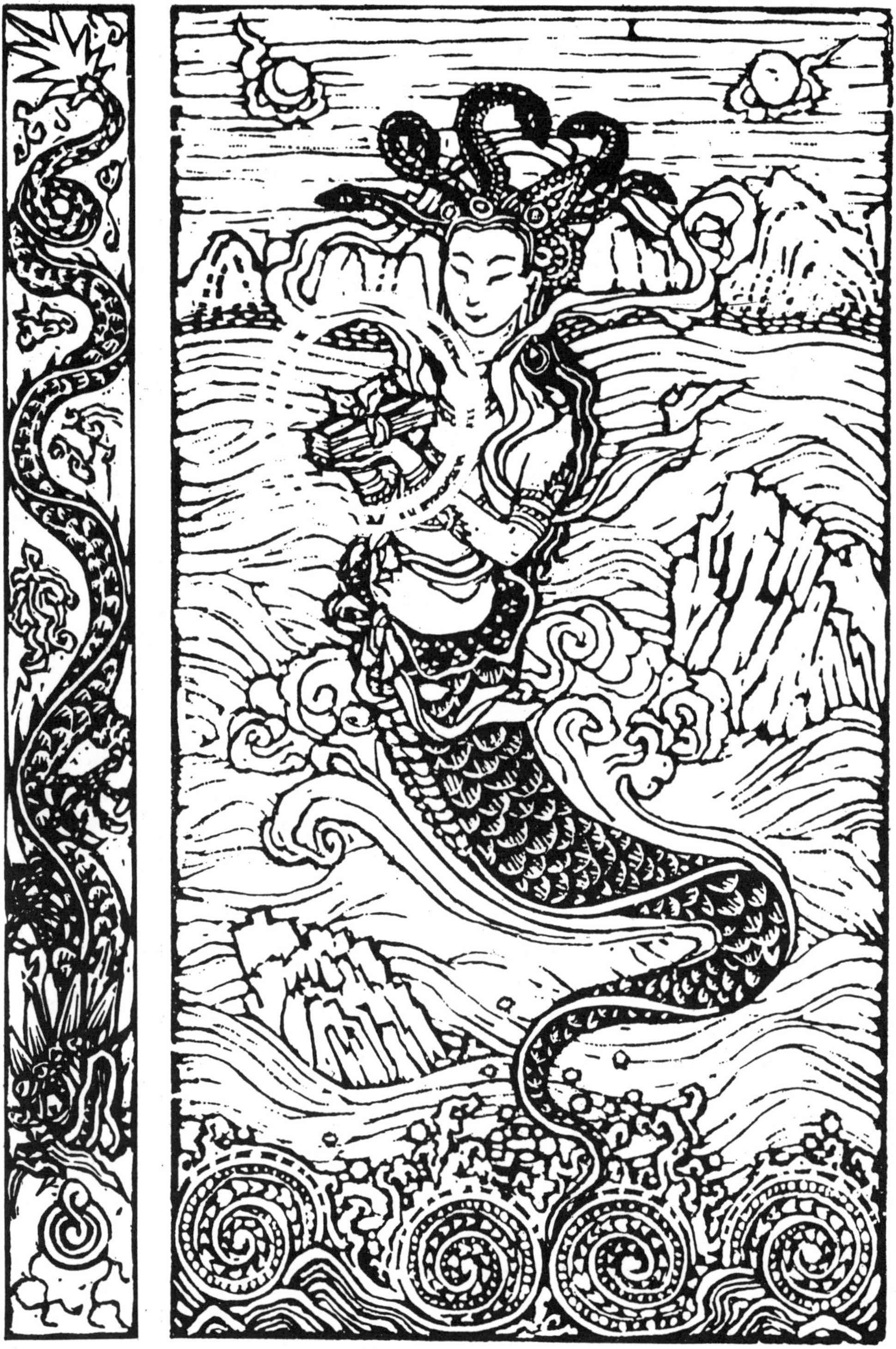

Chapter One

THE UNIVERSAL PERSPECTIVE OF MAHAYANA BUDDHISM

THE MYTHS WHICH Buddhism has inherited from the ancient Hindu tradition tell many stories of Indra, the king of the gods, who lives in a magnificent palace in the Heaven of the Thirty-Three Gods. In his palace Indra has many treasures, and among those treasures, the legends say, is a net. Now this net is no ordinary net. For one thing, it is made entirely of jewels. What is more, this net of jewels has a number of wonderful and extraordinary characteristics. And one of these characteristics is that when you look into the facets of any one jewel, you can see all the other jewels reflected in it. Each and every jewel in the net reflects all the others, so that 'all the jewels shine in each, and each shines in all.'

In the *Avataṁsaka Sūtra*, the Buddha likens the whole universe to Indra's net of jewels.[1] So what is the basis for this comparison? At the simplest level we could say that just as Indra's net consists of innumerable jewels of all shapes, sizes, and degrees of brilliance, so the universe consists of innumerable phenomena of various kinds. But the Buddha takes the analogy further, and in doing so challenges the very way we see things. We usually experience the things that make up the universe as being completely separate and distinct from one another, and we can hardly imagine seeing things in any other way. A mountain, a bicycle, an ant, a block of flats, a policeman—just a mass of separate objects—this is how we see the world. But in reality, so the Buddha says, it is not like that at all. From his point of view—that is, from the point of view of the highest spiritual experience—everything in the universe, great and small, near and far, reflects everything else. All things reflect one another, mirror one another—in a sense they even contain one another. This truth applies not only throughout space but also throughout time, so that everything that happens anywhere is happening here, and everything that happens at any time is happening now. Time and space are transcended, all the categories of logic and reason are superseded, and the world we 'know' is turned upside-down.

Indra's net is not the only traditional illustration of this law of mutual reflection. In the Mahāyāna Buddhist countries of the Far East, a particular teaching from the scriptures has been quoted so often that it has entered deeply and intimately into the literature of these countries, and even into their everyday lives. The saying goes: 'Each and every single grain of dust in the universe contains all the Buddha worlds of the ten directions of space and the three periods of time' (the three periods of time being past, present, and future). This might at first sight seem to be rather a strange and exotic insight, but we do have something like it nearer home, in the poetry of William Blake:

To see a World in a Grain of Sand,
  And a Heaven in a Wild Flower,
Hold Infinity in the palm of your hand,
  And Eternity in an hour.[2]

We are all too likely not to take this familiar verse seriously. If we think about it at all, we probably think 'Oh well, it's not that Blake actually *saw* the world in a grain of sand. It's just a figure of speech, a flight of poetic fancy.' But Blake was not just a poet; he was also a visionary, a mystic. These lines suggest that he really did see, or at least glimpse, the world as it really is, the world as the Buddha describes it through the simile of Indra's net of jewels.

As the Buddha taught that everything is interconnected in this way, it is perhaps not surprising to discover that his own teaching, the Dharma, is itself like Indra's net. The teachings of Buddhism, like everything else, form a network of connections, a net of jewels, and each facet throws light on all the others. This means—to look at it the other way round—that we can't *fully* understand any one aspect of the Dharma unless we understand the whole of it. When we reach some understanding of a doctrine that is new to us, we may think that we can just add it to our stock of knowledge like adding a pebble to a heap of pebbles, but in fact this is impossible. Whenever we encounter a new teaching, we have to go back and look again at everything we already 'know' in the light of our new understanding. Every single insight into the truth that we have modifies, at least subtly, all our previous insights.

So each time we discover a new way of exploring the Buddhist path, our understanding is completely transformed. And the avenues of exploration open to us are numerous. For example, we can see spiritual development in terms of evolution, using anthropology, biology, and history to trace the progress of what I have termed the 'higher evolution of man'.[3] We can bring a Western psychological approach to bear on the practical problems that we encounter in the course of our spiritual development. Western philosophy and the arts also give us rich sources of inspiration; and meanwhile the traditional formulations of Indian Buddhism remain open to us as well. Each exploration of human growth and development sheds light on the whole process.

The *White Lotus Sutra*, which is a product of the Mahāyāna, the second great phase of Indian Buddhism, explores the Dharma through parables, myths, and symbols—in other words, through archetypes, through what Jung calls the collective unconscious. But why does the *White Lotus Sutra* take this particular mode of expression? To understand this, we need to take a look at the history of Buddhism and see how the Mahāyāna developed its universal perspective.

Buddhism began in India some 2,500 years ago. The Buddha, Śākyamuni, was born and brought up as Siddhartha, prince of the Śākyan clan, in what is now southern Nepal. In the years following his Enlightenment, he travelled and taught throughout what was known in those days as the Middle Region, which corresponds to the present day Indian states of Bihar and Uttar Pradesh, an area about the size of England and Wales. And after his death, during the 1,500 years his teaching lasted in India, it spread throughout the whole vast subcontinent and beyond, crossing deserts and seas to penetrate practically the whole of Asia. It even reached westwards as far as Antioch and Alexandria, and this without the benefit of modern transport and communication systems.

As well as travelling so far afield, Buddhism changed greatly during the period of its development in India. The fundamental things, the essential Dharma, remained the same, but the way the teachings were presented and interpreted changed over the years. There were three great phases of development, each lasting roughly five hundred years: the Hīnayāna, the Mahāyāna, and the Vajrayāna. Mahāyāna is a Sanskrit word meaning great way, or great vehicle (from *mahā*, 'great', and *yāna*, 'way' or 'vehicle')—the great way or vehicle to Enlightenment. The Mahāyāna was not a particular school or sect of Buddhism, as some writers make out, but a phase of development which came to represent a certain approach to Buddhism. The term Mahāyāna is often contrasted with that given to the first phase of Buddhism, Hīnayāna, which means little way—and this gives us a clue to the approach that Mahāyāna Buddhism took. Whoever coined the terms 'little way' and 'great way'

was obviously making a contrast. But what is being contrasted? What difference is being pointed out?

According to popular belief, the difference between the Hīnayāna and the Mahāyāna is simple. The Hīnayāna, people say, teaches that you should devote yourself simply to the attainment of your own Enlightenment, completely ignoring the needs of others. The Mahāyāna, again according to popular opinion, teaches the opposite—that you should forget all about yourself, devoting your energies solely to helping other beings to tread the path to Enlightenment. This assessment of the contrast is both crude and misleading. It manages to give the impression that the Mahayanist is a model of transcendental politeness, forever holding the door of Enlightenment open for other people to pass through—a gross distortion of the truth of the Mahāyāna's position. For the Mahāyāna simply—but profoundly—realizes that concern for the welfare and the spiritual development of other people is an integral part of one's own spiritual development. Indeed, to be concerned with one's own development but completely uninterested in that of other people is self-defeating in the long run.

The Mahāyāna vision sees that all forms of life in the universe on all levels, and perhaps especially on the human level, are, like Indra's net, interrelated and interactive. Indeed, the Mahāyāna takes the image a step further. The net is not static, for the individual jewels that make it up are in motion, and the whole net, each and every jewel, is heading in one direction. Admittedly, some jewels are a little further ahead, and some are lagging behind, for the net is after all very large. Some jewels are big and bright, while others are smaller and less lustrous, and some, unfortunately, are even dragging in the mud, so that they seem to have lost their beauty and look more like ordinary pebbles than jewels. But they are all moving towards the same goal, and they are all, directly or indirectly, in contact with one another.

The urge to Enlightenment, the urge to something above and beyond the world, is innate in all life, but it is a blind urge, like that of a plant groping for the light. The Mahāyāna's greatest spiritual hero, the Bodhisattva—a being (*sattva*) dedicated to the attainment of Enlightenment or awakening (*bodhi*)—is one in whom the urge to grow which is present in every living being has become self-conscious. The Bodhisattva is thus the embodiment of the Higher Evolution. Realizing that the urge to develop spiritually is potential in all living beings, a Bodhisattva feels a sense of solidarity with other beings, and could not possibly ignore them and think only in terms of his or her own salvation. Bodhisattvas therefore dedicate themselves to Enlightenment not just for their own sake but for the sake of all living beings whatsoever. For the Hīnayāna, by contrast, the ideal Buddhist is the Arhat, the sage or saint who has destroyed all passions and reached nirvana, but whose spiritual career is at no stage concerned with other beings. Like Bodhisattvas, Arhats have become conscious of the urge to spiritual growth, but their progress is limited because they are unaware that all living beings share the potential for Enlightenment.

Evidence of the contrast between the Bodhisattva and the Arhat is plentiful in the Mahāyāna scriptures, but for a really vivid impression you have only to look at the Buddhist paintings and sculptures produced in India and China, and now preserved in temples and museums throughout the world. The Bodhisattva is usually depicted as a beautiful young man (or woman) sitting on a delicate lotus flower. He has a graceful figure, long flowing locks, and many fine ornaments. The Arhat, on the other hand, is usually an old man with a bald head and bushy eyebrows. Clad in a shabby monastic robe, he leans wearily on a knotted staff. No lotus seat for him—he is usually standing on solid rock, or sometimes, for a change, floating on the ocean. The Bodhisattva represents the ideal in all its perfection and purity, the abstract ideal not stained or touched by anything of the world, but lifted above it. The Arhat, by contrast, represents the realization of the ideal under the conditions and limitations of space and time, the stress of history. No wonder the Arhat has a weather-beaten, worn look.

We can find an interesting parallel to this in the way Christian art depicts the angels and the saints. The angels are usually represented as sleek, graceful, well-groomed young men with long curly hair and wings. They are often playing on musical instruments, and they have sweet, innocent expressions which make it clear that they have never sinned. They don't even know what sin is—they're as innocent as that. The saints, on the other hand, are usually old and worn and rather ugly. They certainly do know what sin is, even if they have succeeded after many struggles in overcoming it or at least in holding it down. And unlike the angels, they suffer; they're usually shown being crucified upside-down, or beheaded, or shot full of arrows, or roasted on a gridiron. Again, on the one hand you have the archetypal, the ideal, and on the other, the realization of the ideal in the concrete conditions of human historical existence.

But contrary to appearances (as depicted in art) Bodhisattvas don't have an easy time of it. They are committed to cultivating spiritual qualities through all sorts of practices, and in particular through the practice of the six *pāramitās*. *Pāramitā* usually gets translated as 'perfection' or 'virtue', but 'discipline for the attainment of Enlightenment' gives a better idea of what the term means.

The first of these disciplines for the attainment of Enlightenment is *dāna*—giving or generosity. According to Mahāyāna tradition you can give in many ways, ranging from the comparatively gross to the comparatively refined and subtle. First, and most obviously, you can give material things—food, clothing, shelter, and so on. Secondly, there's the giving of education and culture. The third kind of giving is psychological—the giving of fearlessness. So many people suffer from profound feelings of insecurity, and the Bodhisattva should resolve those feelings—it's as though the Bodhisattva has to be a sort of psychotherapist on the transcendental plane. Fourthly, the Bodhisattva also gives the gift of the Dharma, the Truth. And this isn't just a matter of handing people a little tract and saying 'Go away and read this.' Giving the Dharma means sharing your own understanding of the truth of things as far as it goes, and pointing, perhaps, to the greater understanding of others with more experience. The final gift—which is also, we may say, the all-inclusive gift—is the giving of yourself in your relationships with other people. You don't just give a part of yourself and hold the rest back. The Bodhisattva can say, in Walt Whitman's words, 'When I give I give myself.'[4]

If there is one teaching of the Buddha that his followers in the East have taken to heart, it is this one—they have learned not just to be generous, but even to be overwhelmingly generous. They usually practise some form of generosity every day. I lived for many years among Buddhists in the East, and I can testify that generosity is one of the most attractive features of life there. When I was first settling in Kalimpong, I stayed with a Burmese Buddhist and his wife, and I soon discovered that I had to be careful what I said, because if I admired anything it was at once given to me—my attempts to refuse were to no avail. This was simply the Burmese Buddhist way of treating a guest. Later on, when I had my own hermitage in Kalimpong, I used to go down to Calcutta and meet up with my old Buddhist friends, especially Buddhist monks from Sri Lanka, Thailand, Vietnam, and Japan. As soon as I came through the door, two or three monks would already be asking 'What do you need?' 'Are you short of anything?—a typewriter, paper, money?' 'Do you need a fountain pen?—Have this one!'

It will perhaps take some time for Western Buddhists to imbibe this spirit of generosity; but generosity is certainly a quality which any practising Buddhist, any would-be Bodhisattva, needs to cultivate. As they sometimes say in the Mahāyāna countries, never mind if you can't meditate, never mind if you can't read or understand the scriptures. You can at least give. If you can't do that, you're not on the path to Enlightenment in any sense.

The second discipline, *śīla*, is often translated—not very fortunately—as 'morality', but the literal translation is 'uprightness'. The aspects of the Bodhisattva's conduct which this discipline deals with are expressed in the form of precepts, or guide-lines, which can be applied to every action of body, speech, and mind. The first of these precepts is an undertaking to refrain from taking life. The Bodhisattva is careful not to injure even the humblest of other living beings, or, to put it more positively, he or she cultivates what Albert Schweitzer calls 'reverence for life'—reverence for the uniqueness of everything that lives. The Bodhisattva reflects 'I have not called life into being, nor can I replace it when it is destroyed, so I have no right to take it, or to harm it in any way.' With this in mind, the Bodhisattva tries as far as possible to be vegetarian. The second precept which the Bodhisattva observes is traditionally phrased 'undertaking to refrain from taking what is not given'—in other words, one abstains from any kind of theft or fraud. In following the third precept, one undertakes to abstain from sexual misconduct. These three are the precepts which concern the ethics of bodily action.

The fourth precept gives guidance on the ethics of speech. The Bodhisattva undertakes not only to be truthful, but to tell the truth with great love and affection, taking into account the feelings and needs of the listener. Also, whether speaking to one person, or to many people, the Bodhisattva speaks in a way that promotes harmony, concord, and unity. In short, the Bodhisattva practises real communication.

Now Buddhist ethics are concerned not just with the actions of body and speech, but also with the actions of the mind. The fifth precept is therefore devoted to the preservation of 'mindfulness' with all that that implies—awareness, vitality, mental alertness, presence of mind, and so on. Practising this precept means avoiding anything which might diminish your awareness. This traditionally refers to over-indulgence in alcohol and drugs, but anything that may be used as a drug can be added to the list.[5]

The third practice of the Bodhisattva is *kṣānti*. It is difficult to translate *kṣānti* by any one English word because it means a number of things. It means patience: patience with people, patience when things don't go your way. It means tolerance: allowing other people to have their own thoughts, their own ideas, their own beliefs, even their own prejudices. It means love and kindliness. And it also means openness, willingness to take things in, and, especially, receptivity to higher spiritual truths. It's very difficult to be truly receptive. Even when we hear something crucial from the spiritual point of view, it's quite likely that we won't really take it in. We may receive it on an intellectual level, but just play around with the idea, not letting it sink into the depths of our being. Prejudices or negative emotions may stop the truth half way. There are so many barriers, so many obstacles, which *kṣānti* needs to overcome.

The fourth *pāramitā* is *vīrya*—energy or vigour, 'energy in pursuit of the good'. *Vīrya* consists primarily in the effort to get rid of negative emotions like anger, jealousy, and greed, and to foster positive emotions like love, compassion, joy, and peace. This means practising the 'Four Exertions': preventing the arising of unarisen unskilful mental states; eradicating arisen unskilful mental states; developing unarisen skilful mental states; and maintaining arisen skilful mental states. *Vīrya* is needed not just for this kind of 'exertion', however, but for the practice of all the disciplines leading to the attainment of Enlightenment, even the practice of *kṣānti*; in fact, without energy we can do nothing.

The fifth *pāramitā*, *samādhi*, presents us with another untranslatable term. It has three distinct levels of meaning. On one level it means concentration in the sense of the unification of all your psychic energies, the bridging of all the schisms in your being. Then there's *samādhi* in the sense of the personal experience of ever higher levels of consciousness, the kind of experience you may have when you meditate. This level of *samādhi* includes the development of what the Buddhist tradition calls 'supernormal powers'—telepathy, clairaudience, clairvoyance, and so on. In the third and highest sense, *samādhi* is the experience of Reality itself, or at least receptivity to the direct influence of Reality. This experience may begin in the form of flashes of insight—perhaps of the kind William Blake had when he 'saw the world in a grain of sand'.[6]

The sixth discipline is *prajñā*—wisdom. Buddhist tradition speaks of three kinds of wisdom. The first kind is traditionally called 'wisdom from hearing'. This is the wisdom we gain by listening to teachers of the Dharma and reading scriptures—wisdom gained at second-hand, as it were. The next kind of wisdom is that which we gain when we reflect on what we have heard and apply our own original thought to it. The third kind of wisdom arises when we meditate on our reflections, and incidentally it coincides with the highest level of *samādhi*.[7] Wisdom in this sense has four levels. The truths it reveals are profound and subtle, and here I will mention them only briefly. Firstly, we develop the wisdom which sees that conditioned existence, the mundane world, is essentially painful and unsatisfactory (*duḥkha*), impermanent (*anitya*), and insubstantial or devoid of selfhood (*anātman*).[8] Secondly, we see that nirvana, the Unconditioned, is devoid of suffering, impermanence, and insubstantiality, and possesses the opposite characteristics—bliss and happiness, permanence (eternity, if you like), and true being, true selfhood. With the arising of the third kind of wisdom, we see that the very distinction between the conditioned and the Unconditioned is only provisional—being part of the structure of thought, it is not ultimately valid. With this kind of wisdom we see the emptiness of the distinction between the conditioned and the Unconditioned. With the fourth kind of wisdom—which has been developed particularly by the Zen tradition—we go even further. We see the emptiness of the very concept of emptiness itself: the emptiness, the relativity, of all concepts, including those of Buddhism.

So these are the disciplines which the Bodhisattva has to practise.[9] Together they make up what is perhaps the noblest way of life ever proposed to humanity, a perfectly balanced and comprehensive scheme of spiritual development. Giving and uprightness provide for the other-regarding and the self-regarding aspects of the spiritual life, for altruism and individualism. Patience and vigour provide for the cultivation of the 'feminine' and 'masculine' virtues. And meditation and wisdom provide for the internal and the external dimensions, the subjective and objective aspects, of the Enlightenment experience.

Despite the guidance which the Mahāyāna gives the spiritual aspirant through the teaching of the six *pāramitās*, you will sometimes hear it said that it is the Hīnayāna which is meant for people who are prepared to make an effort to help themselves, whereas the Mahāyāna is for people who want everything to be done for them by the Bodhisattvas. According to this way of thinking, the Hīnayāna, the 'little way', is so called because it is addressed to an élite group, whereas the Mahāyāna, the 'great way', is addressed to the masses. Again, this distinction is both crude and misleading. As a universal religion, Buddhism addresses itself not to any particular group or community, but potentially to each and every human being. As the Hīnayāna and the Mahāyāna are both stages in the development of Buddhism, both are addressed to all individuals, so we can't distinguish between them in this respect. At the same time, there *is* a difference, which will perhaps become clear with the help of a parable.

Let's suppose that there is a famine somewhere, a terrible famine of the kind that still happens in Africa. People are gaunt and emaciated, and there is terrible suffering. In a certain town in the country which has been struck by this famine there live two men, one old, one young, who each have an enormous quantity of grain, easily enough to feed all the people. The old man puts outside his front door a notice which reads: 'Whoever comes will be given food.' But after that statement there follows a long list of conditions and rules. If people want food they must come at a certain time, on the very minute. They must bring with them receptacles of a certain shape and size. And holding these receptacles in a certain way, they must ask the old man for food in certain set phrases which are to be spoken in an archaic language. Not many people see the notice, for the old man lives in an out-of-the-way street; and of those who do see it, a few come for food and receive it, but others are put off by the long list of rules. If food is only available on those terms it seems less troublesome to starve. When the old man is asked why he imposes so many rules, he says 'That's how it was in my grandfather's time whenever there was a famine. What was good enough for him is certainly good enough for me. Who am I to change things?' He adds that if people really want food they will observe any number of rules to get it. If they won't observe the rules they can't really be hungry.

Meanwhile the young man takes a great sack of grain on his back and goes from door to door giving it out. As soon as one sack is empty, he rushes home for another one. In this way he gives out a great deal of grain all over the town. He gives it to anyone who asks. He's so keen to feed the people that he doesn't mind going into the poorest, darkest, and dirtiest of hovels. He doesn't mind going to places where respectable people don't usually venture. The only thought in his head is that nobody should be allowed to starve. Some people say that he's a busybody, others that he takes too much on himself. Some people go so far as to say that he's interfering with the law of karma. Others complain that a lot of grain is being wasted, because people take more than they really need. The young man doesn't care about any of this. He says it's better that some grain is wasted than that anyone should starve to death.

One day the young man happens to pass by the old man's house. The old man is sitting outside peacefully smoking his pipe, because it isn't yet time to hand out grain. He says to the young man as he hurries past, 'You look tired. Why don't you take it easy?' The young man replies, rather breathlessly, 'I can't. There are still lots of people who haven't been fed.' The old man shakes his head wonderingly. 'Let them come to you! Why should you go dashing off to them?' But the young man, impatient to be on his way, says 'They're too weak to come to me. They can't even walk. If I don't go to them they'll die.' 'That's too bad,' says the old man. 'They should have come earlier, when they were stronger. If they didn't think ahead that's their fault. Why should you worry if they die?' But by this time the young man is out of earshot, already on his way home for another sack. The old man rises and pins another notice beside the first one. The notice reads: 'Rules for reading the rules.'

No doubt you've already guessed the meaning of the parable. The old man is the Arhat, representing the Hīnayāna, and the young man is the Bodhisattva, representing the Mahāyāna. The famine is the human predicament, the people of the town are all living beings, and the grain is the Dharma, the teaching. Just as in principle both the old man and the young man are willing to give out grain to everybody, so in principle both the Hīnayāna and the Mahāyāna are universal, meant for all. But in practice we find that the Hīnayāna imposes certain conditions. To practise Buddhism within the Hīnayāna tradition, even today, if you're taking it at all seriously, you must leave home and become a monk or nun. You must live exactly as the monks and nuns lived in India in the Buddha's time. And you mustn't change anything. The Mahāyāna doesn't impose any such conditions. It makes the Dharma available to people as they are and where they are, because it is concerned solely with essentials. It's concerned with getting the grain to the people, not with any particular manner in which this is to be done. The Hīnayāna expects people to come to it, so to speak, but the Mahāyāna goes out to them.

This difference between the Hīnayāna and the Mahāyāna goes back to the early days of Buddhist history. About a hundred years after the Buddha's death, his disciples disagreed about certain issues so strongly that the spiritual community was split in two. Indeed, they disagreed about the very nature of Buddhism itself. One group of disciples held that Buddhism was simply what the Buddha had said. The Four Noble Truths, the Noble Eightfold Path, the Twelve Links or chain of conditioned co-production, the Four Foundations of Mindfulness; this was Buddhism. But the other group argued that this was not enough. Yes, all of these teachings did form part of Buddhism, but the example of the Buddha's life could not be ignored. The Buddha's teaching revealed his wisdom, but his life revealed his compassion, and both together made up Buddhism.

The Hīnayāna is descended from the first group of disciples, the Mahāyāna from the second. The Mahāyāna derives its inspiration not only from the Buddha's teaching but also from the way he lived his life. This is why the Mahāyāna stresses both wisdom and compassion, saying that compassion inevitably arises from true wisdom. It would be going too far to say that the Hīnayāna is completely without compassion, but the Hīnayāna scriptures rarely mention it, and certainly do not give it equal place with wisdom. But the Mahāyāna scriptures say 'Wisdom and

Compassion are the two wings of the bird of Enlightenment, and with one wing only it cannot fly.'

The life story of the Buddha shows that he didn't wait for people to come to him. He didn't just sit under the bodhi tree and wait for disciples. During the forty-five years following his Enlightenment he travelled far and wide to seek people out and teach them. Time and time again the scriptures report the Buddha as saying 'I went to them and said...' He used to go out to meet people—merchants, queens, goatherds, flower-sellers—and afterwards tell his disciples 'I went to them and said...' And if someone came to see him, the Buddha would take the initiative in the conversation. He would greet the newcomer and put them at their ease, so that they felt welcome. This was the living example of the Buddha.

In the same spirit the Mahāyāna goes out to meet people. For example, in all the Mahāyāna Buddhist countries—China, Japan, Tibet, Mongolia—the scriptures were translated from the Indian languages into the local language from the very first. Tibet didn't even have a written alphabet when Buddhism first arrived there. The first Tibetan Buddhists created a literary language so that they could translate the texts and the Tibetan people could read them for themselves. But in the Theravāda countries of South-East Asia (Theravāda being one school of the Hīnayāna tradition), the scriptures all remained in Pali, the original ancient Indian dialect, which is a dead language, as Latin is. If you wanted to study them you had to become a monk, go and live in a monastery, and learn Pali, before you could read so much as a sentence of the Buddha's teaching for yourself. It's only very recently, under Western influence, that the Pali Buddhist scriptures have begun to be translated into the languages of Sri Lanka, Burma, and Thailand. A Sinhalese monk once told me that he thought English Buddhists were very lucky. 'You have translations of nearly all the Pali texts' he explained 'but we've only just started translating them into Sinhalese'—which does seem quite astonishing.

So the Mahāyāna literally speaks the language of the people it is addressing—Tibetan, Chinese, English, or whatever is appropriate. But more than this, it also tries to speak the appropriate language in a metaphorical sense. Metaphorically speaking, whether we speak English, Hindi, Greek, or whatever, we express ourselves in two main languages: the language of concepts and the language of images. The language of concepts is the language of intellect and rational thought, the language of science and philosophy. But the language of images is the language of the imagination, the language of the emotions. It's the language of poetry, the language of myth and symbol, simile and metaphor. Concepts address the conscious mind, but images appeal to the unconscious depths that—as modern psychology has made us aware—are within us all.

The Buddha himself spoke both the language of concepts and the language of images. Sometimes he expounded his teaching in a highly abstract, intellectual fashion, and sometimes he spoke in beautiful metaphors and parables—the parable of the raft, the parable of the blind men and the elephant, the parable of the ever-smouldering anthill, and a hundred others. But as it developed the Hīnayāna forgot the language of images, and spoke more and more exclusively in the language of concepts, until poetry and metaphor were completely banished. Take, for example, the Abhidharma literature of the Theravādins, which consists of seven massive works, some of them in many volumes.[10] They contain psychological analysis, classification of mental states, descriptions of mental functions, and so on—all in severely conceptual style. It is the proud boast of the Abhidharma that in all those thousands of pages there is not a single figure of speech.

The Mahāyāna, on the other hand, continued to speak both the language of concepts and the language of images, and it spoke them both ever more eloquently, as the hundreds of Mahāyāna scriptures show. Amongst the conceptual works are the Perfection of Wisdom sutras, which number more than thirty, some many hundreds of pages long and others comparatively short. The oldest and most important is probably the *Aṣṭasāhasrikā*, the *Perfection of Wisdom in 8,000 Lines*. The *Hṛdaya*, the *Heart Sutra* ('heart' in the sense of 'essence'—the essence of the Perfection of Wisdom) is well known, and so is the *Vajracchedikā*, the 'Diamond Cutter', and both are much recited in the Mahāyāna monasteries of the Far East. All these scriptures are concerned with one topic—*śūnyatā*, Voidness, Reality—the highest level of Wisdom, the perfection of the sixth discipline of the Bodhisattva. However, *śūnyatā* is presented in these conceptual works not as a concept but as the *absence* of all concepts. In fact, this literature speaks the language of concepts in such a way as to transcend all concepts whatsoever.

There's a mysterious legend attached to the origin of the Perfection of Wisdom sutras. It is said that the great Mahāyāna teacher and sage Nāgārjuna retrieved them from the depths of the ocean, where they had been kept in secret by the nāga kings since the days of the Buddha. This story, which obviously has a symbolic significance, is often depicted in Buddhist art. We see Nāgārjuna floating on a little raft in the middle of the ocean, and a mermaid-like creature with long flowing green hair emerging from the sea with a heavy book in her hands. This is the beautiful daughter of the nāga king who lives in the depths of the sea. She hands over the long-treasured text to the great teacher, and he triumphantly bears it back to dry land, writes commentaries on it, and makes it more and more widely known. This is the legend. We don't know exactly when Nāgārjuna lived—probably in the first century of the Christian era—but it is certain that his teaching of the Perfection of Wisdom was a factor in the rise of the Mahāyāna.

The *Laṅkāvatāra Sūtra*, the 'Holy Entry of the Good Teaching into Lanka', which is set on the island of Lanka, where the Buddha goes to preach to the king of the rākshasas, is also written almost exclusively in conceptual language. This text, popular in medieval times with Chinese Buddhist intellectuals, is one of the most difficult of all the sutras, containing highly abstruse psychological and metaphysical teachings.

Then there's the *Gaṇḍavyūha Sūtra*, the 'Scripture of the Cosmic Array', which is part of a larger work called the *Avataṁsaka Sūtra*, the 'Flower Ornament Scripture', traditionally known as the king of the sutras. The *Gaṇḍavyūha Sūtra* describes the pilgrimage of a young man called Sudhana who visits more than fifty people—men, women, old, young, holy, not so holy—in the course of his search for wisdom and Enlightenment. Sudhana learns something from everyone he meets, until eventually he finds the Bodhisattva Maitreya, who is living in the Vairocana tower in southern India. It is here that Sudhana receives his final instruction, his final initiation. He is admitted to the tower by Maitreya, and inside the tower he has a wonderful vision. He sees that all the phenomena in the universe are contained in the tower, and the tower is contained, or reflected, in every single thing in the universe. Once again, it's Indra's net of jewels. The form of the sutra is all about images—it's a sort of Buddhist *Pilgrim's Progress*—but its content is mainly conceptual.

The *Vimalakīrti-nirdeśa*, the 'Exposition of Vimalakīrti', speaks the language of both concepts and images, maintaining a beautiful balance and blending of the two. It tells the dramatic story of the meeting between Mañjuśrī, the Bodhisattva of Wisdom, and Vimalakīrti, a wise old householder of Vaiśālī, a town of north-eastern India. In a scene which is often depicted in Chinese Buddhist art, the two come together and have a terrific debate, the sound of which echoes down through Buddhist history.

Some Mahāyāna scriptures speak the language of images almost entirely. There's the *Lalita-vistara*, for example—the 'Extended Account of the Sports or Games'. Now we may be forgiven for wondering what kind of spiritual text this might be. And it may come as a surprise to learn that the sports or games are those of the Buddha, that we have here a sutra which offers us what we may say is the Buddha's playful nature. The *Lalita-vistara* recounts various incidents of the Buddha's career which were to him 'child's play', incidents in which he acted freely, easily, naturally, spontaneously—in other words, in a truly spiritual manner. So this sutra is a kind of biography of the Buddha, but it is not biography as we usually understand the term, because it contains a great deal of what scholars like to call 'legendary material'. But this is not just 'false history': the *Lalita-vistara* speaks the language of images, and the events it describes must be taken on a symbolic level.

There are also the three Pure Land sutras, which consist entirely of strings of images, with hardly any conceptual material at all. They describe the Happy Land of Amitābha, the Buddha of Infinite Light, with its deep blue ground and its criss-crossing golden cords, and its wonderful jewel trees, which the sutras lovingly describe, branch by branch, flower by flower, and even petal by petal. One of these sutras is used to aid visualization of the Pure Land in the context of meditation, and all three are the basis of the Shin Shu, or Pure Land School of Buddhism, which prevails in China and Japan; followers of Shin Shu all aspire to rebirth in this archetypal Happy Land.

So to the *Saddharma-Puṇḍarīka*, the *Sutra of the White Lotus of the Good Dharma*. This also speaks almost exclusively in the language of images. Although the sutra is very long, its conceptual content is absolutely minimal. The *White Lotus Sutra*, therefore, appeals not to the head but to the heart, not to the intellect but to the imagination. Its parables, perhaps the most significant in the entire range of Buddhist canonical literature, are famous throughout the Buddhist East, and it is also replete with myths and symbols. In form it's a sort of drama, even a sort of mystery play. It has for its stage the entire cosmos, and the action lasts for millions of ages. The *dramatis personae* consists of the Buddhas and Bodhisattvas, Arhats, gods, demons, and men—in fact, all sentient beings whatsoever. And the atmosphere of the sutra is very strange, an atmosphere of miracle and marvel. In fact, as the sutra unfolds, what we see is a sort of transcendental sound and light show—there seems no other way to describe it. As for the theme of the drama, it is a very great one indeed. It is Enlightenment—not just the Buddha's Enlightenment, or the disciples' Enlightenment, but the Enlightenment of all sentient beings whatsoever. Hence our title: the Drama of Cosmic Enlightenment.

Chapter One

QUESTIONS AND ANSWERS

Is the doctrine of the mutual interpenetration of all phenomena a logical development of the doctrine of conditionality, or does it represent an entirely new vision of existence?

It does not represent an entirely new vision so much as a new *expression* of the Buddhist vision. The doctrine of interpenetration is concerned with the nature of Ultimate Reality, which can be approached in various ways. The *pratītya-samutpāda* (conditioned co-production) doctrine takes a phenomenological approach ('this being, that becomes' and so on).[11] That phenomenology has certain metaphysical implications which are not brought out in the Theravāda but emerge in the Mahāyāna, especially in the Mādhyamika's interpretations of the *śūnyatā* teaching. The fact that all phenomena, all *dharmas*, are reducible to *śūnyatā* was already there in the *pratītya-samutpāda* teaching; the Mādhyamika simply drew attention to it. Multiplicity was thus reduced to unity, for *dharmas* are many and *śūnyatā*—at least for the purposes of discourse—is one. Subsequently, practitioners of the Yogācāra School came to see Reality not in terms of *śūnyatā*, but in terms of the One Mind. In reducing the multiplicity of mental phenomena to absolute mind, however, they too thought in terms of a reduction of multiplicity to oneness, diversity to unity.

The creator of the *Avataṁsaka Sūtra* (which, like all Mahāyāna sutras, is traditionally ascribed to the Buddha) was satisfied neither with the original Hīnayāna position nor with the subsequent standpoint of the Yogācāra. To use Western terminology, he saw that both unity and multiplicity are just concepts. Given that the nature of Reality is ultimately inexpressible through concepts, the question is how to use those concepts at least to hint at its nature. In the *Avataṁsaka Sūtra*, therefore, the concepts of unity and diversity are combined to give at least a more adequate expression of the nature of reality. All things are not seen in the one, nor is the one seen in all things, but rather each individual thing is seen in every other individual thing.

So could the contemplation of the doctrine of mutual interpenetration be more useful to Dharma practice than the doctrine of śūnyatā?
Until you have reached a relatively refined level of spiritual practice, there is little point in exploring metaphysical subtleties. While you are still finding it difficult to concentrate the mind, or practise mindfulness in the affairs of everyday life, it is more important to focus on basic principles. If anything, I would concentrate on impermanence, which does ultimately imply *śūnyatā*, and also has a direct connection with *pratītya-samutpāda*, and therefore with the possibility of spiritual progress. Close study of *pratītya-samutpāda* doctrine inevitably involves arriving at some understanding of *śūnyatā*, because *śūnyatā* is a metaphysical statement of the implications of conditioned co-production.

Does that mean that it is never appropriate to reflect on śūnyatā? *Perhaps the doctrine was only useful as a way of dealing with the highly conceptual state of medieval Buddhism? But if it is redundant, why continue to chant the* Heart Sutra?
If you *do* want to reflect on *śūnyatā*, one way of looking at it is to bear in mind that the word, which literally means emptiness, really means 'empty of all concepts'. It is a reminder to us that ultimate Reality is empty of concepts, in that all our conceptual constructions are inadequate to express it. In that sense, the doctrine of *śūnyatā* is never inappropriate, never out of date. That is not to say, however, that you need to be acquainted with all the highly technical, purely metaphysical expositions of the teaching of *śūnyatā*. You have to bear in mind what the point of it really is from a practical point of view.

Are there any Buddhist practices designed to cultivate the type of vision which Indra's net expresses?
In his book *The Essence of Buddhism*,[12] Suzuki describes a demonstration given by a great Chinese master to explain the doctrine of mutual interpenetration. The master arranged mirrors and candles all round the room in such a way that every mirror reflected all the candles, and also all the other mirrors. The model is inadequate, because it is static, but you could try to imagine all the mirrors and candles in motion—that

would give some idea of what mutual interpenetration is like.

Probably the best way of developing insight into reality through this particular way of looking at it would be to read a text rather than reflecting on the philosophical doctrine. While in a relatively concentrated state of mind, you could read to yourself a chapter of the *Avataṁsaka Sūtra*.[13] The original sutras give a much better feeling for the nature of that particular outlook than any of the more doctrinal expositions.

Apart from the Avataṁsaka Sūtra *and your example from William Blake, are there any significant descriptions of the mutual interpenetration of all phenomena in other cultures and religions?*
The question hinges on what you mean by phenomena. There are certain phenomena within the range of Buddhist experience which do not seem to occur within the range, for example, of orthodox Christian thought or experience, so that the statement that all things are mutually inter-reflecting would have a more restricted meaning within a Christian context than within a Buddhist one. Sometimes Christians speak in terms of Christ bearing all the sins of the world, as though all the sins are reflected in him, but not very much is said about Christ being reflected in every human being, or in material things. It's true that in a verse from a Gnostic gospel, Jesus is represented as saying, 'Split the wood and there am I; lift the stone and there am I', but that text is not included in the Authorized Bible.

So this does seem to be a distinctively Buddhist way of expressing a certain insight, and one which took time to develop. The *Avataṁsaka* teaching of interpenetration comes as the culmination of some centuries of the development of Buddhist thought. There are perhaps analogies in the various mystical traditions. Some of the more poetic Sufi mystics, who think of ultimate Reality in terms of the 'Beloved', speak of seeing the face of the Beloved reflected in all phenomena, which perhaps comes some way towards the Buddhist conception. Plato also gave some thought to the question of unity and multiplicity, and seemed in the *Parmenides* to opt for unity as real and diversity as unreal.

Is there some suggestion of the doctrine of mutual interpenetration in the Hermetic idea 'as above, so below'?[14]
I suppose there is a similarity in a general way, but the Hermetic idea is about correspondence, not mutual reflection. It is perhaps misleading even to say that mutual interpenetration is reflection; it is more that each and every thing is actually present in each and every other thing. Mutual

interpenetration breaks down the whole idea of separate 'thingness', just as the *śūnyatā* concept of Insight does.[15]

Returning to Blake, you have mentioned that his poem in the Auguries of Innocence *is comparable in principle to the theme of the* Gaṇḍavyūha Sūtra. *How closely did his vision approach that of the* Gaṇḍavyūha, *and what particular circumstances or abilities led him to develop such a vision? Did he have access to any concentration or meditation practices, or did he develop any such methods himself?*

As far as I know, Blake never engaged in anything comparable to meditation practice, but we must not forget that he was an artist, and an artist does concentrate very intensely. He also had a natural visionary faculty, and a very positive attitude towards life in a highly elevated sense. How he got the idea of the world in a grain of sand it is impossible to say. Perhaps he just saw things like that, just as he saw the angel in the tree. Perhaps the things he wrote about came directly from his personal experience, even though he was well-versed in the alternative traditions of his day. He seems to have been an unusually gifted person almost from birth.

Much as I admire Blake, however, it seems to me that his vision does not really go very far towards that of the *Avataṁsaka Sūtra*. But you might find the *Avataṁsaka Sūtra* quite overwhelming and baffling; Blake, being more accessible, might be more useful to you. The only way to find out would be to steep yourself in Blake's writings for a while, then do the same with the *Avataṁsaka Sūtra*, and see how you felt. Perhaps you would have a sense of a deeper understanding of things through reading the *Avataṁsaka Sūtra*, or on the other hand you might feel out of your depth, and get more from reading Blake. Perhaps we do need such bridges and links from our own tradition to prepare us spiritually and even intellectually for the Buddhist texts. Without this preparation the deeper insights of Buddhism may remain for us just matters of philosophy in the narrow intellectual sense, with no real bearing on our own lives.

•

You say that there is an urge to Enlightenment which is immanent in all life, and which becomes self-conscious in the Bodhisattva. Is there some conflict between that urge to Enlightenment and the ego's habitual resistance to new experience?—You mention this in The Religion of Art.[16] *It seems to me that much of my behaviour, and that of those with whom I study the Dharma, is motivated more by the ego's resistance than by the urge to Enlightenment. How do we encourage the urge to Enlightenment to become our dominant motivation?*

We know that life on this planet has evolved from lower to higher levels, so we are probably justified in speaking of an urge to progress in this way. A being may not necessarily want to evolve, but it may be virtually forced to in order to survive. This applies to species in the collective sense, and it is similar on the human level. We have an urge to reach higher levels, perhaps produced through the force of circumstances, but at the same time the whole of our past and present experience is holding us back. In the case of the ordinary, worldly person, the urge to progress to a higher level has not become conscious in the individual sense; he or she just goes along with the general tide of humanity. In some people, however, there develops a partly conscious urge to go beyond, to achieve something better. This urge is usually vague and unsure to start with, but the more it develops, the more conflict there is between that immanent urge to grow and the resistance that your being as it already is puts up to further development.

We could perhaps divide people into three categories. There are the Stream-Entrants[17] for whom there is no real conflict. Yes, they may have problems to resolve, but they cannot slip back. At the other end of the scale there are people who are not yet individuals, but just group members who will grow if the group grows but not otherwise. In between are those who have developed some glimmering of individuality, and therewith some individual aspiration to reach a higher level of development. They can be pulled forward by that ideal, but also pulled back by the group working through their own group nature, or their 'ego', as you term it.

The function of the teacher, or spiritual friend, is to encourage individuality and responsibility, to try to detach the nascent individual from the overwhelming influence of the group, and encourage everything in him or her that leads away from the group. That may mean encouraging them to meditate, to develop positive emotions, to free themselves from neurotic and dependent relationships, to go on retreats, to live in a single-sex community, to be open with other people, or many other things, depending on the person and the circumstances. You need to be careful not to develop a formula and apply it to everybody; you should try to respond to the person's actual needs, and help them along the path they have already started to follow, if that is a path leading to growth and development. It feels good to get people going along exactly your own path, but perhaps they need to do things differently. You need to get to know someone quite well to know what their needs are and see clearly what step they need to take next. If you do not think in terms of leading or guiding the other person, but just in terms of being a good friend to them, everything else will grow out of that.

•

You contrast the image of the sixteen-year-old youth, the Bodhisattva, with the battered old monk who is the Arhat, suggesting that the youth symbolizes the ideal in the abstract, whereas the old man symbolizes the ideal in terms of historical limitations. Does that mean that it is impossible to have the fully mature altruism of the Bodhisattva Ideal in concrete historical circumstances?
The Bodhisattva is not young as distinct from being old, but eternally young, which means that the youthfulness of the Bodhisattva represents something outside time and space. In the case of the Arhat, it is scarcely possible to speak of someone as eternally old (unless you think of God the Father, the Ancient of Days), so the Arhat is not just somebody who is old, but somebody who has become old—at least, this is my way of interpreting it. I regard the beautiful, youthful figure of the Bodhisattva as representing the transcendental spiritual ideal as it exists outside space and time, and the Arhat is that same ideal incorporated within the historical process, manifesting under the conditions of space and time.

The very fact of those conditions means that the ideal cannot manifest fully. Even if you have realized that the eternally youthful Bodhisattva represents you as a human being, can you manifest that spiritual ideal fully in your life? Your life has only a certain length, and you have only two arms, two legs, and one pair of hands. There is so much to do, and so much that you cannot do. So within the historical process the ideal cannot actually be manifested fully by any individual, not even by the Buddha. The historical Buddha died. To manifest the ideal fully he would have had to go on living for ever and ever, and living everywhere. A limitation is automatically imposed if you are existing under the conditions of space and time, as an ordinary human being. This is what the Arhat represents, and this is why I speak of him as being a bit battered and bowed. The ideal is there but—from the particular point of view I adopt here—it is there as manifested under the conditions of space and time.

The Mahāyāna usually paints a picture of the Arhat as the spiritual individualist. Is that what you are saying?
No, I am adopting a different point of view, leaving aside the traditional

Mahāyāna way of looking at the Arhat, except in terms of iconography. I am looking at the iconography afresh, and asking myself what it is saying. What does it mean to juxtapose the figures of the Bodhisattvas and the Arhats? In the Christian context, what does it mean to juxtapose these beautiful, youthful angels and these old, emaciated saints? To me, the one is the ideal existing outside time towards which one is striving all the time, and the other is the same ideal as limited by space and time, struggling to express itself despite these limitations. You can see it shining through. Sometimes although the poor old Arhat or saint is so worn down, old and wrinkled, at the same time there is something of the youthful expression of the Bodhisattva there. This is not of course the way the Arhat is viewed within the Mahāyāna tradition, but my own particular interpretation.

The contrast reminds me of the distinction between the different kāyas *of a Buddha.*[18]
Yes. The *sambhogakāya* represents the ideal of Buddhahood as existing without any limitations. The *dharmakāya* takes that process a step further; the limitations disappear to such an extent that the Buddha himself disappears, because even the notion 'Buddha' is a limitation in respect of the ultimate spiritual ideal.

•

I am aware of how much fear affects my behaviour and inhibits me from making contact with other people. Fear seems to affect other people in this way too. Does this explain the emphasis on fearlessness in the list of the things that the Bodhisattva gives?
The Bodhisattva's giving of fearlessness seems to suggest that people are badly in need of it. Fear is produced by a sense of separateness, or ego, for want of a better term. You should not be surprised to experience fear in all sorts of situations. It is just an indication of the fact that you experience yourself as a self, as an ego; whenever you experience yourself in that way there is the possibility of fear. Until you have transcended the sense of separateness there will be fear, because you are bound to be afraid of whatever threatens you. The gift of fearlessness is therefore ultimately the gift of Insight into egolessness, and this is why it is so important. It could even be called an aspect of the gift of the Dharma, in the sense of some actual experience of Insight, not just the words of the Dharma.

Fearlessness is placed between culture and the Dharma in the list of the Bodhisattva's gifts. Is that significant?
Well, fearlessness comes after the gift of culture because it is beyond culture. But if 'the gift of the Dharma' means the Dharma in its fullest sense, I would say that the gift of fearlessness is included in that. Perhaps the two gifts can be distinguished, because whereas the gift of the Dharma is verbal, fearlessness is communicated directly in terms of personality: you give fearlessness to others by being fearless yourself.

Does that mean being egoless yourself?
Yes, exactly. Being brave is something different. Bravery is acting as though you are not afraid even though you are, something we often have to do if we can't manage anything better. It is to some extent a spiritual quality to be able to act as though you are not afraid when you are, because it means that to some extent you have transcended the ego feeling. You are not allowing the fear—the ego sense—to dominate you completely. You may not be able to stop it affecting your emotional experience, but at least you are not letting it affect your behaviour too much.

There are specific practices which address craving and hatred. Would it be useful to address fear in the same sort of way?
Fear would seem not to be a primary emotion in the way that greed and hatred are. In a way, fear is included in them. But there *are* some specific practices for eliminating fear, like the Vajrayāna practices which involve going to meditate in the cremation ground at night. People sometimes keep skulls and bones around them as a reminder, although you can become hardened to their presence, if you are not careful, so that they become mere objects which do not produce any effect.

Perhaps from time to time you should expose yourself to situations of which you are rather afraid. Take the example of giving a talk for the first time. You feel reluctant and nervous. You are afraid of failing, afraid of what other people will say, afraid of making a fool of yourself. But you get over that first experience, and the time comes when you can deliver a talk without any experience of fear at all. And that indicates that the ego has been overcome, at least to some extent.

•

What is the source of the story about the famine, the old man, and the young man?

I think I may have adapted it from a story told to me by a bhikkhu friend in India, so it is semi-traditional.

It is fifteen years since you gave this talk, and during that time the Theravāda has been taught more widely in the West. Would you modify the parable in any way if you were to tell it now? Is there more proselytizing on the part of the Hīnayāna these days?
Things *have* changed over the last few years, partly because Buddhists from different schools have had more contact with each other, at least in the West, and partly because of certain political and cultural events, like the fact that so many Tibetan Buddhists have left Tibet.

But proselytization is not necessarily indicative of a Bodhisattva attitude; indeed, the word itself is slightly pejorative in the same kind of way as 'Hīnayāna'. Very often Buddhist monks and teachers from all Buddhist countries tend to spread just their own culture. Their motives are religio-nationalistic rather than purely spiritual, so their proselytizing cannot really be classified as an expression of Bodhisattva-like outward-goingness.

In fact, in terms of attitudes towards the propagation of Buddhism in the modern world, there is not really much difference between any of the schools, regardless of what they call themselves. They have all got some representatives, whether monastic or lay, who have a genuine feeling for other people and wish to share the Dharma with them, whether they are teaching it in Theravāda, Tibetan, or Zen terms. And I am quite sure that in all the major schools and traditions there are at least a few people who have some spiritual experience, some inner strength, and who go out to others with the Dharma on that basis, just as there are also those who are anxious to gather disciples, or spread their own national Buddhist culture, or even just rake in the money. The important thing to realize is that you can only really go out to others spiritually when you have something to give. It is unwise for any Buddhist to go out to teach others just because he or she feels like it. Your outward-goingness must be a natural expression of your spiritual experience and spiritual strength.

So do you think this difference between a Hīnayāna attitude and a Mahāyāna attitude is mainly a question of spiritual maturity? Is it the case that, whichever school you follow, you will reach a point of spiritual maturity on the basis of which you will want to go out to people?
I think that is true, but there is far greater traditional support for one in that position within the Mahāyāna, in the historical sense, than within

the Hīnayāna. In the oldest Pali texts, which speak of the Buddha's own example, there is the same outward-going basis, at least in principle, that is found in the Mahāyāna. Many Buddhist schools in Theravāda countries, however, do not go back that far, so their followers do not get the support for going out to others that a Mahayanist in a similar position would have. The Bodhisattva Ideal is certainly known in Theravāda countries, but it is an exception to the rule, whereas in Mahāyāna countries it is the rule for spiritual life.

But we must not allow ourselves to be misled by labels. Someone may be teaching the Dharma on the basis of the Pali scriptures, but their teaching may not necessarily be a narrowly Hinayanistic form of Buddhism. In the same way, a lama may be teaching in terms of the Mahāyāna or the Vajrayāna, but he is not necessarily communicating a Mahayanistic or Vajrayanistic attitude. Often there is a correspondence, but equally often there is not. We must be able to read the real message that is being conveyed, regardless of the particular language. You may meet a Theravāda bhikkhu who assures you that you should devote yourself entirely to your own salvation and Enlightenment, and not bother about other people, but he may be most kind and considerate towards you. On the other hand, you may meet a lama who recommends that you should devote yourself, as a Bodhisattva, to saving millions of human beings, but who is very selfish and self-centred in his own behaviour. One must not be misled by words or professions.

•

Obviously 'Hīnayāna' is a pejorative term. What did the Hīnayāna schools call themselves?
Oddly enough, they seem not to have used a collective term to describe themselves. Each Hīnayāna school—the Theravāda, the Sarvāstivāda, the Mūlasarvāstivāda, the Mahāsaṅghikas, and the Bahuśrutīyas—seems to have thought of itself just as that school, so that they had no collective designation to distinguish themselves from the Mahāyāna. Perhaps they just thought of themselves as 'the Buddhist schools'.

Do you think they identified themselves with each other as having certain factors in common at the time, or has that become clear in retrospect?
There must have been some sense of solidarity. They do seem to have been aware that they differed from the Mahāyāna, and from the evidence we have it would seem that they quite consciously refused to accept the Mahāyāna sutras as the word of the Buddha. As they did not use any

collective term, and as we cannot use 'Theravāda' in all circumstances—because the doctrines of the various schools differed—we must make do with the rather uncomfortable word Hīnayāna, even though we are well aware of its limitations and slightly pejorative character.

From a broader point of view, the terms Hīnayāna and Mahāyāna really represent attitudes rather than a particular doctrinal school. How can you say that a Tibetan Buddhist who does not really care for teaching the Dharma to other sentient beings is a Mahayanist, even though he may be well versed in what is technically Mahāyāna teaching? If a bhikkhu from Thailand or Sri Lanka is very concerned with the welfare of others, and with spreading the Dharma, can you really describe him as a Hinayanist? He may be teaching what is traditionally regarded as Hīnayāna doctrine in its Theravāda form, but his attitude is thoroughly Mahayanistic. It is better to try to use these terms Hīnayāna, Mahāyāna, and Vajrayāna in such a way that they become descriptive of attitudes.

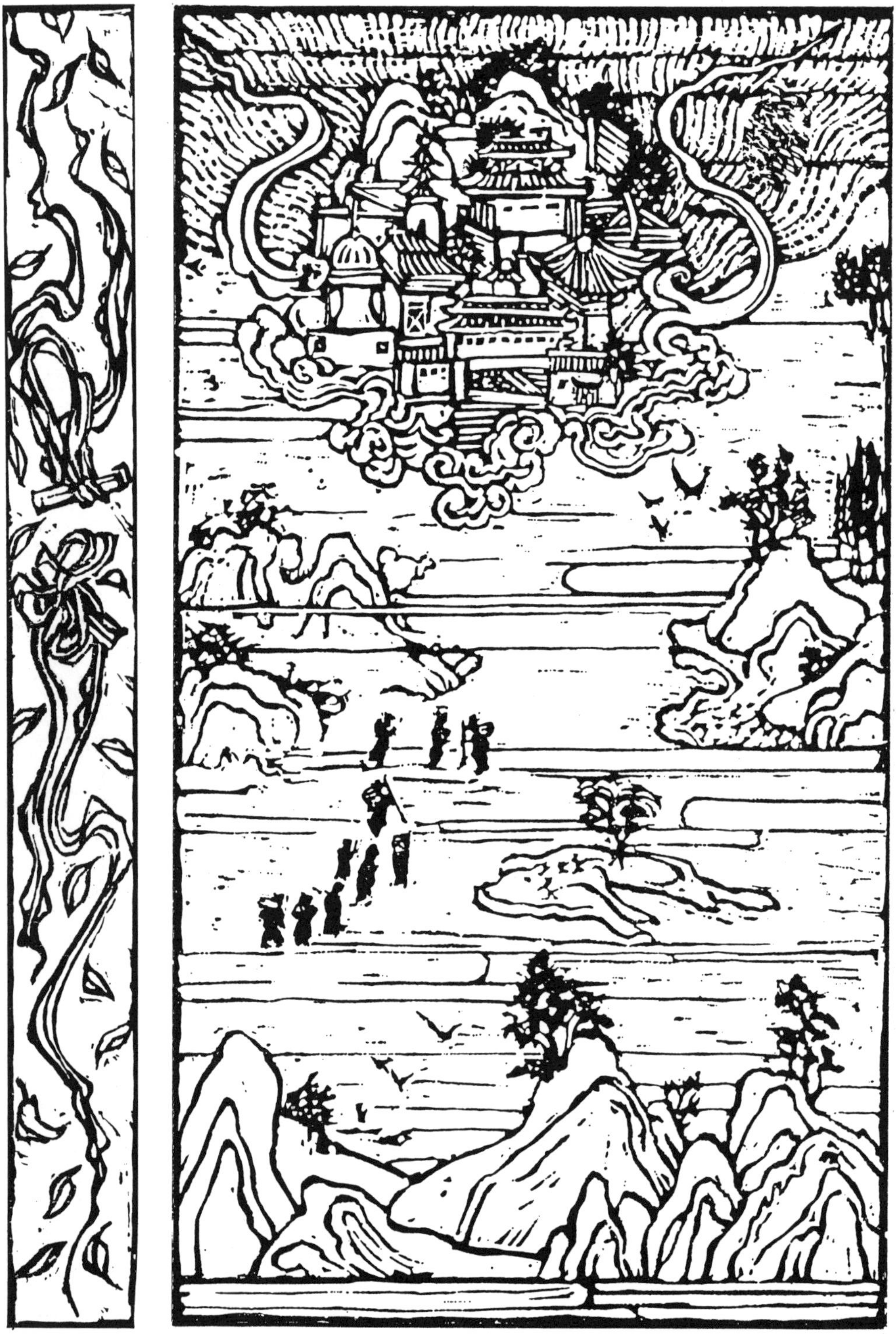

Chapter Two

THE DRAMA OF COSMIC ENLIGHTENMENT

To give a brief idea of what we are concerned with in the *White Lotus Sutra* I have chosen to call it the Drama of Cosmic Enlightenment. But in its own symbolic terms, the title of the sutra, if we attend carefully to it, speaks for itself. It's as though the sutra is bursting with symbolism to the extent that even its title—*Saddharma-Puṇḍarīka Sūtra* in the original Sanskrit—is symbolic. Before we start investigating the symbols within the sutra, then, let's have a look at what the title might mean.

Saddharma is usually translated 'good law' or 'good doctrine'—the doctrine of course being the teaching of the Buddha—but this translation isn't really good enough. *Sat* or *sad* comes from a Sanskrit root which means 'to exist', so it means something more like 'true' or 'real', 'genuine' or 'authentic'. In the same way, although we may be used to translating *Dharma* as 'doctrine' or 'teaching', it is more accurately rendered 'truth', or even 'the ultimate nature of things'. Taking the two together, then, the essential meaning of *saddharma* is 'the real truth', and this is how we can best translate it. Incidentally, the same goes for the Pali equivalent *saddhamma*, which occurs many times in the *Dhammapada*.

Puṇḍarīka means 'lotus' or, more specifically, 'white lotus'. Although we have only one word in English which has to make do for lotuses of all colours, in Sanskrit lotuses of different colours have different names. So we have 'the white lotus of the real truth'. What does this title suggest? Lotuses usually grow in muddy ponds; but although the plants grow in the mud, the flowers bloom out of the water, so that their petals are pure and unstained. Because of this, the lotus has become a symbol of purity—purity in the midst of impurity. It has come to symbolize the presence of the Unconditioned in the midst of the conditioned—if you like, the presence of the spiritual in the midst of the worldly—unstained by the conditions in which it appears. So the title of the sutra is suggesting that although the real truth appears in the midst of the world, it is not tainted by any worldly considerations.

The word *sūtra* is the most common term for a Buddhist scripture, so that Buddhists refer to the sutras just as Christians might speak of the Bible. But although it tends to be used so generally, *sūtra* has a specific meaning. It comes from a word meaning 'a thread', so it suggests a number of topics strung together on a common thread of discourse. The form of a sutra is almost always the same. First you get a description of where the discourse was given, what was going on, and who was present. That is followed by the main body of the text, which usually consists of a teaching of the Dharma, the real truth, by the Buddha himself. The sutra then ends with an account of the effect of the Buddha's teaching on the people listening.

In some sutras, although the Buddha is present, he stays in the background and one of his disciples speaks, in which case the text ends with the Buddha giving his approval to what the disciple has said, thus making the discourse his own, as it were. Sometimes, especially in Mahāyāna sutras, it is not even a question of the Buddha giving his approval. A disciple may be doing the actual speaking, but he speaks under the direct inspiration of the Buddha, so that in truth the Buddha is speaking through him. But however it is spoken, it is important to understand that whatever is said in the body of a sutra is not just issuing from the ordinary level of consciousness. It isn't something that has been worked out intellectually. It isn't a proof or an explanation of something in the mundane sense. It is a truth, a message, even a revelation, issuing from the depths of the Enlightened consciousness, the depths of the Buddha nature. This is the essential content of any Buddhist scripture, and this is its purpose: to communicate the nature of Enlightenment and show the way leading to its realization.

So we can translate the complete title of this particular communication of the Enlightened mind as 'the Scripture of the White Lotus (or if you like the Transcendental Lotus) of the Real Truth'. We could scarcely hope to convey in English all the associations of the Sanskrit words, so the translation is only approximate, but it will do.

As a literary document, the *White Lotus Sutra*—to revert to the short version of the title—belongs to the first century of the Christian era, that is, five hundred years after the death of the Buddha. But although we know when the sutra was first written down, this, of course, does not give us any clue as to when it was first composed. It is hard for us to imagine, but for practically the whole of that first five-hundred year period the Buddha's teaching was passed on by word of mouth. Not a word of it was written down. Indeed, there is no evidence that the Buddha himself *could* read and write. In those days writing was not a very respectable accomplishment. Corrupt businessmen who wanted to keep a record of their international transactions might write things down, but it was not a proper occupation for religious people. So the Buddha just used to teach in the form of discourses, and people would listen to what he had to say, commit it to memory, and then repeat it to their own disciples. In this way the teachings of Buddhism—and of Hinduism too—were passed on from generation to generation, like the lighted torch passed from one runner to another at the start of the Olympic Games.

But eventually Indian Buddhists did start to write down the Buddha's teachings. We don't really know why. Perhaps memories had grown weaker since the Buddha's day. Perhaps people didn't feel so confident, and felt there was a danger that the teachings would be lost if they were not written down. Or perhaps reading and writing had become more respectable, so that it was natural to make the teachings available in written form. But whatever the reason, in the first century CE[19] there was a general writing down of the teachings, and the *White Lotus Sutra* was among the teachings that became scriptures—'scripture' literally meaning a written document—at that time.

The teachings of Buddhism were written down in various languages—Sanskrit, Pāli, Prākrit, Apabhraṁsa, Paiśāci, and so on—and the *White Lotus Sutra* was one of the first to be written down in Sanskrit. But although Sanskrit is the language of ancient India, it doesn't necessarily follow that India was where the text was first written down. By this time Buddhism, especially Mahāyāna Buddhism, had spread into central Asia, and it may have been there that the *White Lotus Sutra* was first recorded. After all, we know that the Pali scriptures originated from Sri Lanka, not India, at around the same time. But wherever the *White Lotus Sutra* was written down, it was written in a mixture of two kinds of Sanskrit: 'Pure' Sanskrit and 'Buddhist Hybrid' Sanskrit. Pure Sanskrit follows the rules laid down by the grammarian Pāṇini, so it is sometimes called Paninian Sanskrit. Buddhist Hybrid Sanskrit (sometimes simply called Mixed Sanskrit) is Sanskrit mixed with Prakritisms to produce a less 'correct', more colloquial language.

So the sutra is written in a combination of these two kinds of Sanskrit. It also combines prose and verse, the prose being in Pure, Paninian, Sanskrit and the poetry in Hybrid Sanskrit. This already makes the text quite distinctive. What makes it curious, not to say odd, from a literary point of view, is its structure. The prose and verse come alternately—first you get a prose passage of a few pages, and then comes a passage in verse. The curious thing is that the verse passage repeats almost exactly what has just been said in prose (with a few contractions and expansions). Some scholars would have it that the verse sections are older than the prose, but there's no real proof of that. The whole work, both prose and verse, is divided into twenty-seven chapters, or twenty-eight in some versions—and makes quite a substantial volume.

The original texts of many Buddhist scriptures have been lost, but in the case of the *White Lotus Sutra* we are fortunate. Copies were discovered in the nineteenth century, and there have been more recent discoveries too—in Nepal, where several copies were unearthed, in the sands of the desert of central Asia, and in Kashmir, where copies were found only a few decades ago. There are also ancient translations of the work into Chinese, Tibetan, and other languages. The standard Chinese translation is the work of Kumārajīva, one of the greatest of all Buddhist translators and scholars, who lived in the fourth and fifth centuries CE, during the T'ang dynasty, a time when Buddhism was thriving in China. For hundreds of years Kumārajīva's translation exerted an influence on Chinese culture comparable to that of the Authorized Bible on English culture, and it is still considered by the Chinese to be a masterpiece of their classical literature. And as well as making such an impact on the literary world, Kumārajīva's great achievement also inspired many Chinese artists, resulting in the development of a whole tradition of illustrating well-known scenes from the sutra.

Until fairly recently, only one complete translation of the sutra had been published in English. This was the work of the Dutch scholar Henrich Kern, published in the Sacred Books of the East series in 1884, and still in print. As this was the first translation, and as in those days people didn't know the real meaning of a number of important Buddhist technical terms, it isn't surprising that Kern's version is less than perfect, although it is very good for its time. It's rather unimaginative, and it contains some extremely odd footnotes. For one thing, the translator seems to be obsessed by the idea that the whole of Buddhism can be explained in terms of astronomy. He also tries to make out that nirvana is quite literally equivalent to the state of physical extinction: Enlightenment equals death, in other words. Very odd. A much more readable, although incomplete, version of the sutra became available in 1930 in the form of a translation of Kumārajīva's Chinese text made by Bunnō Katō and revised by Professor William Soothill, an English missionary who lived for a time in China. Although Soothill was a Christian, he does succeed in conveying the devotional fervour and the spiritual mood of the original text.[20]

The first sentence of the text is translated in the same way in whatever version you read. Indeed, the opening words are the hallmark of any Buddhist sutra, and the English translation, with its distinctive, slightly antiquated form, has a sort of magic about it, like 'Once upon a time'. When we hear or read the words 'Thus have I heard' (*evam mayā śrutam* in Sanskrit), we know at once that a teaching of the Buddha is to follow. But who has 'heard'? Who is the speaker? According to tradition it is Ānanda. Ānanda was the Buddha's cousin, his disciple, and for twenty years his constant attendant and travelling companion. And Ānanda is said to be the principal source of the oral tradition. We are told that his memory was so good that he was able to remember almost word for word whatever the Buddha said, and pass it on to the other disciples. If he happened to be out on an errand when the Buddha gave a teaching, he would get the Buddha to repeat it to him so that he had stored away in his memory a collection of everything that the Buddha had ever said.

I must confess that when I first came into contact with Buddhism, I did tend to wonder whether such a thing was possible. But during my twenty years in India, I certainly did meet both Indians and Tibetans who could reel off hundreds and hundreds of pages of scriptures by heart. And later, when I came back to England, I got to know somebody with a memory almost like a tape recorder. He would say, 'On the eighth of July three years ago, you said…' and would proceed to reel off, word for word, exactly what I had said—the order in which I had touched on certain topics, the logical stages of the argument, all the illustrations I had used, everything—together with the time of day and the circumstances. So I thought to myself, 'If it is possible for someone in London in the twentieth century to have such a phenomenal memory, no doubt it was possible in ancient India too', and I became convinced that the Buddha did have in Ānanda someone with this extraordinary capacity to remember discourses and conversations.

But although these words, 'Thus have I heard', have a literal, historical significance, they also suggest something more esoteric. In reality, the Buddha is not outside us. The Buddha nature is not outside us, but within us—'This very body the Buddha', as the Zen tradition has it.[21] And we could say that there's not just an Ānanda outside, in the realm of history; there's also an Ānanda inside us. And just as the historical Ānanda listened to the Buddha, so the Ānanda inside us hears the voice of truth within. Ānanda, we could say, is our own ordinary mind listening to the utterance of our own Enlightened consciousness. It's as though within us we have two consciousnesses, a lower one and a higher one. The lower consciousness usually ignores the higher one and goes its own way, or maybe doesn't even know that the higher one exists. But if that lower consciousness just stops and listens for a while, if it is receptive, it becomes aware of the voice of the higher consciousness. Like Ānanda listening to the voice of the Buddha, our ordinary mind can be receptive to the higher mind, the Enlightened mind, within us. Taking this line of thought a bit further, we can say that the whole drama of cosmic Enlightenment takes place not only without, on the stage of the cosmos, but also within, in the recesses of our own heart.

Although the opening words of the sutra may be very familiar, once we are past them we find ourselves in a very unfamiliar world indeed. The world of the Mahāyāna sutra is almost the kind of thing you find in science fiction, on a more spiritual, transcendental level. So before we delve into the parables, myths, and symbols of the sutra, we need an introduction to this strange world. You probably won't make much sense of it, and I'm afraid I'm not going to offer much help. I'm just going to relate some of the events described in the sutra and leave them to make their own effect, however strange, however bizarre, however unintelligible. For your part, just read it like a story. And whatever you do, don't think. Don't try to work it all out. Don't ask yourself what it all means. Just let your mind stop ticking and take it all in. If you want to set your intellect to work on it, you can do that later on. For the moment, just absorb the content of the sutra as though you were watching a film in the darkness. This is something transcendentally surrealistic, and you really haven't a hope of working it all out, so just let your rational mind go to sleep for a while and allow the pictures to have their effect.—And don't be afraid of allowing yourself to feel.

The sutra opens on the Vulture's Peak. In geographical terms, the Vulture's Peak is an enormous rocky crag where the Buddha used to stay when he wanted to get away from it all. From there he could see for many miles around. In those days he would have been able to see, far in the distance, the tens of thousands of roofs of Rājagṛiha, the capital city of Magadha, which was one of the great kingdoms of northern India at that time. But there are no roofs there now. You can still visit the Vulture's Peak, and it still commands a magnificent view, but there is no city any more. All you can see is dense leopard-inhabited jungle, and here and there a few ancient Buddhist, Jain, and even prehistoric Cyclopean ruins.

Symbolically speaking, the Vulture's Peak represents the summit of earthly existence. Go beyond it, and you're in the world of the transcendental, the world of the purely spiritual. So when the sutra describes the Buddha as seated on the Vulture's Peak, it is placing him half way between heaven and earth. And he is surrounded there by tens of thousands of disciples of various kinds. We are told that there are twelve thousand Arhats, those who have reached nirvana in the Hīnayāna sense of the destruction of passions, without positive knowledge and illumination. Then there are eighty thousand Bodhisattvas, and also tens of thousands of gods and other non-human beings with their retinues.

And we are told that the Buddha delivers to this huge assembly a great discourse on infinity, a very popular Buddhist topic. He speaks eloquently for a long time, and everybody is deeply moved. Indeed, the effect of the Buddha's teaching is such that beautiful flowers of many colours start raining down from the heavens, and the whole universe shakes and trembles in six different ways. Then, having finished his discourse, the Buddha enters into deep meditation; and while he is meditating, there comes forth from a spot between his eyebrows a brilliant ray of pure white light. It's like a great searchlight sweeping all around the universe so that it is possible to see hundreds of millions of miles into the depths of space. In that intense light innumerable world systems are discovered in all the directions of space. And in every world system can be seen much the same thing as is going on in this one: a Buddha preaching, surrounded by disciples, and Bodhisattvas practising the six great disciplines.

So this is the spectacle revealed by the ray of light which issues from the Buddha as he sits there meditating. Naturally the great assembly is astonished, and everybody wonders what it means, and what is going to happen. The Bodhisattva Maitreya, the future Buddha, as he is sometimes called, enquires of Mañjuśrī, who is the wisest of the Bodhisattvas, traditionally regarded as the incarnation of Wisdom, 'What is going on? What does this great occurrence signify?' And Mañjuśrī says, 'I believe—in fact I'm sure—it means that the Buddha is about to proclaim the *White Lotus Sutra*.'

And as Mañjuśrī says this, the Buddha slowly emerges from his meditation. He opens his eyes and says, as though speaking to himself, 'The Truth in its fullness is very difficult to understand.' So difficult is it, he says, that only the Buddhas, only the fully Enlightened ones, are able to understand it. Only they, *and no one else*, can understand the Truth in its fullness (which may be a salutary reflection for us). Everybody else, the Buddha tells the assembly, has to approach the truth gradually, step by step; and the Buddha takes this into account in his teaching. He takes people by the hand and leads them one step at a time. First he teaches the Arhat Ideal of gaining nirvana in the sense of the extinction of passions, and only then, when that has been achieved and understood, does he expound the higher, more Mahayanistic ideal of the realization of perfect Buddhahood through following the career of the Bodhisattva.

If he revealed the highest truth all at once, the Buddha goes on to explain, people would be so terrified that they would be unable to receive and assimilate it. Incidentally, this is rather like what happens at the point of death, according to the *Tibetan Book of the Dead*. In that instant, Reality in its fullness dawns on the mind in one blinding flash. If the mind could bear it, that moment could be the dawning of Enlightenment itself, but it is too much for the mind to bear, and it just shrinks back, terrified, and falls to ever lower levels of reality until it finds a level where it feels at home. Because people are afraid of Reality in this way, although the Buddha knows the full Truth, he can't take the risk of revealing it to his disciples all at once. He has to take them so far and then show them the next stage, until eventually they reach the ultimate goal. On this occasion, he looks round the assembly and says that he's not sure whether even now everybody present is ready to hear what he has to say. For there is, he now reveals, something more for them to learn. Even the Arhats among them do not yet know the highest Truth.

This revelation provokes a dramatic incident. Five thousand of the disciples present simply get up and walk out. They murmur among themselves, 'Something more to learn? That's impossible. We're Enlightened, we've got nirvana. What more could there possibly be to learn? What is the Buddha talking about? Maybe he's getting a bit senile. Something more to learn?—not for us!' And with that they give the Buddha a perfunctory bow, just for old times' sake, and out they all go, shaking the dust of the assembly from their sandals.

This is a trap into which we can fall only too easily. Mistaking intellectual understanding for true knowledge, we can fool ourselves into thinking that there's no further to go, nothing more to learn. And of course as soon as we start thinking like that, we can't possibly learn any more. This is the biggest danger of all, and many people, like the five thousand disciples, succumb to it. I'm reminded of an episode in English religious history when Oliver Cromwell had dealings with a number of religious sectaries who got into a terrific argument over some knotty points of scripture. They were so obstinate, so immovable, that in the end Cromwell wrote to them, in desperation, 'Reverend Sirs, I beseech you, in the bowels of Christ, think it possible you may be mistaken.'[22]

In the sutra, however, the Buddha doesn't say anything; he just lets the disciples leave. And when they have gone, he simply says 'Now the assembly is quite pure.' In other words, now everyone present is receptive, prepared to consider that there may be something more for them to learn. So the Buddha goes on to reveal the highest Truth to this pure assembly. He tells them that his previous teaching of the three *yānas* is only provisional, an expedient made necessary by the diversity of temperaments among his disciples. Now these three *yānas* are not the Hīnayāna, the Mahāyāna, and the Vajrayāna. I'm afraid that in Buddhism we get lots of terms with double meanings. The *yānas* the Buddha is talking about here are a different set—consisting of the *śrāvakayāna* (the way of the disciple), the *pratyekabuddhayāna* (the way of the 'privately Enlightened' one), and the *bodhisattvayāna* (the way of the Bodhisattva).

I don't want to go into technicalities here[23]—it's more important to grasp the general principle that between them these three *yānas* symbolize different possible approaches to Enlightenment. The first two are different forms of spiritual individualism—the first perhaps being a bit more negative than the second—and the third is of course the Bodhisattva Ideal. When the Buddha says that his teaching of these three *yānas* was only provisional, he means—as he goes on to explain—that in reality there is only one way, *ekayāna*. This is the Great Way, the Mahāyāna, the way leading to perfect Buddhahood. All roads lead to Rome; all the *yānas*, all the different ways—individualistic and altruistic—are useful up to a point, but ultimately they all converge into *the* Way. In other words, there is only one process of Higher Evolution, and all participate in it to the extent that they make an effort to develop. The Buddha tells the assembly that if anyone offers even a flower with faith and devotion, they are already—in principle—on the path to Buddhahood. One thing leads to another. A small act of faith leads to a bigger act of faith, a small practice of the Way leads to a bigger practice, and in this manner, step by step, you gradually begin to tread the Great Way, the one way leading to perfect Enlightenment. There is no good deed, no humanitarian act, that falls outside the scope of the Way.

On hearing this teaching Śāriputra, the oldest and wisest of the Buddha's disciples, is filled with joy. Although he is old, he is prepared to learn. His only regret, he says, is that he has spent so long at a lower level of understanding. But the Buddha encourages him, and tells him that at a time in the distant future he too will realize supreme Enlightenment as a perfect Buddha. He even tells him what his name will be. But not all the disciples are like Śāriputra. Some of them are rather disturbed and perplexed by the new teaching. Have they been wasting their time? Was the old practice completely useless? What should they do next?

To reassure them, the Buddha tells the first of the great parables of the sutra, the parable of the burning house. And we see here for the first time the effect of symbolism. Four leading elders who were still in doubt after hearing the Buddha's abstract statement of the higher teaching are now convinced. They now realize that they can go beyond the stage of eradication of negative emotions, and proceed to positive illumination, supreme Knowledge, Wisdom, Enlightenment … and they are overjoyed. One of them, Mahākāśyapa, gives expression to their joy by telling a parable on their behalf, the parable—or myth—of the return journey.

When the parable has been told, the Buddha praises the four elders, and proceeds to shed more light on the way he leads sentient beings to Enlightenment. We already know that he teaches step by step, holding back the highest truth until his disciples are ready to hear it. Now we learn that he also adapts his teaching to suit the varying capacities of different people. To illustrate this, he tells two more parables: the parable of the rain-cloud and the parable of the sun. He follows the parables by predicting that Mahākāśyapa and the other elders will also become perfect Buddhas, even announcing what their names will be.

Then, turning from the future to the past, and once more addressing the whole assembly, the Buddha tells them about another Buddha, a Buddha who lived millions and millions of years before his own time. The Buddha tells the story because the career of this Buddha in some respects paralleled his own. The majority of the followers of this Buddha, too, had followed the Hīnayāna path of the Arhat. Only sixteen of them—they were his own sons from the period before he became a monk—had aspired to perfect Buddhahood as Bodhisattvas. But sooner or later, the Buddha says, all the followers of this Buddha would enter the Great Way, the Mahāyāna. To illustrate this, the Buddha tells the parable of the magic city—and as we will not be looking at this parable in depth, I will recount it briefly here.

A party of travellers is bound for a place called Ratnadvīpa ('the Place of Jewels'), and has employed a guide to show them the way through the dense forest. It is a very difficult, dangerous road, and long before they have reached their destination the travellers become exhausted, and say to their guide 'We can't go another step. Let's all go back.' But the guide thinks 'That would be a pity. They've come so far already. What can I do to persuade them to keep going?' Well, apparently the guide has some sort of magic power, because what he does is conjure up a magic city. He says to the travellers, 'Look! There's a city right here in front of us. Let's rest there and have something to eat, and then we'll decide what to do next.' The travellers, of course, are only too pleased to stop and have a rest. They have a meal and spend the night in the magic city, and in the morning they feel much better, and decide that they will carry on with their journey after all. So the guide makes the magic city disappear and leads the travellers on to their destination, the Place of Jewels.[24]

The meaning of the parable is not hard to fathom in the context of the sutra. The guide is of course the Buddha, and the travellers are the disciples. The Place of Jewels is supreme Enlightenment, and the magic city is the Hīnayāna nirvana—nirvana as the comparatively negative state of freedom from passions, without positive spiritual illumination. And, as the parable suggests, the Buddha first of all speaks in terms of nirvana in the ordinary psychological sense. Only when this teaching has been assimilated—only when the disciples have rested in the magic city—does he lead them on to the higher spiritual goal of perfect Buddhahood, the Place of Jewels.

We could use the same parable to describe the process of teaching meditation. When people first come along to learn to meditate, they quite often ask 'What is the goal of meditation?' You wouldn't usually reply, straight off, 'Well, the goal of meditation is to become like a Buddha', because that's the last thing most people want to be. They're not interested in anything religious or spiritual; they just want peace of mind in the midst of their everyday life and work. And it's perfectly true to say that meditation gives you peace of mind. But when they've been meditating for some time, and they start to experience peace of mind through meditation, then they might ask 'Well, is this all, or is there something more to meditation?' That would be the right time to say 'Yes, there is something more. Peace of mind in the ordinary psychological sense is not the final goal of meditation, but only an intermediate stage. Beyond it there's a spiritual goal—Enlightenment, knowledge of the Truth, knowledge of Reality—which in Buddhist terms is called perfect Buddhahood.' Here 'peace of mind' is the magic city in which the traveller is nourished and rested for the long journey to Enlightenment.

When the Buddha has told the parable of the magic city, we begin to see the effect of all these parables on the audience. More and more disciples come forward to confess their previously limited understanding and announce their acceptance of the new teaching. The Buddha predicts that the monk Pūrṇa, together with five hundred other distinguished Arhats, will gain supreme Enlightenment, and in their joy these Arhats also tell a parable, the parable of the drunkard and the jewel. More and more disciples are then predicted to perfect Buddhahood, and eventually all the Hīnayāna disciples are converted, and decide to aspire to supreme Enlightenment as Bodhisattvas.

There are, of course, thousands of Bodhisattvas already present, Bodhisattvas who have followed the Great Way from the beginning. The Buddha now turns to them, and impresses upon them that the *White Lotus Sutra* is tremendously important and must be preserved at all costs. The text should be read, recited, copied, expounded, and even ceremonially worshipped, the Buddha says. And all the Bodhisattvas promise to protect the sutra.

Then, suddenly, something extraordinary happens—extraordinary even by the standards of this extraordinary sutra. In the midst of the assembly, from the depths of the earth, there springs up a stupa, a colossal, unbelievably magnificent stupa which towers into the sky. A stupa is a monument which is made to contain the relics—fragments of bone and so on—of the Buddha or one of his disciples. Following a pre-Buddhistic practice, the first stupas were very simple—just a mound of earth, a sort of tumulus. But the stupa which appears out of the earth in the *White Lotus Sutra* is made not of brick, not of stone, not even of marble, but of the seven precious things—gold, silver, lapis lazuli, moonstone, agate, pearl, and carnelian. What is more, it is beautifully decorated with flags and flowers, and it is emitting light, fragrance, and music in all directions.

One can just imagine the scene. There are all these astonished disciples—only the Buddha isn't astonished—and this enormous stupa towering into the sky. And as they all gaze up at the stupa in amazement, from the midst of it there comes forth a thunderous voice which cries 'Excellent, excellent, Śākyamuni! You are well able to preach the *White Lotus Sutra*. All that you say is true.' (Śākyamuni of course is the Buddha, whom we can call 'our' Buddha because he appeared in our world.) At this the disciples are absolutely agog. What does it all mean? Whose is the voice? Whose is the stupa? So the Buddha explains that the stupa contains the preserved body of a very ancient Buddha called Abundant Treasures (*Prabhūtaratna* in Sanskrit), who lived millions upon millions of years ago. During his lifetime Abundant Treasures had made a vow that after his death, the stupa in which his remains were enshrined would spring forth wherever the *White Lotus Sutra* was being expounded. What is more, he had vowed that he himself would bear testimony to the truth of the teaching.

The whole assembly is very impressed by this explanation, and they ask if it isn't possible for the stupa to be opened so that they can see the body of this ancient Buddha, still miraculously preserved after millions of years. But Śākyamuni tells them that it's not as easy as all that. According to another vow which Abundant Treasures made, Śākyamuni has to fulfil a certain condition before the preserved body of the ancient Buddha can be seen. The condition is that Śākyamuni must summon into his presence all the Buddhas who have ever emanated from him, and who are now teaching the Doctrine throughout the universe. And at once Śākyamuni proceeds to fulfil the condition, so that the assembly's wish can be granted. Once more he sends out a great ray of light which reveals the Buddhas in all the universes in the ten directions of space. And at once those Buddhas understand that this is a signal, and tell their own Bodhisattvas 'Now I've got to go on a journey to the Sahā-world, millions of miles across the universe, because Buddha Śākyamuni has sent for me.'

In Buddhism, each Buddha-world, each universe, has got a name. Ours is called the Sahā-world, 'the world of endurance', because here there's a lot to be endured. According to the Buddhist scriptures, our world is not a particularly good one; there are lots of other worlds with Buddhas and Bodhisattvas where conditions are much better. So Śākyamuni doesn't want these incoming Buddhas to see the imperfection of his own little universe, and sets about preparing it for their arrival. He transforms the whole earth into brilliant blue light, like lapis lazuli, with golden cords stretching across it to mark off the blue ground into squares. Inside these squares, we're told, there spring up beautiful trees made entirely of jewels—trunk, branches, leaves, flowers, fruit—and thousands of feet tall. The earth, which is strewn with all sorts of heavenly flowers, smokes with sweet-smelling incense. And to complete the purification process, all the gods and men who are not part of the assembly are transferred somewhere—we're not told precisely where, but they're sort of bundled out of the way—and all the villages, towns and cities, mountains, rivers, and forests, disappear.

Hardly is this transformation completed when five hundred Buddhas arrive from the different directions of space, each accompanied by a great Bodhisattva, and take their seats on five hundred magnificent lion thrones under five hundred jewel trees. Such is the scale of things that they completely take up all the available space, and the Buddhas have barely begun to arrive. So Śākyamuni hastily purifies untold millions of worlds in all the directions of space, and they are all instantly occupied by streams of incoming Buddhas, who take their seats beneath jewel trees and pay their respects to the Buddha Śākyamuni by offering a double handful of jewel flowers.

Now that all these millions of Buddhas, with their attendant Bodhisattvas, are gathered together in one place, the condition laid down by Abundant Treasures has been fulfilled. So Śākyamuni floats up into the sky until he is level with the great door of the stupa, draws back the bolt, and flings open the door with a sound like thunder to reveal the body of Abundant Treasures within. And even though the body of the ancient Buddha is millions upon millions of years old, it is perfectly preserved, seated cross-legged within the stupa. Awe-struck at the sight, the assembly take up handfuls of jewel flowers and scatter them so that they rain down over the two Buddhas.

And it turns out that it is not just that Abundant Treasures's body has been perfectly preserved. The ancient Buddha is actually still alive after all these years, and he asks Śākyamuni to come and share his throne. So Śākyamuni goes to sit next to Abundant Treasures in the stupa—this deeply symbolic and significant scene became a favourite one with Chinese Buddhist artists. The whole assembly, looking up into the sky at the two Buddhas, desires to be raised up to the same level, so Śākyamuni exerts his supernormal powers and lifts all the assembly, all the millions of Buddhas and Bodhisattvas, up into the air until they are level with himself and Abundant Treasures.

At this point, Śākyamuni cries out in a loud voice 'Who among you is able to preach the *White Lotus Sutra* in the Sahā-world? The time of my death is at hand. To whom can I entrust the Lotus of the True Law?' There then follows a whole series of episodes—possibly added to the sutra after the main body of it was completed—which I am going to omit, partly for the sake of brevity, and partly because they rather break up the continuity of the action. After these diversions, two Bodhisattvas come forward in response to the Buddha's demand, and promise that they will preserve and spread the *White Lotus Sutra* after the Buddha's death. And all the Arhats who have been predicted to perfect Buddhahood give a similar pledge.

Attention now turns to two nuns who are present, standing a little to one side. These are Mahāprajāpatī, the Buddha's aunt and foster-mother, and Yaśodharā, his wife in the days before he left home, both of whom became nuns after the Buddha's Enlightenment, under his guidance. They are feeling rather sorrowful because nothing has so far been said about Enlightenment for them, but the Buddha assures them that they are sure of becoming perfectly Enlightened one day. In response, they too pledge to protect the *White Lotus Sutra*.

There are many irreversible Bodhisattvas in the assembly—'irreversible' in that they have gone so far on the path that they cannot fall back into lower states, and are irrevocably bound for perfect Buddhahood. They now announce that they are determined to make the *White Lotus Sutra* known throughout the whole universe, and they join the rest of the assembly in begging the Buddha to have no anxiety about the sutra's future, even in the dreadful days which lie ahead. A dark age is approaching, they say, a time of war and confusion, bloodshed and evil, but they tell the Buddha 'Do not worry. Even in the terrible age that is coming, we shall remember the teaching. We shall preserve it, we shall protect it, and we shall propagate it.'

We are swiftly made aware that the preservation of the sutra will be no easy task. The Bodhisattva Mañjuśrī comments that it is a tremendous responsibility, and the Buddha agrees, and goes on to list four qualities which the Bodhisattvas who want to fulfil this mission must have. First, they must be perfect in conduct. Second, they must confine themselves to 'proper spheres of activity'—which means that they must avoid unsuitable company and dwell inwardly in the true nature of Reality. Third, they must maintain happy, peaceful states of mind, unaffected by zeal or envy. And fourth, they must cultivate feelings of love towards all living beings. The Buddha explains these four qualities in some detail, and then tells another parable, the parable of the wheel-rolling king, or universal monarch. (A 'wheel-rolling' king is one who sets turning the wheel of the Dharma, that is, one who rules according to the Buddha's teaching.)

The story goes like this. There was once a king who went to war because he wished to extend his domain. His soldiers fought so heroically that the king was very pleased with them, and gave them all the rewards they deserved. He gave them houses, land, clothes, slaves, chariots, gold, silver, gems—in fact, everything he had in his palace. The only thing he didn't give away was the magnificent crest jewel that he wore in his own turban. Eventually, however, he was so pleased with the soldiers' bravery that he took the crest jewel itself and handed it over to them. So, as the Buddha goes on to explain, he himself is like the wheel-rolling king. Seeing the efforts that his disciples have made to practise his teachings, seeing how bravely they have fought against Māra, he rewards them with more and more teachings and blessings. In the end, keeping nothing back, he gives them the supreme teaching, the *White Lotus Sutra*.[25]

Having heard this parable, the great Bodhisattvas who have come from other world systems with their own Buddhas offer their services too. But Śākyamuni says 'No, your services are not necessary. I have innumerable Bodhisattvas here in my own Sahā-world, and they will protect the *White Lotus Sutra* after my death.' As he says this, the universe shakes and trembles, and from the space underneath the earth there issues an incalculable host of irreversible Bodhisattvas. One by one they salute in turn all the Buddhas present, and sing their praises. Although this takes an extraordinary length of time—fifty minor aeons, during which the whole assembly stays completely silent—it actually seems, through the power of the Buddha, as though only a single afternoon has passed.

When all the salutations and songs are over, the Buddha Śākyamuni and the four leaders of the great host of irreversible Bodhisattvas exchange greetings. The implication seems to be that Śākyamuni is claiming all these newly appeared Bodhisattvas as his own disciples. The assembly can scarcely believe it. The Buddha assures them 'Yes, these are indeed my own disciples, and they have been following the Great Way for a very long time. You haven't seen them before because they live under the earth.' But this isn't good enough for the perplexed disciples. They say 'Look here. You gained Enlightenment under the bodhi tree at Bodh Gaya only forty years ago. How can you possibly have trained such a fantastic number of Bodhisattvas in that time? A few hundred, a few thousand even, we could believe—but this many? And they seem to belong to past ages and to other world systems too. How can you possibly claim them all as your disciples? It's as ridiculous as a young man of twenty-five pointing to a crowd of wizened centenarians and saying that they are all his sons.'

The Buddha, of course, has a reply to all this scepticism. And this reply is a central revelation, as the Mahāyāna sees it, making this scene the climax of the whole drama of cosmic Enlightenment. The Buddha says that he did not really gain Enlightenment only forty years ago. In fact, he says, he gained Enlightenment an uncountable, incalculable number of millions of ages ago. In other words, he makes the rather staggering claim that he is eternally Enlightened. By now it is obvious that this is no longer the historical Śākyamuni speaking, but the universal, cosmic principle of Enlightenment itself. All these millions of ages, he says, he has been teaching and preaching in many different forms, and in many different worlds. He has appeared as Dīpaṅkara Buddha, Śākyamuni Buddha, and so on. He is not really born, does not really attain Enlightenment, does not really die, but only appears to do so, just to encourage people. If he stayed with them all the time, he says, people would not appreciate him or follow his teaching. And to illustrate this, he tells the parable of the good physician.

This great declaration that the Buddha is eternally Enlightened produces a tremendous effect on the assembly. Hosts of disciples attain various spiritual insights, powers, understandings, and blessings, while flowers, incense, and jewels rain down from the sky, celestial canopies are raised on high, and countless Bodhisattvas sing the praises of all the Buddhas—a display which provides an apt setting for the Buddha's next teaching. For he now explains that the development of faith in his eternal life, faith in the sense of an emotional response, is equivalent to the development of wisdom. Such faith, we may say, is wisdom expressed in emotional terms. If you have this sort of faith, you will see and hear the universal Buddha on the spiritual Vulture's Peak eternally preaching the *White Lotus Sutra*. What is more, the Buddha says, the merits of listening to the *White Lotus Sutra* are very great, and the merits of preaching it even greater—and of course it's very demeritorious to disparage the sutra in any way.

This warning introduces the episode of the Bodhisattva Never Direct. Never Direct, the Buddha says, was a Bodhisattva who lived millions of years ago. He used to go around saying to people 'It is not for me to direct you. You are free to do anything you like. But I would advise you to take up the Bodhisattva career so that ultimately you may become perfect Buddhas.' Now some of the people on the receiving end of this got very fed up with Never Direct. Why on earth should they want to become Buddhas? Many of them became so angry that they abused the Bodhisattva, hit him with sticks, pelted him with stones, and generally gave him a very rough time indeed. Nothing daunted, however, and not bearing his abusers any ill-will, Never Direct would just retreat to a safe distance and continue to cry out 'It is not for me to give you any direction. You will all become Buddhas.' This is how he got his nickname, Never Direct. Śākyamuni ends the story by saying that he himself was Never Direct in a previous life, and some of those who were his persecutors in those days are now his disciples.

At this point it's the turn of the irreversible Bodhisattvas from under the earth to speak. They also promise to protect the *White Lotus Sutra*, and say that they will preach it throughout the whole universe. Their promise sparks off all manner of marvels and wonders. The Buddha-fields in all the directions of space begin to shake and tremble, and all the inhabitants of those distant worlds look down into the Sahā-world and see it revealed, like looking down through the depths of the water and seeing something at the bottom. They see the Buddhas Śākyamuni and Abundant Treasures seated on their joint lotus throne in the middle of the stupa, and they see the countless millions of great Bodhisattvas.

Śākyamuni is joyfully hailed by all the gods, who shower down flowers, incense, and jewels which merge in a huge mass, like clouds massing together, and form a jewelled canopy which covers the whole sky. Marvel upon marvel takes place, until all the worlds in the universe are seen to reflect one another like millions of mutually reflecting mirrors, and interpenetrate one another like innumerable beams of intersecting coloured light. Eventually all these universes, with all their beings, all their Buddhas and Bodhisattvas, are fused into one harmonious Buddha-field, one cosmos wherein the principle of Enlightenment reigns supreme.

For one last time the Buddha extols the merits of the sutra, and reminds the assembly of the importance of preserving it and propagating it. Then he rises from his lion throne in the midst of the sky and places his right hand in blessing on the heads of the countless irreversible Bodhisattvas. At last, requesting the Buddhas present to return to their own domains, he says 'Buddhas, peace be upon you. Let the stupa of the Buddha Abundant Treasures be restored as before.' Everybody rejoices—and thus the great drama concludes.

Chapter Two

QUESTIONS AND ANSWERS

What is the symbolical significance of the name White Lotus Sutra? *Does the title relate to the content of the sutra? Most translators call it simply the* Lotus Sutra—*is this inexactitude?*

When you take the full title, *Saddharma-Puṇḍarīka Sūtra*, the emphasis needs to be on *Saddharma*. It is not just the Dharma, but the real Dharma, the true Dharma, because it contains a higher revelation in respect of the unity of the three *yānas*, and in respect of the eternity of the Buddha. I wouldn't like to say that calling it the *White Lotus* of the true Dharma was *just* a flowery addition, but Indian Buddhists were very fond of that kind of style—there is also the *Karuṇā-Puṇḍarīka Sūtra*, the White Lotus of Compassion Sutra.[26]

You can look at the symbolism of the lotus—that it blooms, that it grows out of the mud, and so on—but that can really be applied to any sutra, because any sutra represents the transcendental truth in that kind of way. So although no doubt you *could* give an exegesis of the title in such a way as to demonstrate the whole teaching of the sutra, in my view that would not originally have been intended to be the case. As I say, the emphasis should really be on the fact that the sutra embodies the *saddharma*, the real teaching of the Buddha; the White Lotus just makes the title more pleasing and evocative.

Strictly speaking *puṇḍarīka* is 'white lotus', just as *utpala* is 'blue lotus', but sometimes *puṇḍarīka* is used simply to mean lotus. I have seen these lotuses growing in India. They are white tinged with pink, bigger than a water-lily, and their petals are large and slightly blowsy, not spiky like the petals of water-lilies.

The sutra is often called the Threefold Lotus Sutra. *What relationship do the preceding and succeeding sutras bear to the* White Lotus Sutra?
They are apparently apocryphal works of Chinese composition. They have their own value—some of the imagery in the introductory sutra is quite extraordinary—but in a way they are superfluous, because the *White Lotus Sutra* stands complete in itself and needs no introduction or conclusion. I have not worked out any doctrinal connection, but no doubt that could be done, or has been done.

You call these two sutras apocryphal. But isn't any Mahāyāna text claiming its descent from the Buddha through some revelation 'apocryphal'?
Chinese works such as these are apocryphal in that they purport to be translated from Sanskrit, and have an array of names of translators, dates, and places of translation, but these details amount to deception, for the works are not in fact translations at all. This distinguishes them from Mahāyāna sutras which are apocryphal in the Indian sense. Unlike the Indians, the Chinese had a highly developed critical sense which they applied to their own literature and to Buddhist works, so they would have been aware of stylistic differences, and that certain words came into use at a certain time. They had a sophisticated ability to discriminate in this way which did not become common in Europe until after the Renaissance.

•

In The Eternal Legacy, *you say that the Mahāyāna sutras are revealed, directly or indirectly, by the Buddha's* sambhogakāya *('body of glory'), and you also say that we are not to think of the sutras as necessarily being delivered at one particular time and place. Were the sutras composed by Enlightened disciples, or do we have to believe that a germ of them at least was uttered by the historical Buddha?*
Well, we cannot regard the Mahāyāna sutras in their present form as having been delivered by the historical Buddha Śākyamuni. It may well be, however, that some of the teachings contained in the sutras do go back to Śākyamuni, and perhaps even some of his actual words are embedded in them. This is noticeable in, for example, the *Lalita-vistara*,[27] in which quite extensive passages of what would seem to be the teaching of the historical Buddha are embedded in this very colourful Mahāyāna sutra. The difference in style and approach can be seen very easily, because the quotations are in rather sober vein whereas the rest of the text is highly mythic and poetic. Although there are examples like this, however, as a whole the sutras cannot possibly be regarded as

representing the actual discourses of the historical Buddha. So what was the genesis of the Mahāyāna sutras? If they were not the utterance of the historical Buddha, whose utterance were they? Certainly they purport to be the utterance of the historical Buddha, though saying that raises all sorts of questions, because the ancient Buddhists did not distinguish the historical from the non-historical, so they would not have been able to think of a sutra as having been given by a non-historical as distinct from a historical Buddha. They did not use those categories. But from our point of view, where did those sutras originate?

If the sutras are a communication from the Enlightened mind, as they appear to be no less than the Pali scriptures, we can only assume that certain gifted disciples had experiences of communication from the Buddha in the sense of the trans-historical essence of Buddhahood. They would then have written down this communication as best they understood it in the form of the Mahāyāna sutras, attributing those sutras in all sincerity to the Buddha himself. It is not that they were deliberately composing something of their own which they proceeded to put into the mouth of the Buddha. That would have been entirely foreign to their way of thinking. Perhaps there were different levels of inspiration, so that sometimes what purported to be the utterance of the *sambhogakāya* actually sprang from a rather lower level of inspiration, but in the case of some Mahāyāna sutras we cannot resist the impression that, as far as we are able to judge, they sprang from as high a level of inspiration as we encounter in the Pali Canon with respect to utterances which seem to be those of the historical Buddha. So it would seem that the Mahāyāna sutras, broadly speaking, originated in the spiritual experience of spiritually gifted disciples who were able to reach a level corresponding to that of the Buddha's own spiritual attainment, and receive there, so to speak, a communication from the Buddha which they thereafter embodied, perhaps sometimes in their own language, in what we know as the Mahāyāna sutras.

So the sutras were esoteric, 'non-public', writings composed by Enlightened disciples?
The impression I have is not that they were withheld from ordinary people or other members of the spiritual community any more than the Hīnayāna sutras were. You must remember that many of the Mahāyāna sutras were produced at a period when writing had become much more common than it was in the Buddha's day. The sutras were committed to writing, or even perhaps originally composed in written form—they do not bear the hallmarks of oral traditions as the Pali suttas do. This means

that they would automatically have had a wider circulation than was possible for a teaching that was transmitted orally and had to be learned from the lips of a teacher with whom you were in personal contact.

Many Mahāyāna sutras have colophons extolling the virtues of copying and distributing the sutra, which would suggest that Mahāyāna sutras were definitely not thought of as esoteric documents in the way that the Vinaya was. According to the Vinaya, it is an offence to teach the Dharma to one who is not a bhikkhu,[28] but the Mahāyāna sutras issue no such prohibition; in fact, you are encouraged to transmit the sutra to as many sentient beings as possible, an attitude which is of course in accordance with the Bodhisattva Ideal.

But the White Lotus Sutra *does emphasize the dire consequences of disparaging the sutra. The Buddha goes so far as to say, 'Those who slander this sutra / If I told the tale of their evils / I could not exhaust them in a whole kalpa. / For this cause and reason / I especially say to you / Amongst undiscerning people / Do not preach this sutra.' Presumably not preaching the sutra to the undiscerning would save them from the consequences of hearing it yet being unreceptive to it, or even disparaging it. The implication is that it is better not to hear the Dharma at all than to hear it and react against it. Is this so? If it is, should all forms of transmission of the Dharma be given only to those likely to be receptive rather than being given indiscriminately in the form of books, public talks, and so on?*

We can't take such an extreme warning at face value. This kind of statement appears in Mahāyāna sutras for a mixture of reasons. Mahāyāna sutras were not accepted by Hinayanists—to use that term—as genuine *Buddhavacana*,[29] and sometimes the Hinayanists seem to have criticized the sutras, or even slandered them, as the Mahayanists would see it. The warnings of this kind which the Mahāyāna sutras contain are therefore partly polemical in intent. At the same time, they are partly the expression of a genuine concern for people's spiritual well-being, a concern that people should not be put in a position of rejecting something which it can only do them harm to reject.

You have to be very careful about this. It is not as though there is some avenging deity waiting to punish you. If you are not receptive to the truth, however, or if you get into the habit of closing your mind to something which you cannot immediately accept and understand, you do come to be in a parlous condition, spiritually speaking. The Mahāyāna sutras are really saying that it is not skilful to present a pupil with teachings which, given their general attitude and mental make-up, they cannot but reject. If those teachings bear the label 'Buddhism', they can only come to the conclusion that Buddhism is not for them. People should not be fed teachings in such quantities that they are quite unable to digest them and are bound to vomit them up.

On the other hand, you also need to be careful in another way. In the last century there was a great controversy in the Church between the Anglicans and the Roman Catholics. A Catholic priest produced a pamphlet called *Reserve in Communicating Religious Knowledge*,[30] which suggested that if, for instance, someone who was interested in Catholicism came round to see a priest, the priest should not talk about Catholic dogmas like the infallibility of the pope all at once, because that would be bound to put the visitor off. The advice was that the priest should say first the kind of thing that the visitor would be able to accept more readily, such as that the Catholic Church teaches that we should love our enemies. The other doctrines or dogmas should be kept in reserve, in recognition of the fact that they were not very acceptable to someone who was just beginning to be interested in the Catholic Church. When the Anglicans got hold of this pamphlet, of course they at once accused the Catholic Church of hypocrisy, of not being open with people about its true beliefs.

In a way, though, the Catholic priest had a point. If you try to explain certain things to people before they are prepared, you may simply scare them away. The fact is that people progress very slowly on the spiritual path, and at the beginning they are just not prepared for the teachings pertaining to the later stages of the path. On the other hand, there is also something in the accusation of hypocrisy. You could use this 'reserve in communicating religious knowledge' in a way that was not quite honest and straightforward. So this is a matter of some tact and delicacy.

For instance, suppose someone at a meditation class asked you 'Do Buddhists not believe in God?' If you replied 'Oh no, lots of Buddhists believe in God,' that would not be straightforward and honest. But suppose you knew that if you were to say that Buddhists do not believe in God—full stop—then that person would never come to the class again, how should you reply? It is a difficult question. I suggest that you should temporize, using that word positively. You could say, for example, 'The word "God" can be understood in a number of different ways. Nowadays there is a lot of discussion even among Christians as to what God really means, even as to whether there *is* a God. In Buddhism we do not pronounce very readily about matters concerning ultimate Reality, and from the Christian point of view God is a statement of ultimate Reality. We prefer to concentrate on the actual practice of ethics and meditation, with a view eventually to having a deeper understanding of these things for ourselves, out of our personal experience.' If you were to answer in this way, you would be neither hypocritical nor untrue to the Buddhist tradition.

Sometimes people want to corner you and force you to make a statement one way or the other, but you should not allow this to happen. Sometimes you have to say 'Buddhism is a vast subject. It is not easy even for those who have been practising it for some time to understand it. Just take it bit by bit. Concentrate on observing the precepts, practising meditation, and reflecting on whatever teachings appeal to you most. Leave the others aside if you find them too difficult or unacceptable. We would not insist that you sign the thirty-nine articles of Buddhism on the spot, even if we had them!'

You said that the White Lotus Sutra *may have been written down in central Asia. How much central Asian influence is evident in the sutra, in terms of its cosmology or even its spiritual content?*
The question is perhaps better applied to Mahāyāna sutras in general than specifically to the *White Lotus Sutra*. It has been suggested that Mahāyāna imagery, particularly the concept of Amitābha and the Pure Land of the *Sukhāvatī-Vyūha Sūtras*, does owe something to Iranian influences. There are anticipations of the jewel trees of the Pure Land in the Dīgha Nikāya of the Pali Canon, for example,[31] and it would seem likely that this idea of jewel trees in magnificent gardens is of Babylonian origin. We know that Aśoka was in contact with the Persian empire, and Persian artisans apparently came to India to build his palace—which seems to have been modelled on that of Persepolis—for those highly polished columns can only have been produced by Persian craftsmen. So it seems quite possible that some of the later, more legendary suttas in the Dīgha Nikāya belonging to that period (one hundred years after the Buddha) do reflect the Persian influence in their imagery.

•

You have referred to the Mahāyāna sutras as works of symbolic religious art, and recommended that we should see them as giving us a glimpse into an archetypal world rather than providing an actual pattern of Buddhist living. So what is the best approach to studying this non-conceptual material?
It is very difficult to say. The main thing is to avoid literalism. You should familiarize yourself with the letter of the text, but not take it too literally. Many people approach almost any Buddhist material in a very literalistic way, grasping the letter tightly and often missing the spirit completely.

I am afraid I will be misunderstood, but I would almost advise that you should not take it too seriously. Read it in the way that you would read good poetry, or a good novel. Enjoy it; immerse yourself in it. You can get down to a study of what the details mean, and what the deeper significance of the sutra might be, later on. To begin with, it is very important to allow the work as a whole to have some impact on you, to try to experience it as a whole rather than getting lost in the details. It is also important to read the sutra itself, and use a commentary to throw light on it, rather than the other way round.

•

The White Lotus Sutra *seems to consist of two main revelations: that there is in truth only one spiritual path, and that what we perceive as the historical Buddha is really an expression of eternal Enlightenment. Chapters 1 to 10 seem to be an independent drama providing a setting for and an amplification of the first revelation; chapters 11, 15, and 16 then provide a setting for the second revelation. Do you think there might originally have been two independent teachings which were brought together to form the twin nuclei of the* White Lotus Sutra*?*

Leaving aside the miscellaneous cluster of chapters at the end, the sutra does naturally fall into these two parts, but that is no reason to regard them as having been originally independent works. Although they have their distinctive themes, the two sections do seem to hang together. One corresponds to the relative bodhicitta and the other to the absolute bodhicitta. One is concerned with the spiritual path which exists in time and is followed in time, and the other pertains to ultimate Reality, as embodied in the Buddha, which exists outside space and time. I do not have an impression of discontinuity or of two independent sutras having been soldered together to make a single work, and as far as I know this has not been suggested by any scholar who has made a study of the work. I think that you are correct in detecting the difference of theme between the two sections, but that distinction represents the basic structure of the sutra, and conveys its twofold message.

•

The sutra talks of faith as the emotional equivalent of wisdom, and recommends worship of the sutra as a practice. Some Buddhists seem to see homage to the White Lotus Sutra *as their only practice. Could this ever be a*

full path to Enlightenment?

I suppose it depends what you mean by worship of the *White Lotus Sutra*. I think that true worship of the sutra could be at least an *approach* to the path to Enlightenment, but I am not sure how easily worship of a text would come to people in the West. It is not impossible, but it is a little foreign to our tradition. Text worship does feature prominently in some religions, particularly in Sikhism. Sikhism has no images, but has as the object of worship the *Adi Granth* (which they call the *Guru Granth*), the volume of the Sikh scriptures. Sikhs place a beautifully printed volume of this text on a silken cushion, or on a canopied throne, and they make offerings to it, just as described in the Mahāyāna sutras, where the practice probably originated.

You could adopt the practice of keeping a scripture open on the shrine, with a little glass case to protect it from incense smoke. It would be suitable for Dharma Day in particular, but it would be appropriate at all times if you wanted to represent all of the Three Jewels in the shrine-room. The symbol of the Buddha jewel is the image, and the symbol of the Sangha jewel is the presence of the spiritual community, but to symbolize the Dharma jewel, a book is needed.

Nichiren,[32] of course, teaches the practice of reverence for the sutra. It seems almost like a form of Pure Land Buddhism, with devotion offered to the White Lotus Sutra *rather than to Amitābha. Could this practice actually lead the practitioner to an insight into the sutra?*

The standard Buddhist teaching is that the Five Spiritual Faculties, which include faith, must be balanced. For a time one particular faculty may predominate, but in the end they need to be in equilibrium. As I see it, there is no question of alternative paths, as is sometimes suggested in Hinduism. If you start off travelling the path of devotion, sooner or later you have to bring in the path of Wisdom; the one reinforces the other.

•

In the sutra the Buddha explains to the assembly that the truth is very difficult to understand, and has to be approached gradually. Do you accept the Mahāyāna's suggestion that its teachings are more profound than those that historically precede it? Are the Heart Sutra *and the* White Lotus Sutra *more profound than the teachings of the Pali Canon?*

That is a very difficult question. Who is to judge what is profound? Someone studying a verse of the *Dhammapada*, for example, might see the whole Truth in that, even though others could not. Sometimes the implications of an apparently simple saying are absolutely vast.

Perhaps you might say that some texts or sayings are obviously more profound than others, but it is very difficult to make a blanket statement. Certainly some Mahāyāna teachings are more *elaborate* than others. For instance, the Mahāyāna sutras have gone into the *śūnyatā* teaching in a much more thoroughgoing fashion than any Pali text. Perhaps you need some acquaintance with the Mahāyāna to be able to appreciate the depths of some of the Buddha's teaching in the Pali scriptures. The depth may be there, but for various reasons it is not so well articulated.

The linguistic resources of the Mahāyāna were far greater, because a Buddhist vocabulary had been developed and refined by that time, and confusions had been resolved. The Buddha had to make do with the language used by the people around him who did not have his Enlightenment experience. He had to use the same language, but try to use it in his own way. When the Mahāyāna sutras were composed hundreds of years later, Buddhists had developed a language of their own which was more adequate to express their insights and intuitions.

So you would not accept the sutra's suggestion that it is explicating a fuller teaching?
It is fuller in relation to the classical Hīnayāna, but the classical Hīnayāna does not necessarily coincide with certain teachings of the historical Buddha as recorded in the existing Pali Canon. Assuming that the teachings of the Pali Canon are properly understood, it could not be said that the Mahāyāna goes beyond them.

•

How radical would the idea of an eternal Buddha have been when it emerged? What stage of development would the trikāya *doctrine[33] have reached at the time of the* White Lotus Sutra?
The distinction between the *rūpakāya* of the Buddha and the *dharmakāya* occurs even in the Pali Canon, although the Theravāda uses the term *dharmakāya* rather literalistically: in their view, the Buddha is the *dharmakāya* simply because he is the embodiment of all the teachings contained in the *tripiṭaka*. So the concept of the *dharmakāya* as distinct from the *rūpakāya* was part of general Buddhist teaching before the *White Lotus Sutra*, but it was the *White Lotus Sutra* which brought it into prominence and placed it at the centre of the teaching, showing how important it was to see that the Buddha was the *dharmakāya* in the fullest sense, not just the *rūpakāya*.

The development of the *trikāya* doctrine seems to have emerged in later Mahāyāna sutras. The earlier ones distinguish between the *rūpakāya* and the *dharmakāya*, but make no mention of a *sambhogakāya*. Sometimes what came to be called the *sambhogakāya* shades into the *dharmakāya*, but there is no sharp differentiation between them as there came to be later in the *trikāya* doctrine, which is associated with the Yogācāra.

In the White Lotus Sutra *it is almost as if the eternal Buddha is both* sambhogakāya *and* dharmakāya.
Yes. If the Buddha is to be an actor in a drama of cosmic Enlightenment, he has to have a form; he can hardly appear as a featureless *dharmakāya*. In that way the Buddha has a *sambhogakāya*-type presentation, although in fact he is the *dharmakāya*. Perhaps it is not advisable to distinguish too sharply between the three *kāyas*.

•

You suggest that the speaker of the sutra could be said to be the Ānanda within. Could this mean that in a sense we have heard the White Lotus Sutra *before because it is an innate memory?*
You could perhaps consider it in terms of the Platonic doctrine of reminiscence, or the doctrine of mutual interpenetration. It is perhaps not too far-fetched to say that there is within you a level of receptivity on which you are listening to the Truth represented by the sutra.

The corollary is that the Buddha is teaching within one's own mind. Given your reservations about any suggestion that one is already a Buddha, is this a useful image?
I think it can be if you bear in mind the limitations of that static way of looking at things. I think such phrases as 'the Enlightened mind within' are to be avoided because they are misleading if they are taken literally. A human being is a potential Buddha in the sense that if he or she makes a sufficient effort, he or she can attain Enlightenment. But it is not as if there is just a thin layer separating you from Buddhahood, so that you have just got to get through that layer and hey presto! there you are, Enlightened. It is a big mistake to think of immanent Buddhahood as any kind of possession.

As far as we know, the Buddha himself did not use the language of potentiality or immanence, and I am very doubtful as to whether it is a skilful language for us to use. No doubt it does express an actual spiritual experience at a certain level, but anyone who is not very spiritually advanced is likely to misunderstand, and would be better off hearing that, by making sufficient effort, they can eventually attain a state called Enlightenment. We are all 'potentially Enlightened', but that is not to say that we are literally Enlightened at this moment in any sense that is comprehensible to us.

The idea of the Ānanda within struck a chord with me. I wonder if identifying with Ānanda rather than with the Buddha gets the benefits of the language of potentiality without some of the risks?
Ānanda is a much more modest figure, because at the time of his association with the Buddha he was only a Stream-Entrant, not yet fully Enlightened; so yes, perhaps you can much more safely identify with Ānanda.

Where did the language of potentiality come from?
It is used in India outside Buddhism—in a way it is the language of the Upaniṣads. One Upaniṣad says 'I am Brahman, I am the Absolute'[34]—there is that direct identification. But whether the Upaniṣads had a historical influence on the Mahāyāna it is difficult to say. It could be that the language of Buddhism was influenced by the thought of the Upaniṣads, or it could be that there was a parallel development.

•

The sutra speaks of three vehicles culminating in one Buddha vehicle. Is this principle of progressive levels unique to this sutra, or is it found in earlier teachings?
It is not really so much a question of levels as of *yānas*. What are thought of as different ways with different goals all merge into one way. They can perhaps be regarded as successive stages of one path, but the point is that it *is* one path—all these apparently different paths are reduced to one path. This is one of the two distinctive teachings of the *White Lotus Sutra* which afterwards became the heritage of the whole of the Mahāyāna.

At the time of the Buddha there was only one path, but in the period before the rise of the *White Lotus Sutra*, the distinction between the Arhat and the Buddha had hardened into separate paths. The *White Lotus Sutra* was an expression of a reaction against this separation, and effectively brought the paths back together again.

In our own day we are doing something similar, on a certain level, in the way in which we bring together the lay and the monastic, which had become so widely separated, into one Going for Refuge.[35]

You mention that the Hīnayāna nirvana is simply the eradication of the passions. Would it really be possible to eradicate all passions without developing Insight?
No, I don't think so. Even if you were to think just in terms of eradicating the passions, and had no thought of gaining *bodhi*, the attainment of *bodhi* would still be part of the process of eradicating the passions, although your mode of expressing that experience would be limited. There is no doubt, however, that when in the Pali Canon Sāriputta is asked to say what *nibbāṇa* is, he gives a purely negative definition, saying simply that it is the cessation of *lobha*, *dosa*, and *moha*.[36] But there are other passages in the Pali Canon which tell a different story.

In fact, the path to nirvana, in whatever formulation, always has both a positive aspect and a negative aspect. In the intermediate stages there is a cessation of something unskilful and also a coming into existence and increase of something skilful. As you progress up the spiral path the positive and the skilful gradually increase as they counterbalance the negative and unskilful. By extension from that, nirvana is certainly the cessation of everything unskilful, but it is also the plenitude of everything skilful. The Hīnayāna often left out the second part of the statement.

Why should they have done that if they had genuine spiritual attainments? Would it have been some sort of skilful means?
That's a circular argument, because you are assuming that they had some genuine spiritual attainment when perhaps they did not. Perhaps there had been a deterioration and on that account they thought just in negative terms. We know so little about the general historical situation, the social and cultural conditions, that it is very difficult to speculate. The fact is that the Theravādins presented the Dharma in increasingly negative terms to the neglect, right down to the present day, of much more positive formulations which are to be found in the Pali Canon itself. A classic example is that of the Twelve Positive Nidānas, which were completely ignored in expositions of the Dharma until the time of Mrs Rhys Davids.[37] Another case is that of the *Itivuttaka*,[38] which tails off at the end into an increasingly negative presentation of the spiritual life, the latter sections being apparently later productions. It is obvious that this tendency to negativity happened, but we are completely in the dark about the psychological, spiritual, and cultural reasons as to why it happened.

At the beginning of the sutra five thousand disciples walk out, and the assembly is thus purified. Why didn't the Buddha just preach to the whole assembly, contacting those who were receptive and not contacting those who were not?
You have to consider what the sutra is trying to do. It is a drama, and in a drama there has to be action. I think the author of the sutra wanted to dramatize the disciples' rejection of the truth offered to them to emphasize that this is what can happen. You can be so full of your own imagined spiritual attainments that you even close your ears to what the Buddha has to say and walk out. As a human being you have that freedom, and some people unfortunately exercise it. This is the point that is being emphasized.

Might the incident also indicate an awareness on the part of the Buddha that it is harder to teach an audience which includes people who are not receptive?
Yes, the fact that there are certain people present who are resistant does affect the atmosphere of a whole group. If you are speaking to a group, it is impossible to ignore a section of it which is in disagreement with the rest of the group. If most of an audience is very attentive and one section is restless, that interferes with the total empathy between speaker and audience.

The Buddha predicts to Enlightenment Arhats such as Śāriputra, numerous bhikṣus, bhikṣuṇīs like Mahāprajāpatī and Yaśodharā, evil doers such as Devadatta, and non-human beings such as a nāga princess, but no lay people. Why is this, and could it be the reason for the emphasis on lay people in the Vimalakīrti-nirdeśa?
You would have thought in view of the universalism of the Mahāyāna that lay men and lay women would also be predicted to Enlightenment, so it *is* rather an odd omission. Perhaps, as you say, the *Vimalakīrti-nirdeśa* makes up for that, although it would not have done so in a conscious way. Perhaps particular Mahāyāna sutras do have responsibility for particular approaches or emphases.

I am sure that the sutra does not intend deliberately to exclude lay people. It is one of the earlier Mahāyāna sutras, so perhaps there is still an over-emphasis on monasticism carried over from the Hīnayāna which has not been fully permeated by the Mahāyāna spirit, as though the author has not completely transcended his Hīnayāna background. It is not so easy to bring everything that you have inherited from the past into line with your real position.

•

The body of the Buddha Abundant Treasures can only be revealed when all the Buddhas who have emanated from Śākyamuni are present. What is the meaning of this episode? And are the emanations people who have become Buddhas as disciples of Śākyamuni, or are they magical emanations?
This coming together of the ancient Buddha and the present Buddha represents Enlightenment's transcendence of time. The coming together of Buddhas (which are magical emanations, to answer your question) is the corresponding transcendence of space. The significance of the episode is that time and space are beginning to be transcended.

When Śākyamuni purifies the whole world and it turns into lapis lazuli ground with golden cords, have we gone up to an even higher level, to enter a sort of Sukhāvatī?
It is more a question of feeling than doctrine. As you read the sutra, what do you feel? Do you feel as though you are rising to a higher level? Later on there is that episode where the Buddha literally raises the whole assembly to a higher level, and the symbolism is obvious, but as you go through the sutra, you must be mindful and examine your own responses. Do you feel uplifted by a certain passage? Does it seem to raise you to a higher level of experience? You must consult your own experience.

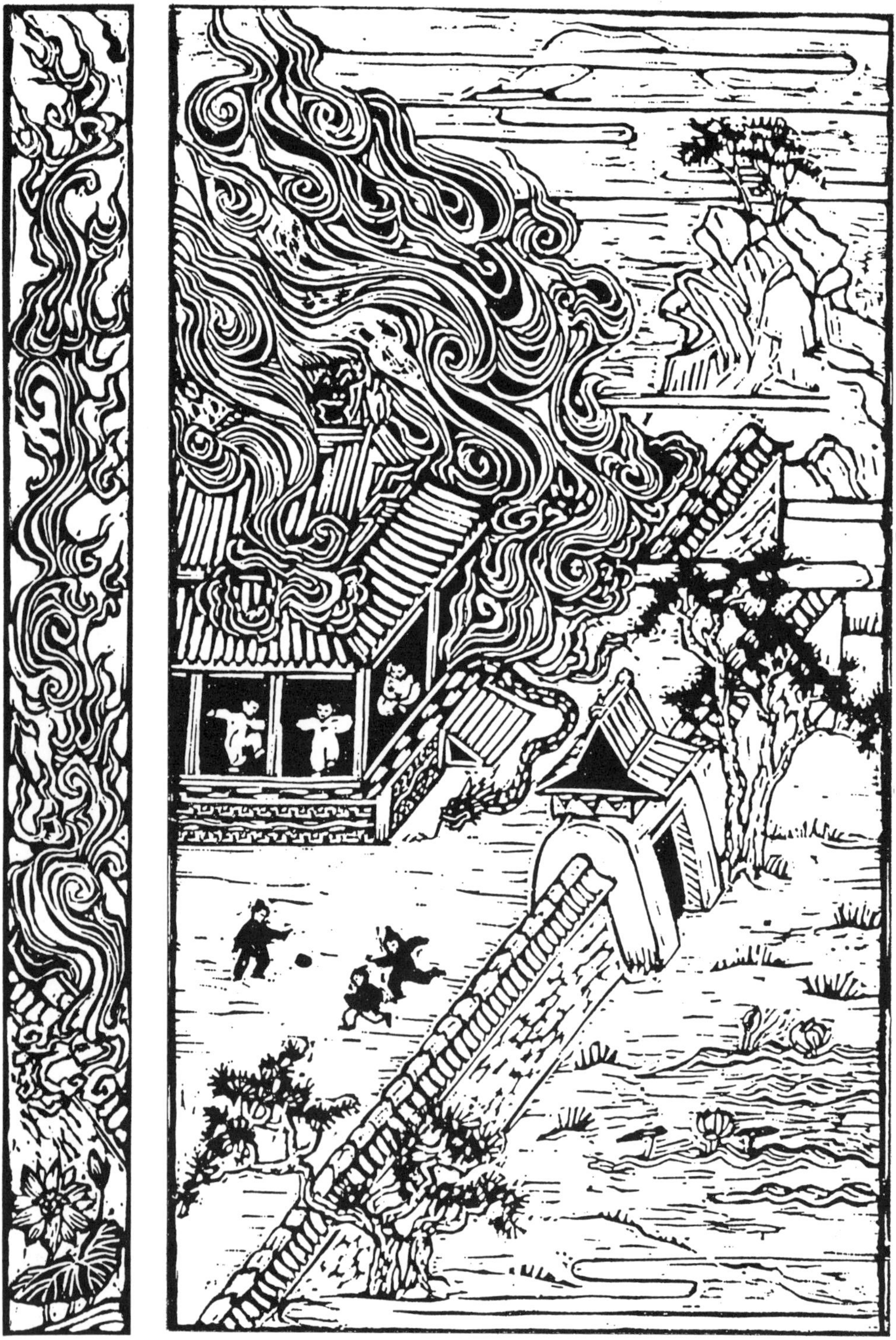

Chapter Three

Transcending the Human Predicament

As HUMAN BEINGS, we live in two quite different worlds. Some of the time we live in the world of rational thought, the world of science, philosophy, concepts, and systematic generalizations from experience. But some of the time we live in a very different world indeed: the world of the unconscious, the world of poetry, myths, and symbols. It is the need for both these aspects of human nature to be involved in the spiritual life which leads to the narrating of the first parable of the *White Lotus Sutra*.

At first, as we have seen, the Buddha is reluctant to speak at all, because the truth of things is so difficult to understand, but at length he is persuaded to attempt an explanation. In clear conceptual terms he tells the disciples that his teaching of the eradication of negative emotions—which they, Arhats that they are, thought was the be-all and end-all of spiritual achievement—is just the start. It's just a way of getting people going on the spiritual path. There is, the Buddha now reveals, a higher spiritual goal which consists not just in the eradication of the negative emotions, necessary as that may be, but in the attainment of positive spiritual knowledge and Enlightenment: Perfect Buddhahood. And the way to attain this higher goal is to practise the Bodhisattva Ideal, working towards Enlightenment not just for the sake of individual emancipation, but so as to contribute to the cosmic process of Enlightenment, the Enlightenment of all sentient beings.

On hearing this, of course, a number of the disciples present simply cannot entertain the idea and leave forthwith—and many of those who stay are thrown into confusion. Will they have to abandon everything they have been taught so far? Have they been wasting their time? They may understand the new teaching in a rational, intellectual way, but their hearts are not convinced. Although he himself wholeheartedly accepts the new teaching, Śāriputra, the greatest and wisest of the disciples, is aware that many of the others are still perplexed, and he speaks on their behalf. Can the Buddha explain things to them in another way? In response to this appeal, the Buddha says that he will tell a story, remarking that 'Through a parable intelligent people reach understanding.' Sometimes it is not easy to understand things when they are put in a dry, abstract, conceptual manner, but with the help of a story much becomes clear. And the story the Buddha tells is the parable of the burning house:

Once upon a time there was a great elder, a very rich old man who lived in a huge mansion with his hundreds of servants and his many children. The story does not speak of wives or mothers, but we know that the elder had as many as thirty children, and they were all quite young. The house in which they lived had once been magnificent, but now it was old and tumbledown. The pillars were decaying, the windows were broken, the floorboards were rotting, and the walls were crumbling. And in the nooks and crannies of this tumbledown house there lurked all sorts of ghosts and evil spirits.

One day the house suddenly caught fire. Because it was so old and the timbers were so dry, the whole building was burning merrily in no time. As it happened, the elder was safe outside the house when the fire started, but his children were playing inside. Too young to realize that they were in danger of being burned to death, they just carried on playing and made no effort to escape.

The elder was very afraid for his children, of course, and wondered how on earth to save them. At first he thought of carrying them out of the house one by one, for he was strong and able, but he soon realized that it would be impossible to get them all out in time. Instead, he decided to try calling out to the children. He shouted 'The house is on fire! You're in terrible danger! Come out quickly!' But the children had no idea what their father could mean by danger. They just carried on playing their games, glancing at the elder occasionally as they ran to and fro, but taking no serious notice of him at all.

The elder saw that there was no time to lose, for the house would crash to the ground at any minute. In desperation he hit upon another plan. He would try to trick the children into coming out of the house. Knowing the different nature of each child, he knew that they liked different kinds of toys, some liking one kind and some preferring another. So he called out to them 'Come and look at the toys I have brought for you! There are all kinds of carts, some drawn by deer, some drawn by goats, and some drawn by bullocks, and they are all standing just outside the gate. Come quickly and look!' And although the children had been deaf to all his warnings, this time they heard him. They all came rushing and tumbling helter-skelter out of the burning house, pushing and shoving each other in their eagerness to get the new toys.

When the elder was sure that all the children were safely out of the house, he sat down with a great sigh of relief; and at once, of course, the children came clamouring round him demanding the toys he had promised them. The elder was extremely fond of his children, and wanted to give them whatever their hearts desired. And, fortunately, he was extremely wealthy—in fact his wealth was infinite—so he could afford to give them the best of everything. Instead of the carts of different kinds which he had promised them, therefore, he gave to each of them a magnificent bullock-drawn cart, bigger and better than they could have imagined in their wildest dreams. Although he had promised them one thing and gave them something else, this was not deceitfulness on his part, because it was motivated by his desire for the welfare and the safety of his children.

So this is the parable of the burning house.[39] In a way there is no need to say any more, because a parable speaks directly in its own symbolic language. It means just what it says it means, and we simply have to let it all sink in. It can be useful, however, to dwell on the events of the story and see what significance they have for us.

The elder, of course, is the Buddha, the Enlightened One, and the mansion in which he lives is the world—not just this earth, but the whole universe, the whole of conditioned existence, all worlds. The mansion—the universe—is inhabited by many beings—not just human beings, according to Buddhism, but beings of all kinds, some less developed than mankind and some even more developed. And just as the mansion is old and decayed, this universe is subject to all kinds of imperfections. For a start, it is impermanent, changing all the time. We cannot stay in it for long; it is more like a hotel than a home. The mansion has ghosts in the corners too, which suggests that this world of ours is haunted. Haunted by what? By the past. We like to think that we live in the present, but more often than not the ghosts of the past are all around us. We may think that we are experiencing objectively existing beings and situations, but often they are really the projections of our unconscious minds, the ghosts of the past that we carry along with us all the time.

In the parable the mansion catches fire at a certain time, but in reality the mansion of the world is constantly blazing and burning. The use of fire as a symbol is very common in Buddhism, and in Indian religion generally. The Buddha used it in a teaching known as the Fire Sermon which he gave not long after his Enlightenment, on an occasion when he was speaking to a company of his disciples who had previously been 'matted-hair' ascetics and whose main religious practice had been fire-worship. No doubt the Buddha was alluding to their previous practice when he led a thousand of them to the top of a hill and said to them 'The whole world is ablaze. The whole world is burning. Burning with what? It is burning with the fire of craving and neurotic desire. It is burning with the fire of anger, hatred, and aggression. It is burning with the fire of ignorance, delusion, bewilderment, and lack of awareness.'[40] This was surely not just an *idea* of the Buddha's, not just a concept he happened to think up. He surely saw the world, as though in a vision, just like this. Perhaps before he spoke he had been looking down from the hilltop into the jungles below, and had seen a forest fire burning in the distance. Then he may have seen, in his spiritual vision, that not only was the forest burning, but the houses were burning, people were burning, the mountains were burning, the earth was burning, the sun, moon, and stars were burning—everything conditioned was burning with the threefold fires of craving, hatred, and delusion.

Fire, incidentally, far from being just a negative symbol in Buddhism, has many positive associations. It is associated with change—in fact fire, the process of combustion, *is* change, and not just change but transformation. In Indian spiritual life fire is therefore a symbol not just of destruction but also of renewal and spiritual rebirth. In Vedic times, long before the Buddha, people placed offerings on a fire altar to ascend in the subtle form of smoke to the realms of the gods. The rite of cremation involves a similar transformation, reducing the physical body to ashes but—or so the ancient Indians believed—sending the subtle aspect of being, the 'soul', to the moon or to the sun, to the world of the fathers or to the world of the gods. In Hinduism the cremation ground is the domain of Śiva the Destroyer, who is the god not only of destruction but also of spiritual rebirth, because before you can build up you must break down. And the flames which surround the wrathful deities of Tibetan Buddhism also symbolize a transformation by fire—the fiery breaking through of the spirit of Enlightenment into the darkness and ignorance of the world.

But fire is a threat to the children in the mansion; in fact they are in danger of burning to death. Who do the children represent? Obviously they represent living beings, especially human beings—that is to say, especially ourselves. In the context of the sutra they represent the Hīnayāna disciples, those who are following lower spiritual ideals. More generally speaking, we can say that they represent all those who have evolved only up to a certain point and have some distance—maybe a great distance—still to go.

The children in the parable are in danger of being burned to death. The implication is that human beings are in danger—*we* are in danger. What does this mean? It could mean that we are in danger of remaining within the world, within the process of conditioned existence, the cycle of birth, death, and rebirth as illustrated by the Tibetan Wheel of Life.[41] The danger is that if we carry on turning round and round within the wheel we must inevitably suffer, at least sometimes. But the symbolism could also mean that we are in danger of getting stuck at a lower level of development. Unfortunately this happens to very many people, and it isn't always entirely their own fault. The human organism, biologically, psychologically, and even spiritually speaking, has a natural tendency to grow. In fact, to grow is the nature of life itself. Life in all its forms wants to unfold its inner potentialities, and if any living thing cannot do this it feels miserable, or at least uneasy and dissatisfied. People are often so restricted by their circumstances that they simply cannot grow—indeed, they sometimes feel that they cannot even breathe. All sorts of unpleasant and uncontrollable factors press in on them from all sides. They strangle them, stifle them, and make them feel that they are not developing as they should and could, so that they feel not only frustrated and restricted, but miserable, resentful, and unhappy in every way.

In the parable, of course, the person trying to rescue the children from danger is their father. If the 'father' here meant the begetter of the children, this might seem to imply that the Buddha is a kind of creator god, the creator of the world, of men and women, and all living beings. But this 'father' simply stands for someone older, more experienced, and more highly evolved. He is like the 'cultural father' of some so-called primitive cultures where you have both a biological father, who begot you, and a cultural father—usually your mother's brother—who is responsible for educating you and bringing you up. (In modern societies the biological father fulfils both roles, but this is not an invariable rule.) So there is no implication of theism here.

The elder's first impulse when the fire starts is to rush into the house and carry the children out—he would be strong enough to do that—but on reflection he dismisses the idea. This goes to show that however willing and able you may be, you just cannot save people, spiritually speaking, by force. You could conceivably drag someone out of a burning building against their will, but it is impossible to make anybody evolve against their will. Yes, you can drag them to meditation classes, you can drag them into church. You can force them to recite the Creed and read the Bible. You can intimidate them into not doing this or not doing that. But you cannot make them evolve against their will. By its very nature the Higher Evolution is a voluntary process, something *you* do because *you* want to do it.

Unfortunately, this is sometimes forgotten. Some religious teachers hold the view that what people really need to make them grow spiritually is discipline—and these teachers are only too willing to dish it out, and give their disciples a very tough time indeed. Of course, there is no shortage of people who are ready to accept this sort of discipline. It is not difficult to find ways of conditioning people along certain lines. This kind of conditioning, however, is a very different thing from real spiritual development. So Buddhism does not force, it does not compel, it does not intimidate, and it doesn't have recourse to discipline in this almost military sense of the term, because trying to force people to develop is self-defeating. Throughout the history of Buddhism, therefore, Buddhist teachers have been very tolerant. Buddhism has never tried to force anybody to do anything.

So in the end the elder gives up the idea of rescuing the children and instead tries calling out to them. Now this call is full of meaning. It represents the call of Truth, the call, if you like, of the divine. Turning to the Hindu tradition again, we find the symbolism of the call beautifully expressed in the medieval Hindu story of Kṛishṇa and his flute. Kṛishṇa is one of the great spiritual figures of Hinduism, a demigod said to be an incarnation of Viṣṇu the Preserver, and he is surrounded by all sorts of myths and legends. The story of Kṛishṇa's flute is set in an Indian village called Vṛindāvana where the people live by herding cows. Just imagine the scene. It is a dark night with no moon and the whole village is sound asleep. The cows are all shut in their stalls for the night, and everywhere —the little thatched mud-walled huts, the fields and the forest—is absolutely still. Then, suddenly, in the midst of the darkness, in the midst of the silence, from the depths of the forest there comes a sound, faint but sweet and shrill, a sound that seems to come from an infinitely remote distance—the sound of a flute. Even now in India you can sometimes have this experience. You can be all by yourself in the midst of the countryside, with no one for miles around, and all of a sudden, out of the dark and the silence, there comes the sound of a flute.

Now although the sound of the flute is very faint and distant, it does not go unheard in the village of Vṛindāvana. Almost as though they have been expecting to hear it, the wives of the cowherds—the *gopīs*—wake up, and know at once that Kṛishṇa is calling them. Without making a sound, without telling anybody, they get up and steal out of their houses, along the streets of the village, and into the forest. Leaving their husbands and their children, their pots and their pans, their cows and their goats, they all go stealing away, rushing away as soon as they are at a safe distance, to dance with Kṛishṇa in the heart of the forest.[42]

In this story Kṛishṇa is a symbol of the divine, and the gopīs represent the human heart, or the human soul if you like; and the sound of Kṛishṇa's flute is the call of the divine, sounding from the very depths of existence. In fact, most of us hear such a call at some time in our lives. It may come in a moment of quietness when we are out in the country, or through an experience of great art, literature, or music. Perhaps we may hear it after some tragic event, or perhaps when we are just rather weary of life. At such a time we may hear the call, the call which is sometimes termed the voice of the silence, the voice of something beyond. But even if we have heard this call very clearly, what usually happens is that we ignore it. Indeed, the very idea that there might have been a voice vaguely worries us. We don't know where it came from, or what mysterious region it might be calling us to. And if we follow it into unknown territory, we are afraid that we will have to give up all sorts of things that we are attached to. So we tell ourselves that we were imagining things, or that it was just a dream, and go on living and working and enjoying ourselves as though we had never heard anything at all.

Quite often, of course, we are much too busy enjoying ourselves even to hear the call, like the children in the parable. They almost completely ignore their father's calls because, the Buddha says—and we can imagine him saying this with a smile—they are absorbed in their games. We are absorbed in our games—the psychological games, spiritual games, and cultural games that we play almost all the time. We are so fascinated by our little games of success, prestige, popularity, ego-tripping dressed up as self-fulfilment, and so on, that even though we hear the call of the divine, the voice of the Buddha, we just go on playing.

And like the children in the burning house, we are not only playing our games, but running to and fro from one game to another. We are restless, anxious, incapable of staying anywhere for long. We constantly want to change the game we are playing or to change our partner—in more ways than one—so we end up running backwards and forwards in desperation. Just one thing occasionally stops us in our tracks. In the story, you may remember, the children just occasionally glance at their father as they run past. Similarly, as we run to and fro playing our little games, we do give the odd glance in the direction of religion.

So what is the elder to do? Force is out of the question and the children will not respond to a direct appeal. In the end his only alternative is to have recourse to a stratagem—in plain words, to play a trick. This kind of 'trick', which benefits the person on which it is played, is known in Buddhism as *upāya kauśalya*—'skilful means'. The elder knows that the children are very fond of toys, so he decides to persuade them to come out of the burning house by promising them carts of different kinds to play with: deer carts, goat carts, and bullock carts. These three different kinds of cart represent, technically speaking, the three 'vehicles', the three *yānas*—the *śrāvakayāna*, the *pratyekabuddhayāna*, and the *Bodhisattvayāna*—that is, the Arhat Ideal, the ideal of private Enlightenment, and the Bodhisattva Ideal.[43] Less technically, the carts stand for different formulations of the Buddha's teaching, or even different sectarian forms of Buddhism adapted to the needs of different temperaments.

Although the children take no notice of their father's warnings of danger, as soon as he promises them all these marvellous toys, out they come rushing. Their eager response to being promised their favourite kind of toy says something very perceptive about how religions appeal to people. It seems to suggest—bearing in mind what the toys represent—that a subjective and sectarian approach to the truth is much more attractive for many people than a more objective, universal approach. And this does seem to be the case in practice. It is certainly the more exclusive forms of religion that exert the most powerful emotional appeal. If your opening gambit is 'Well, look, this is how I see it. Other people see things differently, but we're maybe all right from our own point of view. Let's go forward together,' that is no way to convince the average person. The way to get a following is to put it about that yours is the only true religion and all the others are just plain wrong. This explains why it is that the forms of Buddhism which in the course of history have become the most exclusive—that is, exclusive by Buddhist standards—have become the most popular in the West.

A sectarian approach may be more popular, but does this mean that it is necessary? Do we have to follow a particular path believing it to be the only true way, and only later on in our spiritual experience come to a broader outlook, like the Arhats in the sutra? If we look at our situation it is really questionable whether this is actually possible for us. In the Buddha's day no doubt it *was* possible. His disciples would have been able to learn and practise one teaching at a time. There was no writing in those days, at least not for religious purposes, so the Buddha did all his teaching orally. The disciples couldn't just pick up books about religion, and they certainly didn't go to other teachers, so they knew only what the Buddha taught them.

Even in more recent times, different forms of religion existed independently in different parts of the world—even in different parts of the same country—so it was perfectly possible to stick to one teaching or sect and ignore all the others completely. Until comparatively recently you could be a Christian in the West and never have heard of Buddhism or Hinduism, and you could be a Buddhist in the East and never hear the name of Christianity from one year to the next.

The world is now a very different place. Nowadays, everybody can study everything. All the spiritual teachings are available in written form—'Who runs, may read,' as John Keble said[44]—so it is no longer possible to keep people away from a teaching for which they are not ready. This means that people get hold of all sorts of teachings which, because they are not spiritually developed enough, they can only misunderstand and misinterpret. This just can't be helped. With improved communication and transport, the world is becoming a smaller place all the time. All religions, even all sects, are increasingly to be found everywhere, so it's no longer possible to follow any one and ignore all the others—at the very least we'll know about them from books or hearsay.

In this situation, the only thing to be done is for religions to try to see the parable of the burning house in its universal perspective. We all need to try to recognize that all the ways are different aspects of one and the same path, the path to perfect Buddhahood, the path to Enlightenment. Of course differences of temperament still exist, but sectarianism is no longer needed to cater for them. It is quite enough to choose a method of spiritual practice appropriate to our needs—for example, an appropriate method of meditation. We don't need to belong to a sectarian organization that excludes all the others. We don't need to be 'Theravādin' or 'Zen' or 'Mahayanist'—why not just be Buddhist? And Buddhism itself can be interpreted very broadly. According to the Buddha's own criterion, Buddhism is whatever conduces to the Enlightenment of the individual. The Buddha alone among religious teachers seems to have understood that religion is really the process of the evolution and development of the individual. Sectarian organizations tend to lose sight of this, and in fact many of them express for the most part merely negative emotions, and we would be better off without their exclusivity and intolerance.

You notice that, in their eagerness to get their own particular carts, the children come out of the house pushing and shoving one another. In the same way, in our rush to get out of the house and grab the toy we want, instead of going out side by side or hand in hand, we jostle and shove all the others who are doing the same thing. We may not actually persecute anybody—at least not if we are Buddhists—but at the same time we may not exactly radiate positive feelings towards other people following other paths. This, as we have seen, needs to change, and in fact the parable goes on to show that as you progress on your chosen path it does change. Once the children are all outside, the elder gives each of them the very best kind of cart—or even one and the same cart—bigger and better than anything they could ever have imagined. Here is the indication that the closer people come to the goal, the more their paths converge.

People get into the spiritual life in different ways—some through music, art, or poetry, some through social service, some through meditation, some through the desire to resolve pressing psychological problems. Some people are attracted to Zen, others to the Theravāda. We all have our own personal idiosyncracies, so we are naturally attracted by different things in the beginning. But as we get more and more deeply into our chosen approach, we realize that it is changing us. We begin to notice that our idiosyncracies of temperament—even those which led us to this particular approach—are being resolved. In the end we come to realize through our own experience that all forms of art, all forms of religion, are means for the higher evolution of humanity. By participating in any of them we ourselves are evolving, and other people are also evolving, even though their interests and preoccupations are different from our own. We are all evolving together, all participating in the same process of the Higher Evolution, the process—in Buddhist terms—of cosmic Enlightenment; this is really the message of the parable of the burning house.

So does this mean that the parable is teaching universalism? It is, after all, saying that the distinction between the different *yānas* is illusory, that in reality there is only one *yāna*. But is this universalism? Well, I understand universalism as saying that all religions teach the same thing and that there is therefore no difference between them.[45] The doctrines may appear to differ, but universalists would say that this is only a matter of words—the substance is the same—and they would back this up by trying to equate doctrines from different religions. For example, they would say that the Christian Trinity—Father, Son, and Holy Ghost—corresponds to the Buddhist *trikāya* (*dharmakāya, sambhogakāya, nirmāṇakāya*) and the Hindu *trimūrti* (Brahmā, Viṣṇu, Maheśvara). This kind of wholesale system of equations—the very substance of universalism—often leads to very forced interpretations.

It is clear enough that the parable of the burning house does not teach universalism in this sense. It doesn't say that all religions teach the same thing; they obviously teach different things. Moreover, some religions are more advanced than others—universal religions, for example, being more advanced than ethnic religions. And whereas the universalist would claim that all religions are totally true in all respects, the Buddhist would say that there are some teachings which pass current as religious but—because they are not true—are not really religious at all. The orthodox Christian doctrine of eternal punishment is an example of such a teaching.

The parable is not even saying that all the *yānas* of Buddhism teach the same thing. What it does maintain very definitely is that all the different ways are part of the same 'stream of tendency', to use an expression of Matthew Arnold's. Everyone is trying to get out of the same burning house. Indeed the parable emphasizes movement, escape; it is dynamic, unlike the static teaching of universalism. The universalist fixes systems of belief into patterns which have to rely heavily on intellectual resemblances, whereas the parable of the burning house can rely on the unity of the evolutionary process.

Another general consideration arising out of this parable, and one which must be addressed as it constitutes the main theme, is the idea of escape as a model for the spiritual life. The elder's sole concern is that the children should escape from the burning house. Does this mean that the parable is teaching escapism? Well, obviously enough, it does—in a sense. A lot of people would say that this is typical of the way religions encourage us to run away from the problems of the world, and even from our own problems. And, they would say, this is particularly true of Buddhism. After all, look at the Buddha—leaving his wife and child like that, ducking out of his responsibilities and obligations! Some would say that Christians stay in the world and try to make it into a better place, try to help the sick and care for the needy, whereas Buddhists just sit around meditating, ignoring the sins and sufferings all around them. Pure escapism!

But is escape morally wrong? Suppose you were literally trapped in a burning house. There you would be, standing at the upstairs window, surrounded by smoke and flames. Along would come the fire brigade, and you would escape, either by jumping into a net or by being carried down a ladder. Would your friends say afterwards 'You shouldn't have done that. That was sheer escapism'? Buddhism simply sees that our situation is one of pain and suffering—or at least limitation, imperfection, frustration—and says 'Get out of it.' This is just acting realistically, like escaping from that burning house.

Perhaps the word 'escape' is the wrong one. The word traditionally means 'to gain one's liberty by flight', 'to get safely out of', and so on, but in the nineteenth century it gained a new usage—'mental or emotional distraction from the realities of life'—and it is this which has given birth to the notion of escap*ism*: 'the tendency to seek or practice of seeking such distraction'. The burning house in the parable represents the predicament in which we find ourselves as human beings. Given the connotations of the language of escape, it would perhaps be better to speak of *transcending* this human predicament rather than escaping from it. The parable is showing us how we can transcend our present state, how we can grow from a lower, less satisfactory state of existence to a higher, more satisfactory state.

This is not to say, of course, that there is no such thing as escapism, but we need to understand what escapism really is. Not everybody is prepared to make the kind of effort that the process of growth and development requires—*that* is what we try to escape from. When we try to avoid situations which demand that we go beyond ourselves, when we try to forget our human predicament, when we try to secure an easy life—these are the times when we are really being 'escapist'. Escapism is stagnation, even regression. Sometimes, it is true, religious activity—of the kind which involves lip service but no effort towards personal change—is escapism, though there is less of this these days simply because fewer people are involved in religion of any kind. Nowadays it is more usually non-religious activities that provide outlets for escapism. For many people work is escapism, politics are escapism, even the arts are escapism. Reading is escapism. Watching television is escapism. Sex is escapism. In short, any kind of life that involves no positive, deliberate effort to evolve is escapism—which means, if you think about it, that escapism is the rule rather than the exception. And of course, escapism of this kind is the last thing that the parable of the burning house teaches. It is concerned above all with growth, development, evolution.

Today the burning house is burning more merrily than ever; we only have to open our newspapers or turn on the radio any day of the week to know that. So the whole question of escape—or rather the whole question of transcendence, growth and development into a higher state—becomes more urgent than ever, both for the individual alone and for the individual as part of a spiritual community. Conventional religion as it has come down to us is no longer very useful to us. Even traditional Eastern Buddhism is no longer very useful, either to us in the West or even to people in the East.

Still, there is no need to despair. It is always darkest before the dawn, as the old saying goes. Potentially at least we are on the threshold of an age when the world will be one world, a time when there will be a single world community, a single human culture to which all existing cultures will contribute their best. Enlightenment will be the one universally recognized goal for every human individual, and the way of the Higher Evolution will be the one universally recognized way to reach it. But this will not happen automatically. It will happen only to the extent that the individual human being tries to grow—and we can start to make that effort right now. If we take heed of the message of the parable of the burning house, even here, even now, we can transcend the human predicament.

Chapter Three

QUESTIONS AND ANSWERS

Before hearing the parable of the burning house, Śāriputra says to the Buddha:
   'On first hearing the Buddha's preaching,
   In my mind there was fear and doubt
   Lest it might be Māra acting as Buddha,
   Distressing and confusing my mind.'
Then later he says:
   'It is the World-honored One who preaches the true Way;
   The Evil One has no [such] truths [as] these.
   Hence I know for certain that
   This is not Māra acting as Buddha,
   But because I had fallen into nets of doubts,
   I conceived it as the doing of Māra.'[46]
I wonder if some Hinayanists did think that the Mahāyāna was the work of Māra? Śāriputra represents the Hīnayāna, doesn't he?
Yes. It is quite possible that some followers of the Hīnayāna schools did not merely say that the Mahāyāna sutras were not *Buddhavacana*, but went so far as to say that they were the work of Māra. There is no direct evidence, but this could be indirect evidence.

But what sort of person thinks in this way, considering the matter more broadly? After all, you are quite right to be on your guard against misrepresentations of the Buddha's teaching; there is nothing wrong with that. But the type of Hinayanist represented by Śāriputra here would seem to be the sort of person who is so desperately afraid of not getting it right that he clings fast to his own particular orthodoxy and is closed to any other way of looking at things, even within his own spiritual tradition, and very quick to suspect that some other way of looking at his own tradition is the work of the devil. This suggests great insecurity.

Many people in the Western world during the Middle Ages and even during the Reformation had this sort of attitude. They were so afraid of falling into heresy, so concerned to be completely orthodox Catholics, that they would sometimes say to the Church 'Just tell me what to believe.' Sometimes dogmatic Communists behave in this way too. They are so anxious to follow the exact party line that they are even prepared to change, believing one thing one day and another thing the next as the party line changes. This does suggest great personal insecurity, and a lack of faith in one's own powers of judgement.

•

When Śāriputra receives his prediction to Enlightenment, and in the later predictions, the Buddha foretells the duration of what is called the 'counterfeit Dharma'.[47] *What does this mean? Does it correspond to anything in the history of Buddhism, or point to any real future danger?*
To the best of my knowledge the counterfeit Dharma is that form of Buddhism in which the outward appearances are kept up but the inner spirit is lost. It is tempting to identify that with the Hīnayāna, and perhaps the Hīnayāna did exemplify it in some respects, but in some cases you find Mahāyāna practitioners also just keeping up appearances and losing the spirit. It happens in Zen; it can happen in any form of Buddhism. It is not possible to point to any particular period, although perhaps it has happened in some periods more than others.

We may find personally that there may be times when what *we* are practising is a counterfeit Dharma; we are going through the motions but the spirit is lacking. At other times our heart may really be in it, and then it is the real Dharma. It is not a fixed thing. It is akin to the third fetter, reliance on rules and rituals as ends in themselves.[48] So you can't say that any one particular form of Buddhism represents a counterfeit Dharma. Any individual Buddhist can practise his form of Buddhism in such a way that so far as his life is concerned it is a counterfeit Dharma.

•

The Buddha asks Śāriputra if the elder has been guilty of a falsehood in giving the great carts of the precious substances to his children equally. Śāriputra replies 'Even if the elder did not give them one of the smallest carts, still he is not false. Wherefore? Because that elder from the first formed this intention: 'I will by tactful means cause my children to escape.' For this reason he is not false.'[49] *Is this more or less saying that the end justifies the means?*

No, I don't think it means that at all. Suppose someone comes along to a Buddhist centre to learn meditation. If they ask whether meditation will give them happiness, you are likely to say that it will. The centre does not exist for the sake of making people happy in the limited sense that the person had in mind when they asked the question, but it is not untrue to say that if you practise Buddhism it will make you happy, even in the sense that that person understands that particular term.

It is that sort of point which is being illustrated here. If you give someone more than you had promised them, you are not failing to keep your promise. If you told someone that if they came outside you would give them a bag of sweets, and you actually gave them two bags of sweets, would you have told a lie? Technically you would have, perhaps, but not ethically. You have given more than you promised; you have more than kept your word. Certainly this passage is not to be understood as condoning lies, even in a good cause.

Śāriputra does say that even if the elder had not given the children any carts at all, he would still not have been lying, because his intention was to help the children to escape.

Yes, because the escape was what he really gave them—a greater gift than any cart.

•

The previous chapter of the sutra says 'All things abide in their fixed order, hence the world abides forever.'[50] *What does this mean?*

The Sanskrit here is *dharma-sthitiṁ*, 'dharma' in this context meaning 'cosmic law'. The cosmic law is established according to a certain order; it is not random or fortuitous, but proceeds in certain ways. So this phrase does not mean that the Dharma is fixed in the sense of eternalism, but that its proceeding in a certain way is fixed. The speaker is seeing existence in terms of a certain undeviating order, seeing it especially, perhaps, in terms of the cyclical order and the spiral order. These are fixed in the sense that if you develop a mental state which pertains to the round you will not experience the fruits of the spiral, and vice versa. You can rely on that just as you can rely on the law of gravity. If you jump into the air, you will come down. The law of gravity will not suddenly be suspended so that you go floating up into the air—it is a fixed law, a determinate law, a law that endures. So this is an affirmation of Buddhism's faith in the Dharma, or cosmic law, for want of a better term. You can think of it in terms of the five *niyamas*;[51] they too can be depended upon not to change.

In a footnote to the text, the Chinese master Chih-i is quoted as saying '*Dharma-niyāmatā*, law-order or fixed position, indicates suchness. Because of standing on reality, all laws (or beings) abide forever, and therefore every phenomenon also has an unshakeable and everlasting existence.' Of course you must not think of the thing as separate from the Reality or Suchness in which it is said to abide—that would be to abstract and reify the concept of Suchness. And the phenomena are not unchanging—that is the area of possible confusion—but fixed only in that the process which they represent can be relied upon to go on in that particular way.

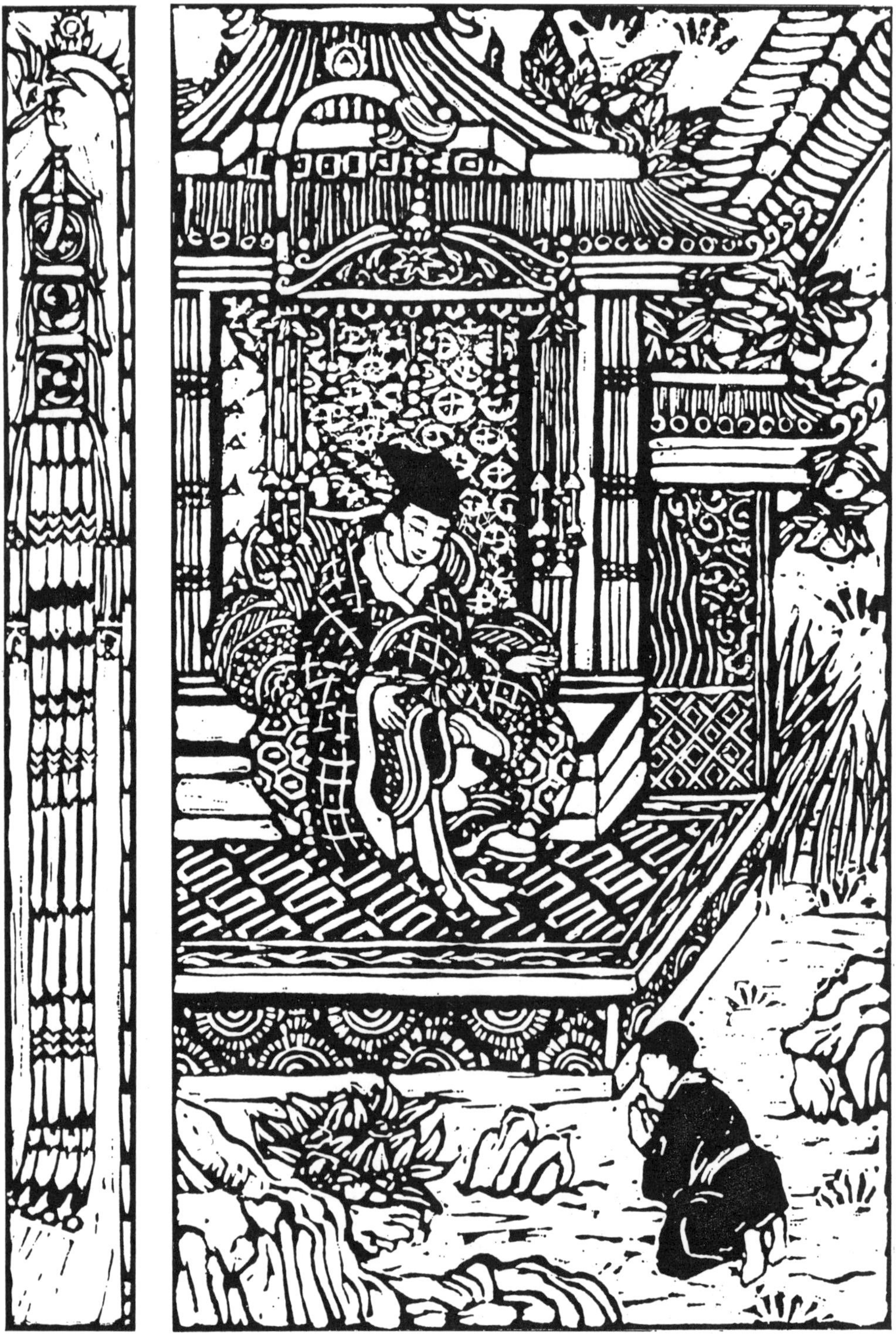

Chapter Four

THE MYTH OF THE RETURN JOURNEY

THE PARABLE OF THE BURNING HOUSE gives us the metaphor of life as predicament, or even as trap, but this is of course only one way of looking at it. Human existence is multi-faceted, deep and mysterious, difficult to understand. 'Wonders are many, and none is more wonderful than man' chants the chorus of Sophocles's play *Antigone*.[52] Throughout history, facets of the nature and purpose of human life have been reflected by symbols and similes from which have arisen myths, legends, and stories—and these in turn have crystallized into epic poems, novels, dramas, and parables. The mystery of human life always having been the compelling preoccupation of humanity, the great works of ancient and modern literature which concern some aspect of human existence are read and reread, even after hundreds and thousands of years.

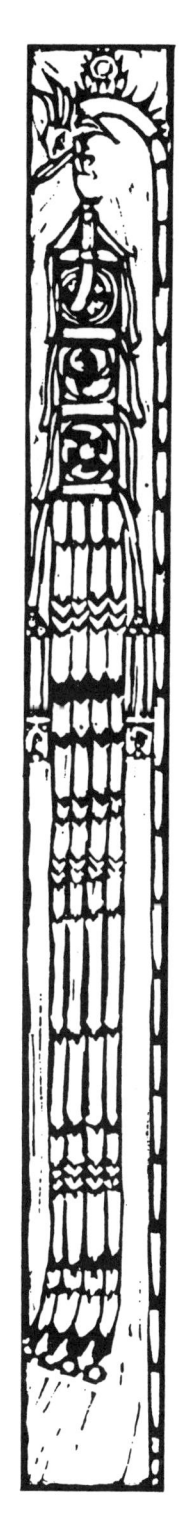

Some of these great works see human life in terms of conflict, or even warfare. Homer's *Iliad*, for example, tells the story of the battle between the Greeks and the Trojans over Helen of Troy, a battle involving not just men and women but even gods and goddesses. Two or three hundred years after the *Iliad* another epic was written, perhaps not so eminent from a literary point of view, but very, very much longer: the *Mahābhārata*. This was composed by the Indian poet and sage Vyāsa, and gives an account of the battle between the Kauravas and their cousins the Pāndavas for possession of their ancestral kingdom. Northern Europe produced the anonymous eighth century Anglo Saxon epic *Beowulf*, which recounts the battles of the hero Beowulf against three terrible adversaries: the fiendish monster Grendel, Grendel's still more fiendish mother, and the dragon. Even from comparatively modern times we have one of the very greatest of all epic poems, Milton's *Paradise Lost*, whose main theme is the War in Heaven, the battle between Satan and the Messiah. In all these works life is seen in terms of conflict. Life is a battle—between right and wrong, between light and darkness, between heaven and hell, between conscious and unconscious—and the battleground is the human heart.

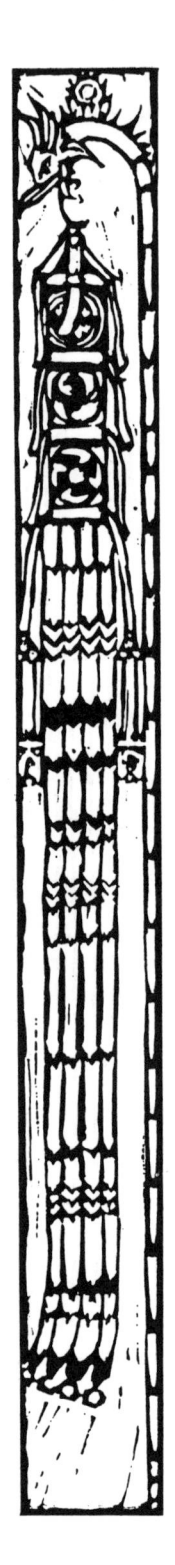

But human existence can also be seen as a riddle, a mystery, or even a problem, and this is how the book of Job in the Bible sees it. Job has been brought up to believe that God rewards the good for their virtue—and punishes the wicked—here in this very life. But although Job is conscious of no evil in himself, he suffers, and it seems that his suffering is the punishment of God. Why should the just man be ground into dust while the unjust man 'flourishes like the green bay tree'? To make sense of life Job needs to know the answer. The same kind of question plagues Shakespeare's Hamlet, confronted with the murder of his innocent father by his villainous uncle. When Hamlet asks his famous question 'To be or not to be?', life itself has become a problem.

There are many other ways of viewing human existence. However, of all the symbols and similes for life, perhaps the most popular and significant is that of the journey or pilgrimage. Life is not only a battle, not only a problem. It is a journey: a journey from the cradle to the grave, from innocence to experience, from the depths of existence to the heights, from darkness to light, from death to immortality. We find life seen as a journey in a great number of works: the *Odyssey*, the *Divine Comedy*, *Monkey*, *Pilgrim's Progress*, *Wilhelm Meister*, *Peer Gynt*, and countless others.

The *White Lotus Sutra* gives its own account of human life as a journey. The parable of the return journey, which occurs in chapter 4, is related not by the Buddha but by four great elders. They have heard the Buddha tell the assembly that Śāriputra is now so far advanced on the path that he is sure to reach the highest goal of all—not just emancipation from his own individual sin and suffering but Buddhahood itself. Amazed and delighted to learn that the spiritual life has a higher aim, the existence of which they had not hitherto suspected, the four great elders say they feel as though they have quite unexpectedly acquired a priceless jewel, and in chorus they give expression to their feelings in a parable.[53]

They say that once upon a time there was a man who left his father and went away into a distant country. He lived there for a long time—perhaps as long as fifty years—and during all that time he was miserably poor. Roaming around, doing a job here and a job there, he lived from hand to mouth, and all he ever possessed were the clothes he stood up in.

Meanwhile, his father was leading a very different kind of life. He was a businessman, and he met with such success in his various trading ventures that he became extremely rich. His trade took him from place to place until he finally settled in another country, where he continued to heap up riches—gold, silver, jewels, and grain. He had slaves and workmen and journeymen, horses and carriages, cows and sheep. He even had elephants—and in the East if you possess elephants you really are rich. He also, inevitably, had dozens of dependants and followers clustering around him in the hope of some reward. His influence in business—money-lending, agriculture, commerce—spread far and wide, and he lived the life of a merchant prince.

But despite his growing wealth and all his business activities, the rich man never stopped missing his son. How was the boy? Would they ever meet again? Sorrowful at their long separation, his one hope was that one day his son would come home to inherit the wealth due to him. 'After all,' the rich man thought, 'I am getting old, and one day I must surely die.'

All this time the son continued to roam from one town to the next, from one kingdom to the next, until one day, quite by chance, he came to the place where his father was living—although of course he had no idea that he was anywhere near his father. As he was passing, or rather skulking, through the streets keeping a lookout for odd jobs which would earn him a few coppers for food, he saw an enormous house, and sitting in the doorway he saw what seemed to be a very rich man. He was surrounded by an enormous company of people, all waiting on him, or waiting for him. Some had bills in their hands and others had great bundles of money that they wanted to give him. Others had presents, and maybe some had bribes.

The rich man was sitting in the gateway on a magnificent throne—even his footstool was ornamented with gold and silver. He was handling millions of gold pieces, just running his fingers through them, and someone was standing behind him fanning him with a yak's tail. In India a yak's tail is one of the symbols of royalty and divinity, so you would only be fanned with one if you were very, very rich indeed, and had been exalted almost to the plane of divinity. Not only that, he was sitting under a magnificent silk canopy which was inlaid with pearls and flowers, and hung all round with garlands of jewels. He really was a magnificent sight.

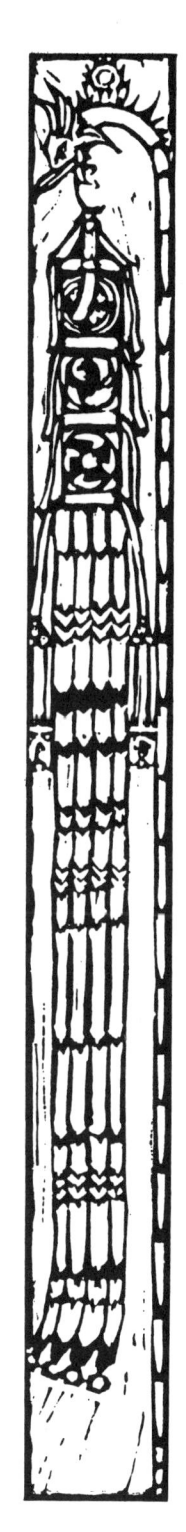

When the poor man saw this rich man seated there on his throne, in all this state, he was absolutely terrified. He thought he must have come upon the king, or at the very least some great nobleman. 'I'd better be off,' he said to himself. 'I'm much more likely to get work in the streets of the poor. If I stay here they might make me into a slave.' And he hurried away, without the faintest idea that the rich man was his own father.

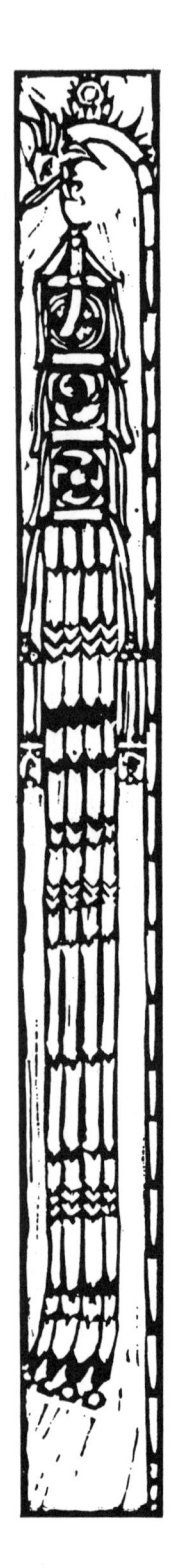

But the rich merchant no sooner saw that wretchedly poor man at the edge of the crowd of followers than he knew that this was his son, come back after all these years. What a relief! Now he would be able to hand over his wealth to its rightful inheritor and die happy. Joyfully he called a couple of servants and told them to run after the poor man and bring him back. But when they caught up with the poor fellow he was more terrified than ever. 'They've been sent to arrest me. I'm probably going to have my head cut off!' he thought—and he was so afraid that he fell to the earth in a dead faint.

His father was rather surprised at this, but he began to see that all those years he had been living in riches, his son had been living in poverty, and this had created a great psychological difference between them. The boy was obviously not used to being in contact with the rich and powerful. But the faithful father thought 'Never mind. However low he may have sunk, he is still my son,'—and he resolved to find a way of restoring their relationship. In the meantime, things being as they were, he decided that it would be better to keep his son's identity secret. He therefore called another servant and instructed him to tell the poor man that he was free to go. Hardly believing his luck, the poor man went off with all speed to seek work in the poorest quarter of the town.

But he was followed by two of his father's men, chosen for their humble appearance. When they caught up with him, the men offered him work, as the rich man had instructed them to do. The job would be to clear away a huge heap of dirt that had accumulated at the back of the mansion, and the wages would be double the normal rate. The poor man accepted this proposal at once, and went off to work with the two men. Day after day he shovelled the heap of dirt and removed it in baskets to a distant place. He found lodging in a straw hovel right next to the mansion, so close that the rich man could see it from his window. The rich man would often look out and think how strange it was that he should be living in a beautiful mansion while his son lived in squalor so near by.

One day, when the poor man had been working at the mansion for quite some time, the rich man put on dirty old clothes and, taking a basket in his hands, managed to have a talk with his son. 'Don't think of working anywhere else', he said, 'I'll make sure you've got plenty of money. If there's anything you need—a pot, a jug, some extra grain, anything like that—just ask me. I've got an old cloak in the cupboard; you can have that if you like. Just don't worry about a thing. You've been working well and I'm pleased with you. You seem honest and sincere, not like some of the rogues I've got working for me. In fact—well, I'm an old man—you look to me as your own father, and I'll treat you just like my own son.'

So for a number of years the poor man carried on clearing away the heap of dirt, and he got into the habit of going in and out of the mansion without thinking twice, although he continued to live in his old straw hovel. Then it happened that the old man became ill, and knew that he was soon going to die. He called the poor man and said 'I feel that I can trust you completely now, just as I would my own son, so I'm going to hand over to you the management of all my affairs. You'll do everything on my behalf.' And from that day onward the poor man was the rich man's steward, and looked after all his investments and transactions. As before, he went freely in and out of the mansion but continued to live in his old hovel. Even though he was handling all this wealth, he continued to think that he was poor, for as far as he knew the money was not his, but his master's.

But as time went on, the poor man changed. His father, who watched him constantly, saw that he was gradually becoming accustomed to handling riches, and feeling ashamed that in the past he had lived so miserably. It became obvious that the poor man had begun to want to be rich himself. By this time the rich man was very old and weak indeed, and he knew that his death was near. So he sent for all the people in the city—the king's representative, the merchants, his friends, his distant relations, ordinary citizens, and country folk from round about—and when they were all gathered, he presented his son to them and told them the whole story. When he had finished, he handed over all his wealth to his son, who, of course, could hardly believe his good fortune.

In the context of the *White Lotus Sutra*, this parable has a specific meaning which the four elders explain as soon as they have finished telling the story. Until now, they confess, they have been contented with an inferior spiritual ideal. Now, in his kindness and generosity, the Buddha has revealed to them the ideal of attaining supreme Enlightenment not for themselves alone but for the benefit of all sentient beings, and in this way has made them heirs to all his spiritual treasures. Like the son in the parable, the four elders feel overjoyed at the wealth which they have so unexpectedly gained.

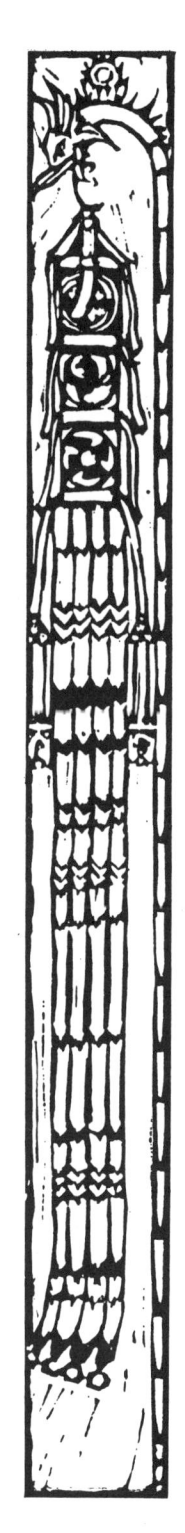

The four elders' explanation takes us quite a long way, but with a little imagination we can go much further, even much deeper. We can start by reflecting on the strangely familiar ring of this story. You may well be thinking 'I'm sure I've heard that story somewhere before.' Thinking back, you may be pretty sure that you haven't read the *White Lotus Sutra*—it isn't the sort of thing you can read one weekend and then forget about—so why does the parable of the return journey seem so familiar? The reason, as you may have realized, is that it resembles a much more widely known parable: Jesus's parable of the prodigal son.[54] This parable is told by Jesus of Nazareth to elucidate a different point, and it has a different ending, but in general outline the two stories are the same. In both parables there is an affectionate father and a son who runs away; in both parables the runaway son lives miserably for a while before returning to the bosom of his father; and in both parables the position of servant is contrasted with the position of son.

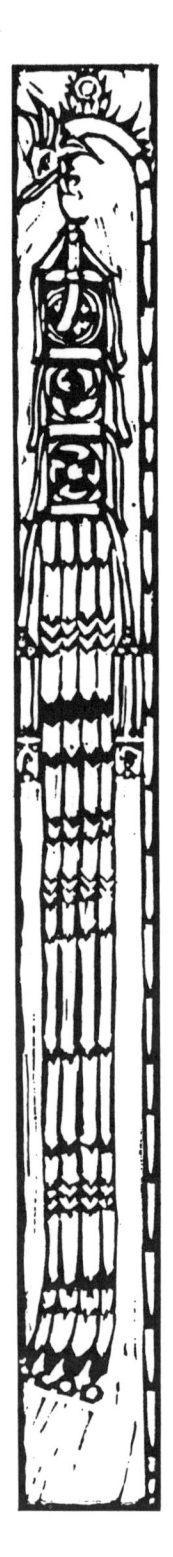

These are the similarities between the parables; there are also significant differences between them. Perhaps the most important of these differences is that in the Gospel parable the prodigal son appears to be guilty of wilful disobedience, whereas in the *White Lotus Sutra* the son seems to go astray just through carelessness and forgetfulness. This illustrates a crucial difference between Buddhism and Christianity, Christianity seeing the human condition in terms of sin, disobedience, and guilt while Buddhism sees it more in terms of forgetfulness, unmindfulness, and ignorance.

Another parable about a father and a son, belonging to roughly the same period as the parable of the return journey, constitutes an even more interesting parallel. It occurs in the apocryphal Acts of the Apostle Thomas, an essentially Gnostic work extant in Greek translation as well as in the original Syriac. Modern translators call the story the 'Hymn of the Pearl', but the text gives it the title 'Song of the Apostle Judas Thomas in the Land of the Indians.'[55] Saint Thomas, one of the twelve Apostles, is traditionally known as the Apostle to India because he is supposed to have visited India soon after the death of Jesus, and this parable is said to have been composed while he was imprisoned there. Whether he had much contact with Buddhism, and whether the 'Hymn of the Pearl' owes anything to the parable of the return journey, we can only speculate.

The parable says that in the East there live a father and his son. The son is quite happy living in the wealth and splendour of 'the kingdom of his father's house', but one day his father sends him on a mission to the land of Egypt, to bring back the one pearl which lies, encircled by a great dragon, in the midst of the sea. When he reaches Egypt, the son finds the dragon and waits for him to go to sleep so that he can take the pearl. But the Egyptians become suspicious of this stranger, even though he is disguised in Egyptian garments, and they give him a drugged drink which causes him to lose his memory. Forgetting that he is the son of a king, forgetting all about the pearl, he enters the service of the king of Egypt. And eventually, living with the Egyptians, eating their food and drinking their drink, he becomes more and more like them. In the end, we are told, he falls into a deep sleep. His father in the East, who knows what is happening, becomes anxious, and sends his son a letter—in the form of a bird—reminding him of his mission. And as soon as he receives the letter, the son comes to his senses, enchants the dragon, and seizes the pearl. He returns home in triumph, and his father receives him with great joy.

Each of these parables, the return journey, the prodigal son, and the 'Hymn of the Pearl', has its own wealth of symbolism, but they all share the same central symbol. They all begin with a separation between a father and a son; this is the event from which everything else follows. So what is meant by this separation of father and son? Who or what are the father and the son?

Well, we could say that the father represents what may be called the higher self (although we need to be careful not to take the expression too literally), and the son is the lower self. And just as the son is separated from his father, the lower self is separated—or, in more contemporary language, *alienated*—from the higher self. Here, by the way, is another metaphor for the human condition: alienation. We are alienated from our own higher selves, our own better natures, our own highest potentialities. We are alienated from Truth, from Reality. And just as the son went not just a short distance away from his father, but to an altogether different part of the world, so the alienation between the higher self and the lower self is severe. Indeed, the schism between the two is complete; there is no contact of any kind between them.

We may say that the condition of the human race is one of alienation from Truth, but when did this condition begin? The son lives in a distant country for many years, which suggests that the alienation is of long standing. But if we take the parable literally, the implication is that although it may have happened a long time ago, it did happen at a certain point in time. This is the view of orthodox Christianity, which teaches that Adam and Eve lived happily in the garden of Eden, in harmony with God and in obedience to his commands, until Adam took a bite of the apple, at which point mankind fell from grace and became alienated from God.

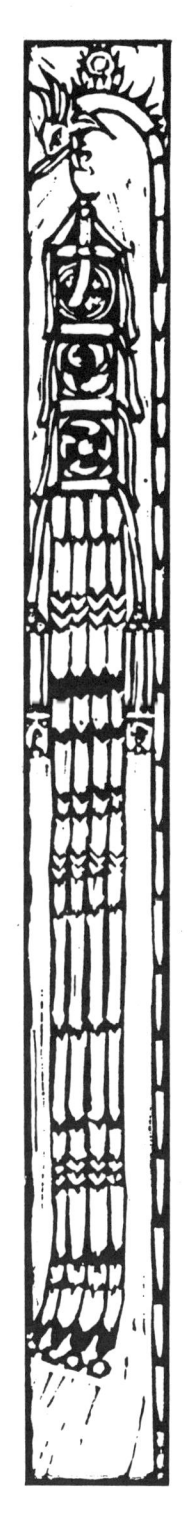

Buddhism holds a different view. According to the Buddha you can go back and back in time for millions of years, millions of ages, but you will never come to an absolute first beginning of things. However far back you go, you can still go further. You will never get back to a point before the point at which time begins. So the beginning of the parable is not in time at all, but completely outside time. This means that the 'return journey' is not a journey back into the past, but a journey out of time altogether, a journey which transcends time. It is very important to understand this.

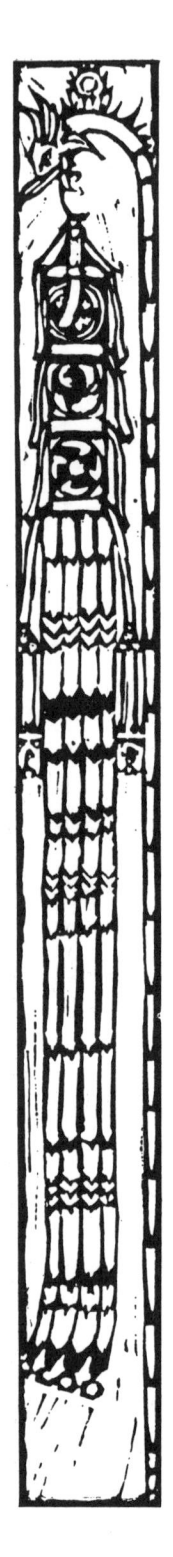

In the books about Zen which people are so fond of reading, there are all kinds of strange and wonderful—and apparently meaningful—expressions, all kinds of appealingly snappy little mondos and koans. One of these Zen sayings—which is of course absolutely true—speaks of 'your original face before you were born'. The Zen masters are apparently rather fond of asking their disciples, at a moment's notice, to show them their original face before they were born. 'Come on!' they demand, 'Show it to me. I want to see it.' Of course the hapless disciple usually fails miserably, as hapless disciples tend to in these stories, written as they apparently are by the masters. The disciple tends to tackle the problem by sitting down and thinking about yesterday, the day before, the week before, a month ago, two months ago, a year ago, two years ago, twenty years ago, thirty years ago—until they get back to the day they were born. If they can get back past *that*, they think, they will encounter their original face.

This is all wrong. To think that before a certain point in time there was the original face and after that there was no original face is a complete misunderstanding. The expression may seem to mean this, but if we go trying to track down the original face in the past, if we take this expression 'original' or the word 'before' literally, we are not really practising Zen, but just regressing in the psychoanalytical sense. The past is no nearer to Enlightenment than the present or the future, because time has nothing to do with Enlightenment. We are 'born', in the Zen sense, out of time, and our original face also exists out of time, so the Zen expression 'seeing your original face' has nothing to do with going back in time, or with going forward in time, or with standing still at the present moment of time. When Zen speaks of seeing your original face before you were born, it means going outside time altogether, rocketing through time and coming up on the other side in a dimension where there is no time at all, no past, present, or future. That is where the original face is to be seen, and nowhere else. That's where it 'is' all the time.

So there is no question of going back in time to enquire into the beginning of our state of alienation. We are alienated from reality here and now, and all we have to do is overcome this alienation from reality.

And we can't do that just by going back and back into the past because we are still running on the rails of the alienation itself. We have to take a leap, a crosswise leap—a jump from the top of the pole, to use another Zen expression—to land, if we're lucky, in the absolute.

This is the point of the Buddha's famous parable of the poisoned arrow—another parable connected with war—which is told in the Pali Canon.[56] The Buddha says that a soldier was wounded in battle by a poisoned arrow. Fortunately there is a surgeon on hand, but when he tries to take the arrow out, the wounded man says 'Just a minute! Before I let you take out that arrow I want to ask a few questions. Who shot this arrow? Was he a brahmin, a kṣatriya, or a vaiśya? Was he dark or fair? Was he young or old? What sort of bow was he using? And what sort of arrow is it?—A wooden one? An iron one? If it's wood, what sort of wood is it made from?—Oak? Cedar? Where does the feather come from? Is it a goose feather or a peacock feather? Answer all these questions, and then you can take out the arrow.'

Long before his questions were answered, of course, the soldier would be dead from the poison in the arrow. The important thing is to get rid of the arrow, not to enquire where it came from. In the same way, if we try to go back and back all the time—'How did the world begin? How did we get into such a mess? What was I in my last birth? What are the roots of my neurosis?'—there is no end to it. We could go step by step back into the past and still be walking in millions of years. What we need to do is just see our present alienated, neurotic, conditioned, negative state, and rise above it, go soaring up into eternity, into a spiritual dimension. This is the message of the poisoned arrow. Likewise, the 'return journey' of the son is not about going back in time, but about going beyond time.

The son, who represents the lower self, wanders from place to place looking for work, for the simple reason that he needs food and clothing. He has no higher ideals. He has none of his father's ambitions of succeeding in trade and commerce. Translating this into modern terms (borrowed from Abraham Maslow's book *Towards a Psychology of Being*),[57] the lower self is 'need-motivated'. Everything the son does is out of his subjective need, out of his craving. By contrast, the father—the higher self—is 'growth-motivated'. The parable expresses this in terms of his accumulation of riches, but this is in no way to imply that it is glorifying capitalism or anything like that; as a parable, its meaning is symbolic. The father, the higher self, accumulates wealth until he possesses all conceivable spiritual riches and qualities.

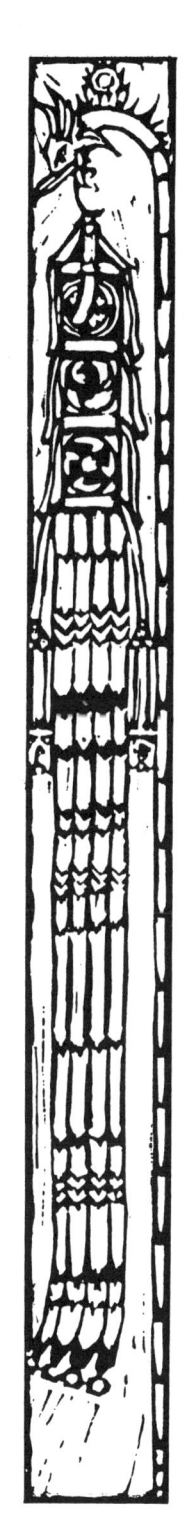

Although he is so rich, the father is not happy because he is thinking of his son *all the time*. What can we infer from this? It tells us that the higher self never loses its awareness. It's conscious all the time. Although we may completely forget the higher self, the higher self never forgets us. But at the same time—this is the mystery—we are it. An image may help to make this clear. Imagine an enormous subterranean chamber all lit up from within. We are living in a tiny chamber next to—indeed part of—the big one. A pane of glass which is transparent only from one side separates the two chambers, so that although someone in the large illuminated chamber could see everything going on in the little chamber, from the little chamber we can see nothing at all of what is going on in the large chamber. In fact, we have no idea that there *is* a large chamber. But although cramped in our little chamber we may forget, even be oblivious to, the existence of the large chamber, the large chamber always has a window onto the little chamber. Even though the lower self forgets the higher self, the higher self is the higher self *of* the lower self.

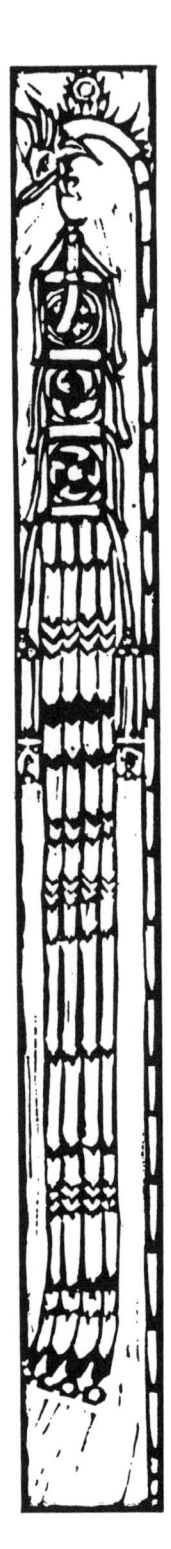

The parable says that the poor man roams from one town to another and one country to another until he eventually reaches the place where his father is living. So he is already on his way back to his father, although he does not know it. It is his need for food and clothing, his craving, which drives him from place to place and brings him almost to his father's door. What are we to make of this?

Let's look at an example. A man has a certain psychological problem. He's so worried about it that he just can't sleep, and sleeping tablets don't help. He is really getting desperate for some peace of mind. One day he meets a friend who says 'I know what will help you. You need to meditate.' By this stage the man is ready to try anything, so he asks where he can learn to meditate and goes along to a class. His only concern is to get rid of the problem and get some sleep. But at the meditation classes he starts to hear about something new: Buddhism. At first he is not particularly interested, but after a few months—rather to his surprise—he finds himself not just trying to get peace of mind but trying to follow the spiritual path. After a while he even starts thinking in terms of Enlightenment. So when did he take the first step in that direction? It was when, driven by his need for peace of mind, he joined the meditation class. In the same way the poor man, driven by his basic needs, made his way to his father's door without knowing it. This is the first stage of the return journey.

When the poor man eventually arrives at his father's door, his father is sitting outside surrounded by gold, jewels, and flowers. The poetic description of the rich man—who represents the higher self—is highly significant. He is a glorious archetypal figure, a god, even a Buddha, so he is described with light and colour, jewels and brilliance. But how does the poor man react? He is so terrified at the sight that he wants to run away. He thinks that he has come upon a king or nobleman, not recognizing in this glorious figure his own father. This goes to show that the alienation between the lower self and the higher self is quite severe. Even when the two confront each other, the lower self does not recognize the higher self as its own higher self, but thinks it is something strange and foreign. Such a confrontation occurs when we come face to face with an embodiment of the spiritual ideal. Whenever we read a description or see an image of the Buddha—or some god or saint—we think, or our lower self thinks, 'This has nothing to do with me. I'm down here, poor and humble. I'm not like that. I don't have those qualities.' The theistic systems which believe in a personal creator god, and indeed all dualistic systems, encourage this attitude.

We could call this the stage of religious projection. We project outwards all the qualities which are buried deep down in the depths of our own nature, not realizing that they are our own. As we see it, these glorious external figures are endowed with all the qualities which we lack. We are poor and they are rich. This religious projection is a step in the right direction; indeed, it is the next stage of the journey. It is a positive thing because it enables us to see spiritual qualities in a concrete way. But the projection must be resolved. These qualities belong to us—not to our ego, but to the deepest and truest depths of our being—and we must claim them as our own.

As yet, however, the son does not recognize his father, although his father immediately recognizes him and sends messengers to bring him back. But the poor man is terrified, thinks he is going to be arrested, and faints away. This reminds me of the account of the death experience given in the *Tibetan Book of the Dead*. At the time of death, so the text says, the Clear Light, a white light of absolutely unbearable brilliance, like a million suns, suddenly bursts on the vision of the dying person.[58] This light is the light of Reality, the light of Truth, the light of the Void. If we recognize that this is no light bursting upon us from without, but the light of our own intrinsic mind, our own true self, unfolding from deep within, if we can realize our oneness with that light, then we gain Enlightenment on the spot. But what happens? The light comes—blinding, terrible, overpowering—and most dying people shrink back in fear. 'Human kind cannot bear very much reality.'[59] This is true not only at the moment of death, but at all those moments when we encounter a truth that seems more than we can possibly bear.

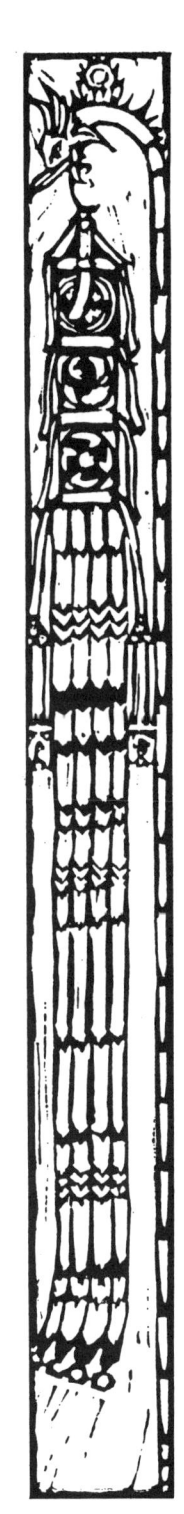

The poor man, you notice, is not just terrified. His imagination is working overtime. He thinks that he is being arrested: already in his mind's eye he can see the block and the executioner's axe. His first thoughts are of imprisonment, slavery, violent death. Only too often when we come in contact with the Truth, it seems not liberating but an imprisonment, a limitation, or at least a nuisance. We do not want to change our ideas, or to change ourselves, and in that diseased state the liberating truth seems to us confining and narrow. Not only that, like the poor man in the parable we are afraid of dying. When the lower self—the I, the ego—comes in contact with Reality, it thinks, as it were, 'I'm for the chop. I'm finished; this is the end of me,' and so it shrinks back.

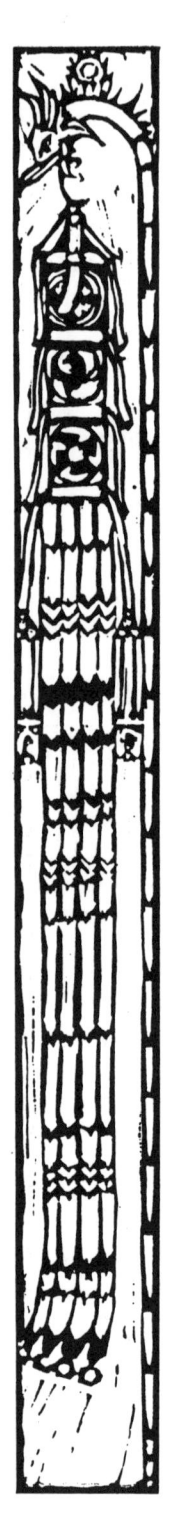

So the rich man lets his son slope off, but of course he has not given up hope, and by some clever planning he manages to get his son clearing away the heap of dirt at the back of his mansion. Now according to the interpretation of the parable which the four elders give, the son's clearing away dirt represents the narrow, selfish type of religious life which is aimed at individual development to the exclusion of any concern for others. The four elders identify this sort of approach with the Hīnayāna, the lesser teaching which they have so recently renounced, but this is perhaps a little extreme. A better—or at least more contemporary—interpretation would suggest that the clearing away of the dirt represents the process of psychoanalysis, the heap of dirt representing all the repressions which the alienated person uncovers during analysis. The sutra mentions that it takes twenty years to clear away the dirt, which seems rather a long time, but resolving repressions, negative emotions, complexes, and all the rest of it is rather time-consuming, so analysis does sometimes take as long as that.

And eventually, while the process of removing the dirt-heap continues, the father manages to speak to his son, and confidence springs up between them. As this trust develops, the poor man begins to enter the rich man's mansion without hesitation, but he continues to live in his own hovel. So what does this mean? On one level it refers to the scholar, the academic specialist in comparative religion. He knows the texts, sometimes in the original languages, and he knows the teachings, even the higher teachings. Sometimes he even claims to know the esoteric teachings. In other words, he goes in and out of the mansion without hesitation, knowing exactly what is there—but he does not live there himself. He still lives in the straw hovel which represents all the things he is really interested in as an academic: promotion within his department; his annual increment; prestige within his profession; controversy and brisk exchange of articles and opinions with other scholars.

On a higher level, the poor man's going in and out of the mansion without hesitation refers to the average follower of religion. Such people are undoubtedly sincere and have perhaps had genuine religious experience—they go in and out of the mansion, as it were—but their home is elsewhere. Even though they have some spiritual experience, maybe during the weekly meditation class, they are preoccupied most of the time with mundane things. In one of his books William James, the great psychologist and author of *The Varieties of Religious Experience*, discusses the question 'What is a religious person?' He says that a religious person is not one who has religious experiences—anybody can have those—but one who makes religious experiences the centre of their existence. It is not important where we visit; what is important is where we permanently live, or at least where we live most of the time—in other words, where our real centre of interest lies. As the Gospel says, 'Where your treasure is, there will your heart be also.'

When the rich man falls sick, he hands the management of his affairs over to the poor man, who thus becomes familiar with riches but still continues to live in the hovel. This element of the parable represents the theist, or the theistically inclined mystic, and the dualistic approach in general. Such a person may have great, overwhelming, uplifting spiritual experiences, but they all seem to come from outside, not from within. The mystic says 'These experiences are not mine; they are the gifts of God.'

Once you reach this stage of the journey, only time is required. The rich man sees that his son is becoming used to riches and ashamed of his poverty, that he aspires to be rich himself. In other words, the alienation of lower self from higher self is becoming less and less. When the rich man is at the point of death, the alienation is practically over, with just a thin thread remaining; the lower self and the higher self are almost one. And when at last the rich man acknowledges the poor man as his son, he dies, and there are no longer two—father and son, rich man and poor man—but only one, a rich man who was once a poor man. In other words, unity between the lower self and the higher self has been completely restored. The return journey has been accomplished.

Our journey also is nearly accomplished. The four elders who have told the parable compare themselves to the son—and the Buddha, of course, is the father. Formerly, they say, they had not dared to think in terms of becoming like the Buddha, thinking only of following his verbal teaching, which had seemed to indicate a lesser goal, the goal of individual emancipation, the goal of the destruction of negative emotions. But they now realize, they say, that that is not enough, for there are all sorts of positive qualities to be developed. It is not enough to have

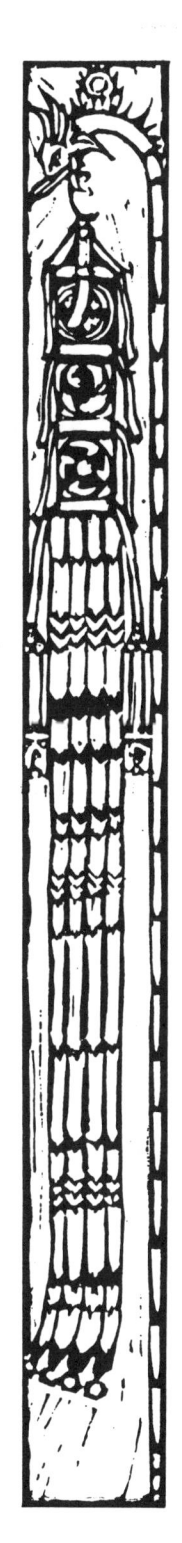

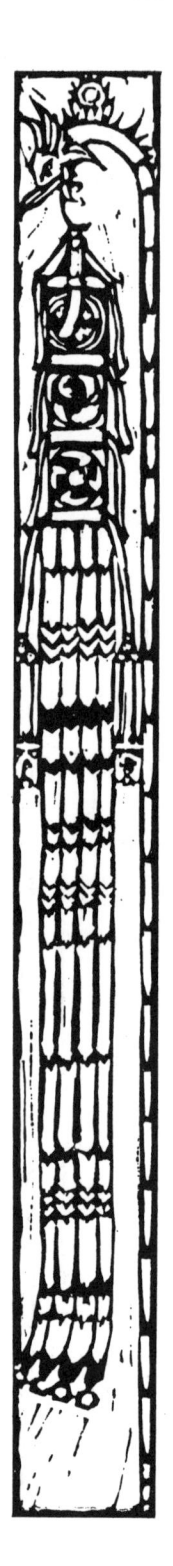

Wisdom; you need Compassion too. It is not enough to be an Arhat; you can become like the Buddha himself. You can follow the Bodhisattva Path; you can aspire to supreme Enlightenment.

In other words, the four elders wake up to the truth of the Higher Evolution of man. They realize that the Buddha is not something unique and unrepeatable, but a forerunner, an example of what others too can become if only they make the effort. They realize that the religious life is not just a personal affair in a negative limited sense, but part of a cosmic adventure—and this is what we too have to try to realize. Religion, when properly understood, is not something remote from life, not just a dull, churchy little backwater, but life become conscious of its own upward tendency, its own tendency to grow and develop. And whether we know it or not, we are all involved, directly or indirectly, in this upward tendency of life. Each one of us is the poor man in the parable, the son who has run away; but each one of us also, if we only knew it, is the rich man, the father. And each one of us is making, even at this very moment, the return journey.

Chapter Four

QUESTIONS AND ANSWERS

It seems to me that there are two complementary models which describe the predicament of man: the conceptual, linear model of the Higher Evolution, and the cyclical myth of the Fall, of descent and return, the latter developed, for example, by Blake in the Four Zoas. To what extent is the myth of the Fall in accord with the Dharma?

It is *not* in accord with the Dharma. There *is* a myth of a fall in Buddhist literature, in the *Aggañña Suttanta* of the Dīgha Nikāya in the Pali Canon,[60] but that is not a fall from the absolute, so to speak, but from a higher to a lower plane of being within the mundane sphere. The sutta describes how at the beginning of the world period beings remaining from a previous cycle of evolution and involution, attracted by the evolving material universe, descend and become merged with it. So far the picture is identical with that of other traditions. The difference is that Buddhism does not regard this fall as a fall from a state of perfection. Indeed, in Buddhism there can be no question of such a fall. By definition a Buddha *cannot* fall; there is no fall from the state of Enlightenment. There can only be a fall from relatively higher to relatively lower states within the *saṃsāra*.

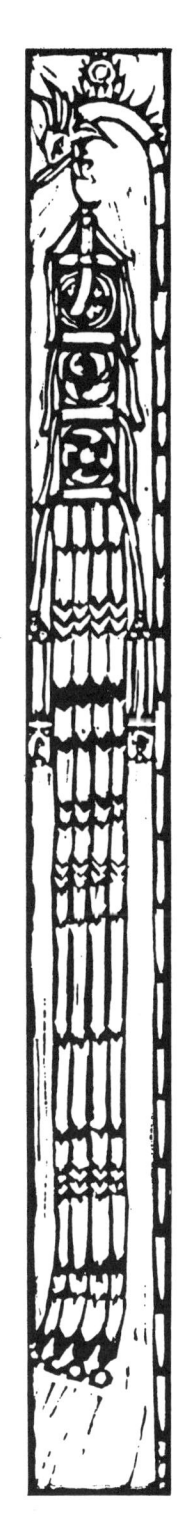

Buddhism does not recognize an ultimate first beginning, so there can be no question of everything starting with an original fall of man. There is also no question of a return journey in the sense of going back into the past. It is going 'back' to something which is outside time. You can think of the absolute as being above you, or as being deep within you, or even as something which you have left behind, but you cannot help putting it in some relation to space and time. Within the Buddhist context, therefore, the return journey is not literally a journey to something which was there in the beginning. You return to it not by travelling backwards in time but by going out of time altogether. We can think of the absolute as being 'above' the temporal process, which is spatial terminology, or we can think of it as being 'before' the temporal process, which is temporal terminology. If one of these ways of thinking has more emotional resonance for you than the other, make use of whichever is appropriate—but be careful how you interpret it in conceptual terms.

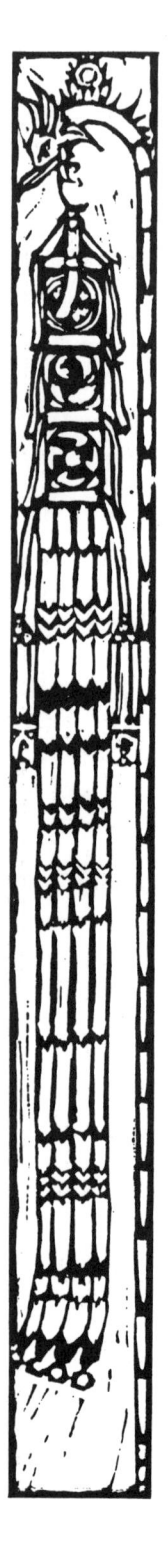

But if you take the myth of the fall not literally or as doctrine but symbolically, is there anything wrong with that approach?
Well, you can think of the fall as occurring outside time. Really the fall occurs at every instant. There is a fall every time craving arises in dependence on feeling, instead of faith.

Why does the idea of a return journey have such a strong emotional appeal?
One reason might be that it suggests the real possibility of contact between yourself and what you are seeking, or even that you are in contact with the ideal already in a vestigial way. Perhaps also it has something to do with the experience of very early childhood. Maybe you unconsciously hearken back to those very early days of 'oceanic oneness'.

But surely it is not just a matter of 'going back to the womb'? Isn't it more that you make use of that impulse but turn it around and allow it to move you in the direction you really need to take?
When you get in touch with the emotions bound up with that very early state, that must be a positive thing, because you can then link something very deep and basic in yourself with your spiritual quest, your spiritual aspirations.

Perhaps from time to time it would be a good thing to try to get back in contact with those early childhood feelings. I think in almost all cases they must have been intensely pleasurable, though perhaps they were all too quickly overlaid with much less pleasurable experiences. A baby gets immense emotional satisfaction from the experience of relative oneness with its mother; in fact, our relationship with our mother is probably the most important emotional experience in our life, leaving aside spiritual developments. This is perhaps not a very popular point of view, but I think that in the course of our adult relationships we are often only trying to recapture that early pleasurable experience, which in almost all cases was so intensely blissful, so secure, so satisfying, so uncomplicated. We could probably not have survived very long without it.

How might one get back in touch with those early feelings?
You can just try to remember them. It is not really a question of remembering specific experiences; that is perhaps not possible unless something traumatic happened to you. It is more like recollecting the feeling of the state before anything traumatic happened. There is a theory that your first really traumatic experience occurs when you are weaned, and this is not surprising. Watch a mother and you will see that she is totally absorbed in her baby; it is almost a lover-like relationship. On the receiving end of that, the baby probably feels great, and really enjoys the experience. Everybody has gone through that at some stage, and it must have left a trace in the psyche which perhaps still persists. It is good to get in touch with that.

So the return journey myth could be a synthesis of those early feelings and the feeling of wanting to be an individual, wanting to develop spiritually?
Yes. It is important to carry your emotions, especially your more basic and primitive emotions, along with you.

•

The Christian religious tradition gained inspiration from earlier literature by interpreting the myths and parables of that literature allegorically. I have in mind the Christian interpretations of the Greek myths as they came down to them particularly through the Metamorphoses *of Ovid.*
Well, I think that usually Christian thinkers were more concerned with giving allegorical interpretations of Old Testament myths and legends. Some took the view that the gods and goddesses of Greek and Roman mythology were simply demons. It was the Greeks themselves, the Neoplatonists, who started the allegorization of their own myths.

What is the function of allegory?
Strictly speaking, allegory means the personification of certain abstract qualities which are then made to behave in a way that illustrates the relationships between those qualities. Suppose, for example, that you want to describe some sort of moral conflict. Perhaps you call your hero Everyman. Someone called Temptation comes along and tries to persuade him to do something, but then another character called Good Counsel advises him not to do it. Conscience might intervene and reinforce what Good Counsel says, but then Pleasure comes along and Everyman is swayed in the other direction. That is the distinct literary form called allegory. One of the best-known allegories in English is the

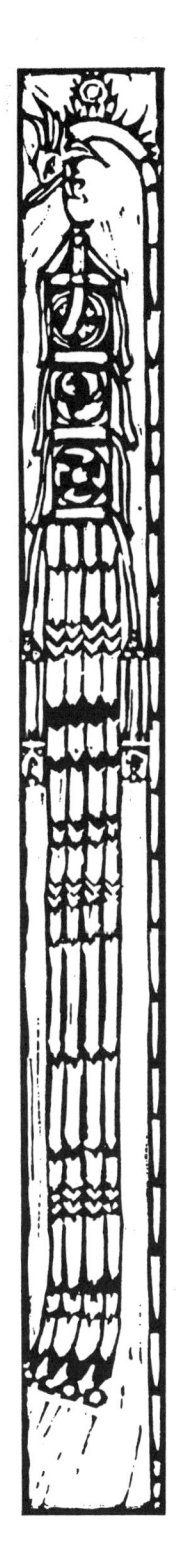

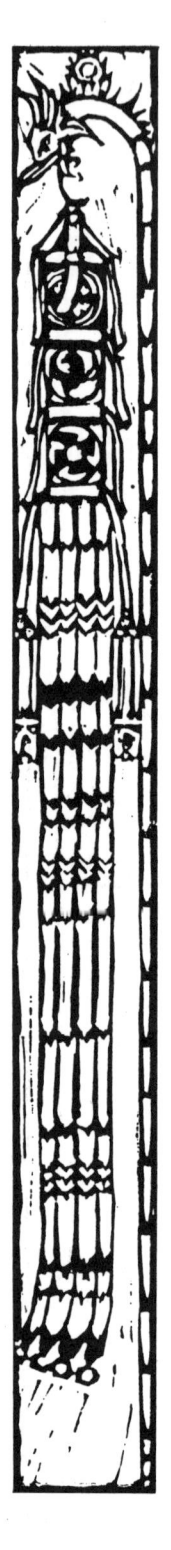

Pilgrim's Progress.

When we speak of the allegorization of myths and legends, though, we are not really thinking of that specific form; we are using the term in a very loose, perhaps even incorrect, way. The basic purpose of the so-called allegorization of myths, legends, and symbols is to try to evoke from them a meaning which is deeper and more acceptable than the surface meaning. This kind of allegorization is extremely important as a means of preserving continuity of tradition and reflecting the developing spiritual consciousness of the individual or group. Suppose, say, as an ancient Greek you know various stories about the gods and goddesses, but some of the actions of the gods and goddesses are in conflict with your own moral sense. What are you to do? At first sight it seems that the options are either to stifle your moral sense and continue to take those stories literally, or to heed the dictates of your moral sense to such an extent that you reject the myths and legends on moral grounds. But there is a third option, a middle way. You can interpret the myths and legends in such a way that your moral sense, your developing spiritual sense, is no longer offended. That is really what this type of 'allegorization' is all about. It enables you to stay in touch with your own tradition and faithful to it while not having to accept it in a literal sense which is offensive to you. You are able to grow and at the same time you stay in contact with your tradition. This is an almost universal process, because as people develop, the old myths in their literal forms become unacceptable.

For instance, at one point in the *White Lotus Sutra* we find the Buddha putting out his tongue and encircling the universe with it.[61] This is really quite grotesque, and offends our aesthetic sense, but can we take it literally? We could say that the sutra is illustrating the power and importance of speech in a way that the ancient Indian mentality evidently found acceptable, but that we cannot accept. We are not happy with the imagery, and certainly cannot take it literally, so we have to do the best we can with it by allegorizing it.

To what extent are the parables found in the White Lotus Sutra *intended by their author to be interpreted allegorically?*
It is very doubtful whether the authors of parables consciously distinguish their many different levels of meaning. To take another example, commentators on Shakespeare's plays have read all sorts of profound meanings into them, interpreting their imagery and the significance of the various characters, but it is very doubtful whether those meanings were consciously present to Shakespeare's mind when he composed the plays. That is not to say that those meanings cannot validly be found

there; it is almost as though Shakespeare had a higher perception which included those meanings in a non-conceptual way.

It is much the same with the author of the parables, myths, and symbols of the *White Lotus Sutra*. You *can* construct a myth or legend, but that is an artificial procedure which probably will not have the same kind of impact. Some poets have tried to create myths of their own, but they are usually not very successful. Most poets wisely prefer to give some shape to traditional material.

So to what extent can the sutra be interpreted allegorically after perhaps first absorbing it on a more imaginative, non-rational level?
You will start interpreting it, allegorizing it, when you feel a need to do so. If you don't feel a need to do so, don't bother. I think a lot of people reading the parables, myths, and symbols of the *White Lotus Sutra* will quite spontaneously start trying to interpret them as a means of engaging with the material at a deeper level. And if you do this you do reach a deeper and fuller experience of those parables, myths, and symbols. It is not that you cease to experience them as parables, myths, and symbols—indeed, after allegorizing them you should experience them more profoundly and more strongly.

Has Buddhist tradition had recourse to allegory in any particular texts?
I don't think that Buddhist myths and symbols have been studied in this way in the East, as far as I can recollect. More often than not they were just taken literally. Eastern people did not feel any incongruity; they could perhaps take quite literally the statement that the Buddha protruded his tongue and it encircled the universe. Not having that sort of faith, we are obliged to allegorize so that we don't feel alienated from the sutras. Allegorization usually comes with a certain amount of intellectual sophistication.

Is there a risk of losing something of the complexity and ambiguity of an image by going for one-to-one correspondences?
It is not such a simple matter as a one-to-one correspondence. The more deeply you go into a myth or symbol the more you realize how multi-faceted and multi-layered it is. It is not a question of saying it means this, so you can forget about the myth itself because now you have grasped in conceptual terms what it was trying in its inadequate way to say. That is much more like allegorization in the strict sense: a woman *en déshabillé* represents Temptation with a capital T, full stop. In the case of real myths and parables it is not as simple as that.

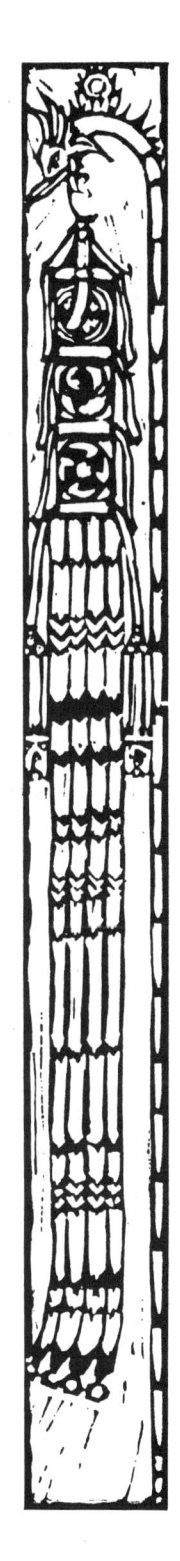

This parable introduces the symbolism of the servant and the son. In the West being a servant has become quite discredited, and the relationship between son and father is not flourishing either. What do servants and sons symbolize in a spiritual context?

A servant is one who serves. Why should you serve, from a spiritual point of view? What does service mean? Service means that you do something for somebody else, more often than not something which he could just as well do for himself. In the old days a servant polished his master's shoes. The master was presumably capable of polishing his own shoes, but the servant did it. So why is one the servant and the other the master? You could say that it is because one has more money than the other, but I would say that that is not a real servant and master relationship. Such a relationship really implies that the master is superior and perhaps the servant even gains by serving him. The servant cannot do what the master is able to do, so he does for him things which he could perhaps do for himself but which he should not be allowed to do because he has more important duties to perform. Understanding this, the servant gladly serves him so that he can devote himself to something which the servant is incapable of doing. If servant and master share the same ideals, service to the master is the servant's way of serving those ideals. Without the servant, the master could not devote himself to the ideals so fully. This is the *natural* servant–master relationship. If it is based merely on economic considerations, it can obviously be exploitative.

In the old days the bond between master and servant was bound up with feudal loyalty, and that had many positive elements. As the servant you did not have the resources and strength to protect yourself, but you placed yourself under the protection of your feudal superior and he guarded your life, perhaps with his own life sometimes. In return for that, you placed yourself at his disposal in certain other respects. It was a natural relationship in which you recognized his superiority in a certain sense.

In India, even in pre-Buddhistic times, the disciple served his teacher, living with him—in his house if he was a householder and in the monastery if he was a monk—and serving him. The Tibetan language has a word which means both 'disciple' and 'servant'. That was also the custom in some of the Western monastic orders, and the system survived in some of the English universities of medieval foundation; there were 'sizars' who served in the college in return for free board, lodging, and tuition. Going back to India, under the Vedic tradition, if you wanted to be accepted by someone as a disciple you went to his house, gathering some sticks on the way which you offered to him on your arrival. This expressed your readiness to serve the teacher, because you would expect to serve him if he taught you. You would go and fetch water, gather sticks, perhaps take the cattle out to graze. Only when you had done all that would you sit down at the teacher's feet and listen to him expounding the Vedas.

Clearly we are out of touch with that tradition. These days, influenced by the predominance of egalitarian ideas, people don't like to think that anybody is superior to them in any essential way, and therefore they don't like to serve in this basic, genuine sense. This kind of service was the rationale behind the relationship between the *upāsaka* and the *bhikṣu*, but unfortunately in recent times this has developed into a situation where the *bhikṣu* lives the Buddhist life vicariously on the layman's behalf, and the layman just makes merit by serving the *bhikṣu* instead of trying to follow the spiritual path himself.

As far as the relationship between father and son goes, I think that in modern times very few people know what it means to be a son. In ancient times the man regarded his son as himself reborn, as his heir, even as the one whose services after his death were going to ensure that he went to heaven. People did not understand the nature of conception; it was thought that the impregnation of the female was like planting seed in a field. Not being regarded as a joint product of both parents, the child, especially the son, had a very close relationship with the father. This emerges in ancient literature, and sometimes even in more recent writing. In some Victorian novels the deep attachment of the father to the son, sometimes in an unhealthy way, is very evident.

It is the instinct of the father to have a son like himself, in whom he can see a continuation of himself. Sometimes, therefore, fathers are very attached to their sons—often without the son's realizing it—trying to live their lives and fulfil their ambitions through them. These days fathers are often denied that sort of satisfaction. Sometimes their sons even take a delight in doing the very things their father does not want them to do, and of course this results in a loss of contact between father and son.

The man—or woman—who wants to be an individual has to make a break, in a sense, with both father and mother. At the same time, he or she needs to try to maintain some kind of positive connection without forfeiting his or her individuality, and that is not easy. There is sometimes a struggle between parents and children—the children wanting to be individuals, and the parents wanting to dominate the children and live their lives through them. We are in a difficult position these days.

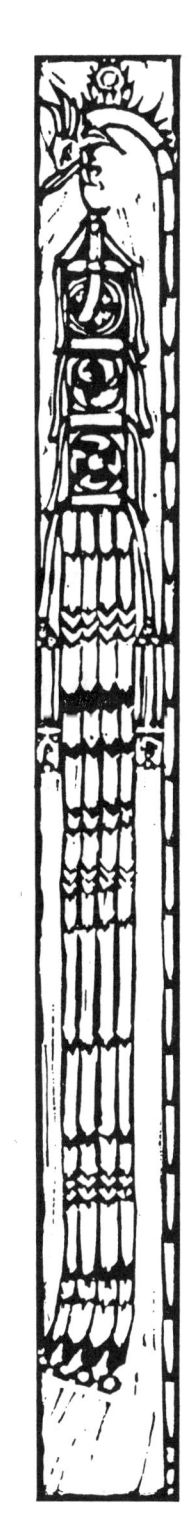

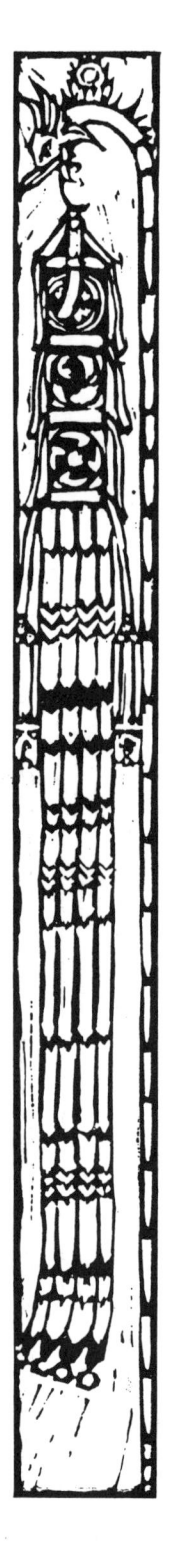

Perhaps in the old days, when it was inevitable that the son would follow in the father's footsteps, things were more straightforward.

•

Is the teaching of the Tibetan Book of the Dead *to be taken literally, or as a symbolic account of the psyche shrinking from reality, regardless of the after-death state?*
I think it can be taken in both ways. Govinda makes the point that the so-called *Book of the Dead* is also a book of the living, something that in principle can be practised in the present life.[62] With regard to the after-death experiences I think there are certain details which need not be taken literally; for instance, the 'seven times seven days' is clearly symbolical. But from the accounts in various traditions, and even the modern secular accounts of people coming back from death-like experiences, it seems that something like the brief contact with Reality described in the *Tibetan Book of the Dead* does take place. There are even descriptions of contact with what seem to be angels, spiritual guides, Buddhas, and so on. We can thus take the content of the after-death experience as described in the *Tibetan Book of the Dead* as broadly corresponding to the facts, though we do not necessarily have to accept all the details, some of which may be symbolical or pertaining more to Tibetan culture than to the actual spiritual experience.

You mentioned in passing the Clear Light of the Tibetan Book of the Dead. *In some texts the Clear Light is taken to be synonymous with* śūnyatā. *What is the correspondence?*
The expression śūnyatā is not to be taken literally. The Unconditioned is empty with regard to the conditioned, but it is not literally void, literally empty. One of the ways of expressing that is by thinking in terms of light, thinking of the Void as a luminous void—though of course that sort of thinking also has its limitations, because it encourages us to think of Reality as being something like the sun, to put it crudely. The sun is a very good symbol—our experience of the sun is a very positive thing—but as a symbol it has its limitations. The light of the sun shines from a definite limited area, but when we speak of the Clear Light of the Void, do we really mean that Reality is circumscribed in space and rays are coming out of it? It is just not possible to take the image literally without limiting the Reality itself. It has therefore sometimes been described in terms of pure light without any actual source, light of the highest possible intensity distributed equally everywhere. The light of the sun

diminishes the further away it is from its source, and presumably we cannot think of the light of *śūnyatā* in that way.

Are there sources within other religious traditions which speak of Reality in terms of light?
In Sufism Reality is often spoken of in terms of light, and the approaches to it in terms of stages of increasing brilliance. There are also some verses in the Koran which speak of light upon light, and in one of Saint Paul's epistles he speaks of going from glory to glory. In the Pali Canon too there is the idea of the higher heavenly realms as being realms of increasing brilliance, with presumably the top, the transcendental, having the greatest brilliance of all.

So would Reality still have that expansiveness, like the sun's radiance which expands outwards?
Yes, but into what would Reality expand?

The image of an evenness of light seems a bit flat—it has no dynamic quality.
I suppose it does seem flat—but why do we need to feel that dynamic quality? Perhaps we need both evenness and expansiveness. One is Reality in terms of space; the other is Reality in terms of time. Perhaps we need the idea of light without any boundary, with a high degree of brilliance evenly distributed, but we also need within that the light which is increasing in brilliance all the time. That does sound logically contradictory, but perhaps that cannot be helped. It's a bit like the difference between the relative and the absolute bodhicitta.

•

In the parable the son is afraid when he first encounters his father with all his wealth. In connection with this, you say that that which is liberating seems to us confining. How can we overcome the fear of change?
You need the help and encouragement of your spiritual friends. When I was staying in Wales, I was watching the baby lapwings learning to fly. The babies were scared of flying, but in the end they would flap their miserable wings and get airborne, and then there would be a terrific flurry of wings as they were caught up in an air current and swept away. All the time the parents would be hovering nearby uttering cries of encouragement until the baby got the hang of it and began to enjoy soaring around. The parents sometimes needed to give vigorous encouragement for quite a long time before the baby took to the air.

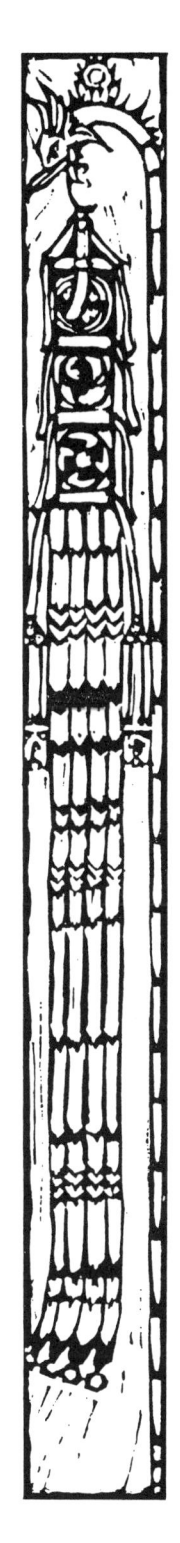

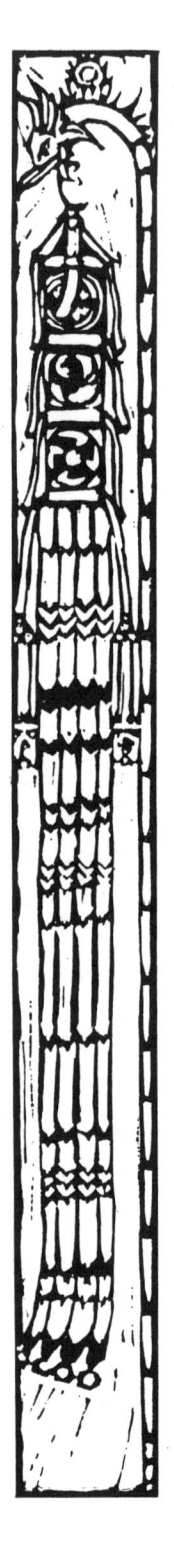

Your spiritual friends need to function in the same sort of way. They need to say 'Come on, you can do it! You're not going to kill yourself! Give up that habit. Move out of that situation. It's OK, you'll survive.' This is where spiritual friends can be really helpful, especially spiritual friends who have already gone through the same kind of experience and know what it's like.

Do you think that one of the functions of puja is to help to overcome this kind of fear?
It's one of the functions of all spiritual practices. The difference is that it is possible to resist a spiritual practice and not let it take its effect, whereas a spiritual friend will not necessarily tolerate that kind of resistance.

•

In the lecture you speak of a higher self and a lower self, and say that the lower self can forget the higher self but the higher self will not forget the lower self. In what sense will the higher self not forget the lower self?
Although I have used those expressions, you mustn't think of the higher self as being really separate; this kind of language is not very Buddhistic, although I think I am justified in using it. The higher self is aware of the lower self in the sense that you are aware of yourself at a deeper level, a level at which an experience of something like Reality, or at least a higher level of consciousness, still persists. Since it is higher, it can, so to speak, look down on the lower. It's rather like a one-way mirror; you can look through and see another person, but they can't see you.

Does that higher self have a guiding function in your life even though you are not aware of it? I have heard of people having experiences in which they felt they had met spiritual guides which they took to be an aspect of themselves which was guiding them.
Yes, you can think in those terms. There is the guardian angel, the genius (in the Roman sense), the patron saint—these are all ways of looking at that particular experience. The important thing to realize is that the 'guardian angel' is really you—and that is extremely difficult to realize, because the mere fact that you think of it as something objective means that you don't experience it as you. You can *think* that it is you, but that is a completely different thing. The minute that you start to really *feel* that it is you, very strange things start happening within you. The 'he' or the 'it' becomes 'I', which means that it is transformed at least to some extent.

If the higher self has, as it were, paternal feelings towards the lower self and therefore appears in the form of a guide, why does it only appear occasionally in a definite form? Why do we not hear that voice more often?
Because the lower self is the lower self—and some selves are lower than others. In some people the lower self is further removed from the higher self, and hears its voice less clearly or frequently. This is really just a question of spiritual status. Why are you not Enlightened? Why do you not normally dwell in the third dhyāna? There are ten thousand reasons. Why are you what you are?

Bearing in mind the dangers of using the language of potentiality and immanence, in what respect can the higher self be said to be there if you are not actually experiencing it?
The language which speaks of thinking that you are already a Buddha is dangerous and to be avoided, but it is quite positive to think in terms of a guardian angel (rather than a Buddha or even a Bodhisattva) which is invisible but hovering near. There is a very real possibility of contact with that. The possibility of contact with the Buddha, on the other hand, is rather remote for the time being; thinking of yourself as being Buddha can only be purely abstract and theoretical. Thinking that you have an angel which is your slightly higher self is much more real and accessible, something you can really have some feeling for.

Is it good actually to invoke your guardian angel?
It could be. You will just have to try it and see whether it works for you. Some people might feel a bit foolish invoking their guardian angel, or, to use a Buddhist term, their *punya devatā*. But a Sinhalese Buddhist friend of mine often used to say, when things were going well, 'Ah, that must be my *punya devatā*,'—this being a personification of one's own previous good karma helping one out in the present. He seemed to think of it very much as a sort of guardian angel.

How does this idea fit in with the practice of visualizing a Buddha or Bodhisattva? When you visualize your yidam, *are you really coming into contact with an inferior emanation of the Buddha or Bodhisattva?*
Yes, you could look at it like that.

When you are visualizing, is it appropriate, then, to feel that this is your guardian angel?
If you visualize successfully, it is formally (in both senses of the term) a Buddha or Bodhisattva, but your actual experience is much more akin

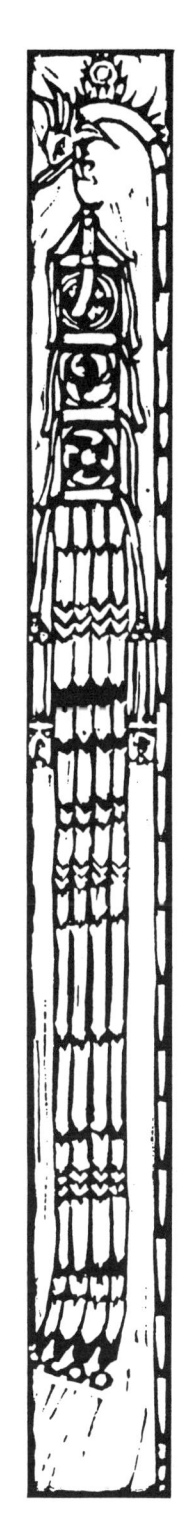

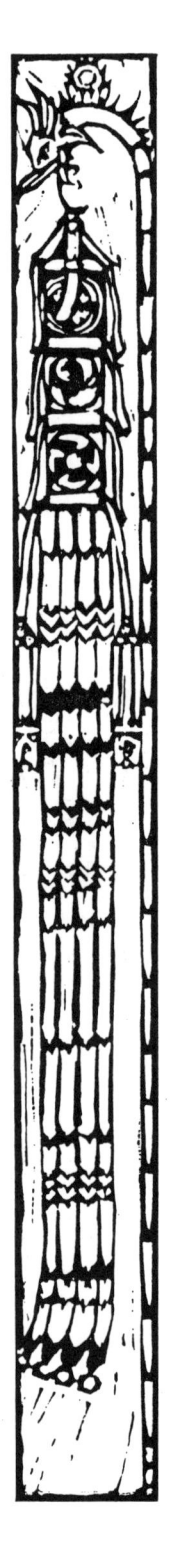

to an experience of your guardian angel. It is sometimes said that Buddhas and Bodhisattvas have three forms—a *devatā* form, a Bodhisattva form, and a Buddha form—so perhaps you could think of the *devatā* form as corresponding to the guardian angel.

Fear of meeting Reality directly could perhaps inhibit the visualization of the form as Buddha or Bodhisattva. But I would rather like to meet a guardian angel...
Yes. For many people the danger is not shrinking from Ultimate Reality but continuing to think of it in purely conceptual terms to such an extent that they are cut off from any slightly higher experience at all. It is much better actually to experience your guardian angel on a comparatively low level than just to have highly abstract thoughts about Buddhahood and Ultimate Reality. An ounce of practice and experience is worth a ton of theory and conceptualization.

Do you have any suggestions about how to contact a guardian angel?
You have to find a point of contact. Look in literature and art, and see whether there is any figure of that kind that attracts you. It might be a figure from Egyptian mythology, or even from a novel or a painting. Take that as your starting point. If it attracts you, you must have some affinity for it; it must mean something to you.

•

You said of the stage of the parable at which the son is becoming familiar with the riches of his father that this was the stage of religious dualism, and that from now on the final stages of the son's journey were 'just a matter of time'. How can the transition from dualism to Insight be said to be just a matter of time?
I didn't mean that it is an automatic process. It is just a matter of time assuming that you are keeping up your spiritual practice, at least from a Buddhist point of view. If your spiritual practice is Christian, you may just remain stuck in that duality and think that the riches that you are observing don't belong to you but to somebody else. Within the Buddhist context, however, if you keep up your practice, it will gather momentum and you will find yourself moving from the stage of dualism to the stage of oneness, so to speak.

Using the Buddha's story of the man with the arrow in his eye, you say that there is no point in trying to go back to the roots of our neuroses; the important thing is to transcend them here and now. Later, commenting on the son shifting the pile of dirt, you suggest that this could refer to the psychoanalytical process. This shifting of the dirt does seem to be a useful preparatory stage in breaking down the son's alienation from the father. How useful are psychological techniques in the context of spiritual practice, and what are their limits and risks?

I think such techniques may be useful within the context of spiritual life. Outside that context, however, they don't seem to do much good, perhaps because they have become ends in themselves. If human beings are basically spiritual, no method or technique that doesn't recognize that is going to help very much. Some useful preparatory work may be done, but even that will be vitiated by the fact that there is no recognition that we are basically spiritual beings.

You can't say 'Let's deal with these mundane problems and leave aside any sort of spiritual consideration.' Indeed, you can't ignore the basically spiritual nature of human beings when dealing with them in any way, perhaps not even the physical. Can you really help people even to a limited extent by treating them as machines?

The great risk is simply that of losing sight of the ultimate spiritual objective. If a psychoanalyst is trying to help someone to be happy, but thinks of happiness in purely mundane terms, perhaps they can't really do all that much for the person. A lot of people seem to have an analyst not as someone who is helping them to get over their problems so that they will be in a better state of mind, but as an ongoing institution, like having a doctor or a lawyer. To think that you will always need your analyst isn't very encouraging from the Buddhist point of view. Perhaps in that case you might suspect that the analyst also needs you.

So if you don't have an intuition of a higher spiritual reality towards which to grow, you can't really successfully engage in psychological techniques?

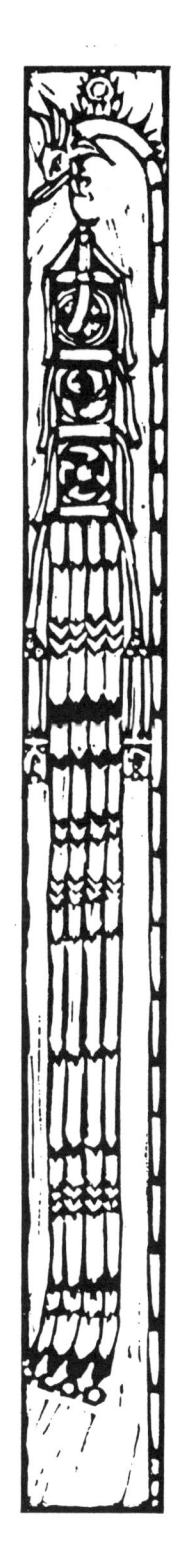

Well, sometimes so-called psychological problems are spiritual problems. Someone may go to the doctor apparently with some sort of illness, but perhaps what they are really suffering from is malnutrition. In the same way someone may come along with what seem to be psychological problems, but what they are actually suffering from is spiritual starvation. In that case there is not much point in trying to tackle the psychological problems in terms of psychoanalysis without spiritual nourishment. It is spiritual nourishment and friendship that they really need; then at least some of the problems may go away.

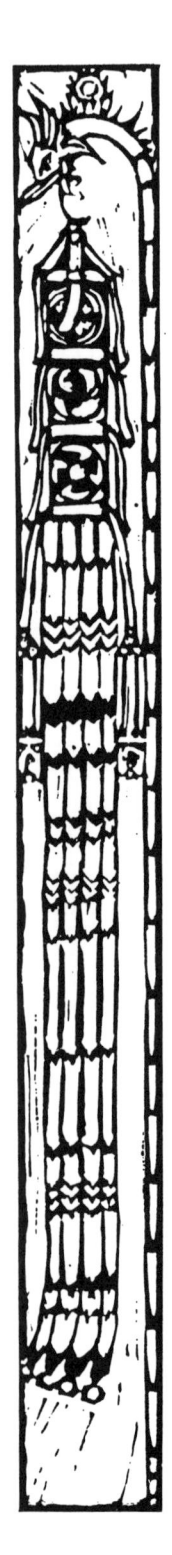

When I hear about counselling and other techniques, I notice in myself both a definite interest in them and a feeling that what is really lacking is a more whole-hearted use of the more obviously spiritual practices that we already have: puja, confession, recitation of sutras, spiritual friendship. I do feel attracted to these psychological techniques, but I suspect that it is not an entirely healthy attraction.

That suspicion is probably justified; it's all too easy to wander off along bypaths. If there is some method or technique we know that we can bring in, well and good, but we should not start to have wholesale recourse to these things, giving meditation and puja a minor place. The danger is that we may start relying more on these techniques than on the Dharma and traditional Buddhist practices.

But even when people have built up authentic meditation experience through years of practice, they often seem still to have deeply rooted reactive patterns of behaviour which are at odds with their meditation experience. Year after year these patterns seem to go untouched and unchanged. Are there areas, in our communication with other people for instance, that meditation doesn't affect?

I think meditation does resolve such areas if you can get into it deeply enough and for long enough, but this is often not possible. If your circumstances are not conducive to intensive meditation, you may need to tackle your problems on their own level. Your spiritual friends may be the best people to help you do that, pointing out things that you can't see yourself. Perhaps in extreme cases professional help may be needed, but as far as possible you should look to your friends. Of course, for a friend to be able to point out basic patterns in this way they need to know you very well, and have a strong positive feeling for you; and you need to be able to trust them too. This implies a considerable degree of friendship. If you don't normally function in this way as a friend, it is perhaps because you are not yet sufficiently a friend. We could do a lot more for one another in this way.

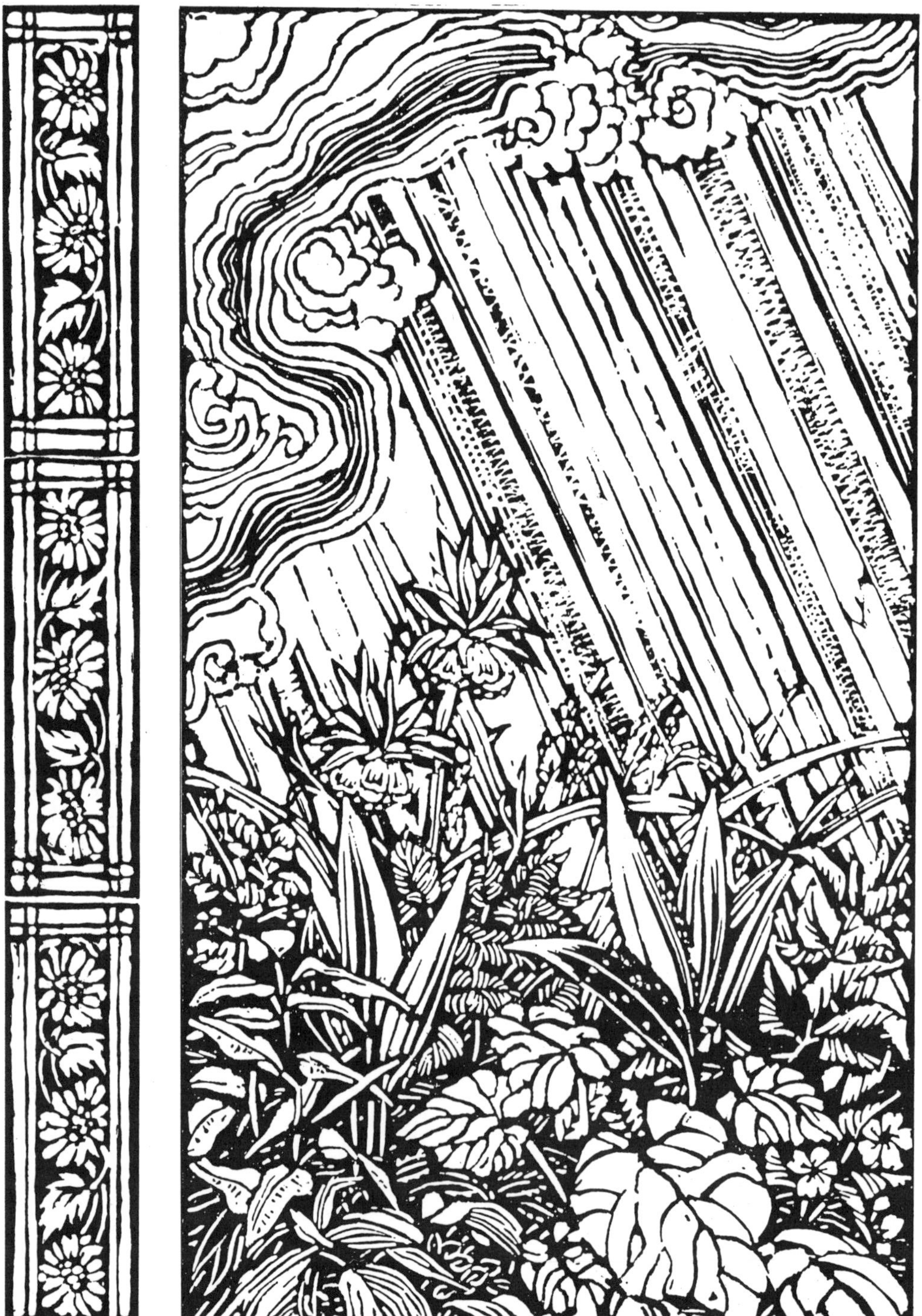

Chapter Five

Symbols of Life and Growth

In England we have four distinct seasons—spring, summer, autumn, and winter—but this particular pattern is not universal. In northern India, which provides the backdrop for the *White Lotus Sutra*, there are three seasons in the year, of about four months each. There's the cold season, when by Indian standards it's cold all the time, a bit like an English summer without the rain. Then there's the hot season, which is very hot indeed. There's no rain at all, not even a drop, and it seems to get hotter and hotter and hotter. The leaves drop off the trees, and all the vegetation turns brown and dry; the earth is baked brick-hard; and towards the end of the hot season great fissures appear in the ground, some of them so wide and deep that you have to be careful as you walk along not to fall into them. Cows wandering in search of food kick up a thick dust which turns the whole atmosphere a dull yellow.

Then, come July, before your very eyes the rainy season begins. One minute the weather is hot and bright, the next, with miraculous speed, a huge dark cloud appears, blotting out the sun, and within a few minutes the whole sky is overcast, deep greyish-blue turning almost black. On every side lightning flickers and flashes, and terrible crashes of thunder roll from one end of the sky to the other. Then you hear a great sound, like the rushing of a tremendous wind, and down comes the rain. It comes down in great bucketfuls for days and days and days. Water swirls underfoot all the time, and the ground is a great sea of mud. The rivers turn yellow and overflow their banks. Here and there in the villages the mud walls of the huts collapse, and sometimes whole villages are swept away.

But then, just a few days after the rainy season has begun, a wonderful thing happens. Just like magic, the yellow, parched land suddenly becomes entirely green, and vegetation of every kind springs up. The rice fields are filled with emerald shoots, and even the most stunted bushes and shrubs burst into leaf. The bamboo and the plantain shoot up inches in a single night. Every shrub, every tree, every bush, every plant, starts to grow.

After so many months of intense heat and dryness, the start of the rainy season in India is greeted with a joy which it is hard to imagine English people feeling for April showers. The Indian monsoon comes as a tremendous relief, the worker of a magical transformation. The scene is often represented in art, especially in the Moghul miniature paintings, and described in Pali and Sanskrit literature. It is also depicted in the parable called the rain-cloud, also known as the parable of the plants, which occurs in the fifth chapter of the *White Lotus Sutra*. In Soothill's translation from Kumārajīva's Chinese version, this is what the Buddha says:

It is like unto a great cloud
Rising above the world,
Covering all things everywhere,
A gracious cloud full of moisture;
Lightning-flames flash and dazzle,
Voice of thunder vibrates afar,
Bringing joy and ease to all.
The sun's rays are veiled,
And the earth is cooled;
The cloud lowers and spreads,
As if it might be caught and gathered;
Its rain everywhere equally
Descends on all sides,
Streaming and pouring unstinted,
Permeating the land.
On mountains, by rivers, in valleys,
In hidden recesses, there grow
The plants, trees, and herbs;
Trees, both great and small.
The shoots of the ripening grain,
Grape vine and sugar-cane.
Fertilised are these by the rain
And abundantly enriched;
The dry ground is soaked,
Herbs and trees flourish together

*From the one water which
Issued from that cloud,
Plants, trees, thickets, forests,
According to need receive moisture.
All the various trees,
Lofty, medium, low,
Each according to its size,
Grows and develops
Roots, stalks, branches, leaves,
Blossoms and fruits in their brilliant colours;
Wherever the one rain reaches,
All become fresh and glossy.
According as their bodies, forms
And natures are great or small,
So the enriching (rain),
Though it is one and the same,
Makes each of them flourish.
In like manner also the Buddha
Appears here in the World,
Like unto a great cloud
Universally covering all things;
And having appeared in the world,
He, for the sake of the living,
Discriminates and proclaims
The truth in regard to all laws.
The Great Holy World-honoured One,
Among the gods and men
And among the other beings,
Proclaims abroad this word:
'I am the Tathāgata,
The Most Honoured among men;
I appear in the world
Like unto this great cloud,
To pour enrichment on all
Parched living beings,
To free them from their misery
To attain the joy of peace,
Joy of the present world,
And joy of Nirvāṇa.
Gods, men, and every one!
Hearken well with your mind,*

Come you here to me,
Behold the Peerless Honoured One!
I am the World-honoured,
Who cannot be equalled.
To give rest to every creature,
I appear in the world,
And to the hosts of the living,
Preach the pure Law, sweet as dew;
The one and only Law
Of deliverance and Nirvāṇa.'
With one transcendent voice
I proclaim this truth,
Ever taking the Great-Vehicle
As my subject.
Upon all I ever look
Everywhere impartially,
Without distinction of persons,
Or mind of love or hate.
I have no predilections
Nor any limitations;
Ever to all beings
I preach the Law equally;
As I preach to one person,
So I preach to all.
Ever I proclaim the Law,
Engaged in naught else;
Going, coming, sitting, standing,
Never am I weary of
Pouring it copious on the world,
Like the all-enriching rain.
On honoured and humble, high and low,
Law-keepers and law-breakers,
Those of perfect character,
And those of imperfect,
Orthodox and heterodox,
Quick witted and dull witted,
Equally I rain the Law-rain
Unwearyingly.[63]

There is no need to comment on the specific details of this parable; the general meaning is obvious enough. But before moving on to consider the parable's implications, I want to comment on the kind of symbolism it introduces, the symbolism of life and growth. Now clearly the parables which we have met so far are also symbols of life and growth. In the parable of the burning house, the children—that is to say sentient beings—are depicted as moving from a state of potential suffering to a state of everlasting bliss, peace, and happiness. In the parable of the return journey the poor man comes closer and closer to the rich man, becomes more and more like him, and is in the end acknowledged as his son and heir. So in both these parables there is growth, onward and upward movement. In fact, we could say that the whole *White Lotus Sutra* is a symbol of life and growth, for it depicts a universe in which every living thing is moving upwards. Arhats are becoming Bodhisattvas, Bodhisattvas are becoming Buddhas—all individual beings whatsoever are moving in the direction of Enlightenment. However, the parable of the rain-cloud can be singled out specifically as a symbol of life and growth for an obvious reason—because it compares the whole process of spiritual development to the unfolding of a plant.

Plant symbolism is much more common in Buddhism than is generally supposed. In fact, the first symbol for humanity to emerge from the Enlightened consciousness of the Buddha was a symbol of this kind. If we go back to the time just after the Buddha's Enlightenment, we find that he was at first hesitant about going out to teach the truth he had discovered. It was so difficult and subtle—would anyone else ever be able to understand it? The scriptural records tell us that at that point the Buddha looked out over the world and saw a vision of the whole mass of humanity just like a great bed of lotuses.[64] Many of the lotus plants were not just deep down in the water, but right deep down in the mud, so submerged that you could hardly see their buds. But others, the Buddha saw, had begun to grow, so that at least the tips of their buds had emerged above the surface of the water. Other buds stood free of the water and were starting to unfurl their petals. And a very few were on the point of bursting into bloom. Through this beautiful vision of the different stages of development, the Buddha realized that there were at least some individuals who could flower in the sunlight of his teaching, and set out to share his vision of reality.

If we turn to a period much later in the Buddhist tradition, we find in Tibetan Buddhism a similar sort of symbolism. According to Tibetan tradition there are a number of psychic centres (which the Tibetans call 'wheels')—four, five, or sometimes seven—situated at different points along the median nerve within the human body: one at the stomach, one at the solar plexus, one at the heart, one at the throat, one at the head, and so on. These psychic centres are symbolized by lotuses of different sizes and colours, and with different numbers of petals. Practitioners who use this symbolism say that in meditation—especially in certain esoteric meditation practices—a powerful current of upward-moving energy is generated within the body. This current is called in Buddhist Sanskrit *chandali*—'the fiery one'. It corresponds to the Tibetan *tummo*, usually translated as 'psychic heat', and the Hindu *kuṇḍalinī*, 'the coiled-up one' (an evocative term for 'coiled-up' potential energy). In all these traditions this potential energy is often represented as a serpent. As the energy passes up the median nerve, it activates the different centres, and the lotus flowers open—the higher up the centre, the bigger and more beautiful the lotus. Leaving aside the question of whether we can take the symbolism of the psychic centres and the current of energy literally or whether it is metaphorical, the lotus here clearly symbolizes the whole process of spiritual development.

White Tārā is one of the most popular of the archetypal Bodhisattvas of Buddhist tradition. As her name suggests, she is completely white in colour—a beautiful, graceful, smiling figure, usually seated in *siddhāsana* and clad in the silks and jewels of a Bodhisattva. In her left hand she holds a whole spray of lotuses. And here there is a very interesting point to notice. The spray of lotuses consists of a closed lotus bud, a half-open bud, and a fully open flower. Now these lotuses could represent, for example, the Buddhas of the three times—the past, the present, and the future. No doubt the symbolism is rich and capable of many interpretations. But the simplest and most obvious meaning is that White Tārā's three lotuses represent the process of growth and unfoldment which is the spiritual life.

This kind of symbolism, then, is frequently found in the Buddhist tradition. But why—in chapter 5—does the *White Lotus Sutra* suddenly start talking in terms of plants and their growth? Well, you could say that it just happened like that—it was an accident—but I don't personally believe that. I believe that this kind of symbolism is introduced at this point in the sutra for a very definite purpose. It is there to correct a mistake which it is only too easy to make if we take certain details of the previous parables—the burning house and the return journey—too literally, a mistake which may lead us to misinterpret the whole process of the spiritual life.

In the parable of the burning house the children are persuaded to come from the inside of the building to the outside. In the myth of the return journey the poor man comes from a distant country to his father's city, and then to his father's mansion. In both parables, then, there is a change of place, a journey, a movement in space. Now the characteristic feature of movement in space is that the moving object changes its position but does not itself change. In other words, the change that takes place is external, not internal. So if we take the parables literally, the danger is that we will understand the process of spiritual development not in terms of internal change, but in terms of external change. This means that—consciously or semi-consciously—we will think of the self as having experiences, traversing changes, but itself remaining unchanged.

This misunderstanding does represent a very real danger, and one that we are all likely to encounter or even succumb to. It is easy enough to study the history of Buddhism. It is easy enough to become acquainted with all the doctrines and study the different stages of the path. The danger is that we may start to mistake our intellectual journey through those stages for real experience. We may be aware that our understanding of nirvana itself is only theoretical, but it may not be so obvious that our knowledge and understanding of the earlier stages is also quite theoretical. If we are not careful we will not be aware that we are not passing through them in actual experience, but only mentally, that is, externally. There's no internal change taking place at all.

For example, many books on Buddhism refer to the Buddha's Noble Eightfold Path—there's no getting away from it, and quite rightly so—but it is very often misrepresented. We are given a picture of a path divided into eight stages, and encouraged to think of ourselves traversing it stage by stage. But it isn't like that at all. Following the Noble Eightfold Path is in practice much more like putting forth, one after another, eight successive shoots or branches. This is reflected in the term for the Eightfold Path in Pali (*aṭṭhāṅgikamagga*) and Sanskrit (*aṣṭāṅgikamārga*). *Aṅga* does not mean a step or stage, but a limb, shoot, or branch, so following the Eightfold Path is not at all like climbing a ladder rung by rung, but more like rising up as the sap rises up through a tree when the rain falls.[65]

Taking the analogy further, we could say that the first of these shoots, Perfect Vision, or transcendental consciousness, is like the rain. When you get your first glimpse of transcendental consciousness, your first experience above and beyond the limitations of your ordinary self, like rain spreading through the soil it gradually permeates and influences all other aspects of your being. It spreads to your emotional life, your speech, your activities, your way of earning a living, your mental state—your whole way of life.

So practising the Noble Eightfold Path is not a matter of following a path step by step, but of imbibing a certain inspiration, having a certain experience, and then allowing that to permeate all aspects of your being until you are permanently saturated in that experience at all levels. At that point of perfect and complete transformation, you reach the eighth step of the transcendental Eightfold Path, the Perfect Samādhi, and you attain the Enlightenment of a Buddha.

It is to stop us from mistaking external change for internal change, from mistaking intellectual understanding for personal experience, that the *White Lotus Sutra* adds to the symbol of the journey the symbol of the plant. The symbol of the journey apparently has two factors: the path itself and the person treading the path. In the symbolism of the plant, however, these two factors come together to produce a single factor. The plant itself is the process of development, so there is no possibility of any misunderstanding. Instead of thinking of ourselves as traversing the path, we now think of ourselves as plants, as living, growing things. The only question that arises is that of what stage we have reached. Are we still buds, submerged in the water or the mud, are we half-open flowers, or are we even in full bloom?

Whatever stage a plant has reached, it needs both rain and sun to help it to grow. It is appropriate, then, that sun imagery is also introduced in the *White Lotus Sutra*, in a parable which follows directly after the parable of the rain-cloud: the parable of the sun and moon. The Buddha does not elaborate upon this parable, and it is so short that it is in fact more like a simile than a parable. This is Kern's translation from the Sanskrit:

> *And further, Kāśyapa, the Tathāgata, in his educating creatures, is equal and not unequal. As the light of the sun and moon, Kāśyapa, shines upon all the world, upon the virtuous and the wicked, upon high and low, upon the fragrant and the ill-smelling; as their beams are sent down upon everything equally, without inequality; so, too, Kāśyapa, the intellectual light of the knowledge of the omniscient, the Tathāgatas, the Arhats, &c., the preaching of the true law proceeds equally in respect to all beings in the five states of existence, to all who according to their particular disposition are devoted to the great vehicle, or to the vehicle of the Pratyekabuddhas, or to the vehicle of the disciples. Nor is there any deficiency or excess in the brightness of the Tathāgata-knowledge up to one's becoming fully acquainted with the law.*[66]

The sun and moon are of course universal symbols, and like plant and flower symbolism they feature frequently in Buddhist tradition. In Tantric Buddhism, the sun is embodied especially in the figure of Vairocana, who occupies the centre of the mandala of the Five Buddhas.[67] His name means simply 'illuminator'. In the Vedas, the pre-Buddhist scriptures, Vairocana is one of the names of the sun, and in Japanese Buddhism he is known as Dainichi, 'the great sun Buddha'.

Iconographically he is represented as being brilliant white in colour, like the sun at its midday brightest, and he is shown holding his emblem, the eight-spoked golden wheel of the Dharma. His fingers make the 'wheel-turning gesture', the *dharmacakrapravartana*, which is associated with the Buddha's first teaching at Sarnath, and represents the dissemination of the truth in all possible directions, just like the beams of the sun shining in all directions of space. The lotus throne on which Vairocana is sitting is supported by lions, the lion itself being a solar symbol. Furthermore, according to Indian mythology, when the lion roars in the jungle at night, all the other beasts fall silent. The Buddha, we are told in the scriptures, preaches his Dharma with a lion-like roar, *singha-nāda*; when Truth is given utterance by the Buddha, all partial truths or untruths fall silent.

In the *White Lotus Sutra* too, the sun is a symbol for the Buddha's teaching. In some respects the meaning of its symbolism in the sutra is identical to that of the rain-cloud. Both are indispensable to the life and growth of the plant. And both are absolutely impartial; this is stressed in both parables. The rain-cloud gives the same moisture, and the sun gives the same light and heat, to each and every plant on the Earth. The cloud doesn't give some plants a heavier shower of rain than others. The sun doesn't treat some plants to a purer or a brighter light. In the same way, in principle the Buddha gives the same teaching, communicates the same reality, the same higher state of consciousness, to all living beings. The teaching has different forms, just as the rain consists of individual drops and the sunshine of individual rays, but all the forms have one and the same meaning, just as each raindrop is made of water and each sunbeam is made of light.

The quality of impartiality is particularly drawn out in the parable of the rain-cloud. The word which the Buddha uses to describe the rain is *ekarasa* (*eka* meaning 'one', and *rasa* meaning 'taste', 'juice', or 'essence'). This same word is used in a similar connection in another parable, one which occurs in the Pali scriptures: the parable of the great ocean.[68] The Buddha says that wherever you go in the great ocean, you can scoop a handful of water and it will have the same taste: the taste of salt. Likewise, whatsoever part of his teaching you take up, it will have one taste: the taste of freedom. In other words, whatever aspect of the Buddha's teaching you practise, it has one essence, one purpose, one effect—to help you to get free from your conditioning. There are many different presentations of the Buddha's teaching. There are the lists: the Eightfold Path, the Five Spiritual Faculties, the Three Refuges. There are the teachings about suffering, impermanence, and no-self. And there are all sorts of methods of practice: the mindfulness of breathing, the mettā bhāvanā, the contemplation of the impurities, the *brahma vihāras*. But all these many teachings, traditions, and practices have just one aim: to help individual human beings to become free from their conditioning.

From this the important corollary follows that the Buddha's teaching is not to be identified with any one formulation. It is not possible to say that the Buddha's teaching is the Noble Eightfold Path and just that, or the contents of the Pali Canon and just that. The Buddha's teaching is not just Zen, or just Theravāda, or just what Professor so-and-so says it is. Buddhism cannot be identified with any one individual formulation, much less with any one individual school or sect. The Buddha's teaching or message can only be identified with that spirit of liberation, of freedom from conditionedness, that pervades all these formulations, just as the taste of salt pervades all the waters of the ocean. Whether it is the teaching of the Eightfold Path or the teaching of the Bodhisattva Ideal, whether it is this meditation practice or that, if it helps us to become free from our conditioning, it is part and parcel of the Buddha's teaching.

When we read about Buddhism, it is very important not only to remember this but to try really to feel it; otherwise all our studies and knowledge will be in vain. When we read the scriptures or hear about the Buddha's teaching, it is not enough just to pay attention to the words, the ideas and concepts. What really matters is to feel, through the concepts, through the images and symbolism, that which informs and gives life to them all—the experience of emancipation from all conditions whatsoever. In other words, we are trying to feel at least to some degree the absolute consciousness of the Buddha, the Enlightened consciousness from which all the teachings originally came.

Now, although the rain falls on all alike, and the sun shines on all alike, the plants themselves are all different and they grow in different ways. A nut grows into a tree, and a seed into a flower; a rose bush produces big red blossoms whereas a crocus bulb produces small yellow ones. Some plants shoot up in the air, others creep along the ground, and others clasp bigger and stronger plants. They all grow according to their own nature. And it is just the same, the parable suggests, with human beings. They all receive the same truth, they all hear what is in principle the same spiritual teaching, and they all grow. But the strange, astonishing, and wonderful thing is that they all grow in different ways. They all grow according to their own nature. People may all hear the same teaching, believe in the same teaching, and follow the same path, but they do what seem to be completely different things. Some become more and more deeply involved in meditation, so that in the end they are spending most of their time meditating and have hardly any contact with other people. Others take up social work. Others burst into song, write poetry, or paint pictures. And others, perhaps the majority, simply go on being themselves. They do not display any specific talent, but just become more and more individual. The paradox is that although we each become more and more different from one another as we grow and develop, at the same time we also become more and more like one another: more aware, more sensitive, more compassionate; in a word, more alive.

This means that in the spiritual life there can be no question of regimentation. It is reasonable to expect that, with a little endeavour, all human beings will grow, but it is unreasonable to expect all human beings to grow in the same way. This, unfortunately, is often forgotten. When we discover something that we ourselves find very helpful to our own development, we tend to think that everybody else should also find it helpful. Indeed, if we are not careful, we even start insisting that they must find it helpful. Or, conversely, we discover that something is not helpful to us, at least at present, and therefore refuse to recognize that it is helpful to other people.

It is this kind of fixed attitude which leads to sectarianism in Buddhism. When people hit upon a helpful approach to their spiritual development, rather than just making use of it, they are quick to declare that the school or method they have discovered *is* Buddhism. If you don't follow this school, they say, you can't really be a Buddhist. This is just as bad as orthodox Christianity, and indeed represents a carrying over of Christian attitudes into Buddhist life.

I must confess that I found a lot of this sort of thing in the English Buddhist movement when I came back in 1964 after spending twenty years in the East. For instance, there were some people who—quite rightly—found meditation very helpful indeed, and devoted a number of hours every day to practising it. And because they found meditation so helpful, they used to declare that the practice of studying the scriptures—or reading about Buddhism at all—was completely useless. In their opinion, nobody who called themselves a Buddhist should be expected, or even allowed, to do anything other than meditate.

But there were other people, I found, who preferred to study. And these people, who tended to be rather bookish, would say that people in the West, being tense and full of problems, and rather difficult in all sorts of ways, were simply not ready for so sublime a spiritual practice as meditation, and ought to stick to reading books. Some people went so far as to say that meditation was dangerous, and that if you insisted on doing it at all, five minutes at a time was quite enough. Other people again were against anything ceremonial or colourful. They did not find ritual helpful themselves, for one reason or another, so they tended to say that it was bad for everybody.

We need to be careful not to get stuck in fixed ideas about which particular Buddhist school is best, or which kind of Buddhist practice is best. Furthermore, we need to examine our fixed ideas about what 'Buddhism' is, and even what 'religion' is. Again we can take as our reference point the parables of the *White Lotus Sutra*, which say that the rain falls and the sun shines on the good and the bad alike. But in applying this to our own situation, I want to put it rather differently: the rain falls and the sun shines on the *religious* and the *secular* alike.

For a couple of thousand years in the West, all cultures and communities were 'officially' religious. This meant that you could only develop higher states of consciousness through traditional religious means: prayer, meditation, the sacraments, and so on. If you wanted to evolve, you had to be a religious person and do it in the religious way. You had to be a pious church-goer, or a religious scholar, or a mystic.

But a great change has taken place. It began at the time of the Renaissance, when thinkers, philosophers, and artists started separating—some would say emancipating—themselves from the tutelage of religion. Then, after the Industrial Revolution, the whole process speeded up, and today in most Western countries—and the change is spreading to the East as well—communities and cultures are secular rather than religious. Art is secular art; it has no direct connection with conventional or traditional religion. And literature is very definitely secular literature.

But despite this split between the religious and the secular, the Higher Evolution is still possible. In the modern world, especially in the West, it can take place not only in religious but also in secular terms. Indeed, in the West today spiritual progress is more likely to take place within a secular context than within a conventional religious one. All that is traditionally or conventionally associated with the word 'religion' has little appeal now for the vast majority of thinking people. One can even go so far as to say, to put it bluntly, that those who go to church are probably not very interested in religion, and those who are very interested in religion are unlikely to go to church.

It might be better, therefore, to present the Higher Evolution of man not in conventional religious terms at all, but in secular terms. Perhaps more people would then be attracted to the teachings and benefit from them. It may be that one day we shall have to conclude that in sticking to traditional religious forms, including Eastern religious forms, we are being unimaginative and unrealistic, and perhaps even excluding—or at least not encouraging—some people who could benefit from the teachings of the Higher Evolution.

The rain falls and the sun shines on the religious and the secular alike. Both rain and sunshine help all plants to grow in their own way. In everything that we have seen so far, the two parables are similar. But there *is* a distinction between them, although this distinction does not exactly amount to a difference. The symbolism of the rain-cloud and the symbolism of the sun are complementary. The rain-cloud gives moisture, whereas the sun gives light and heat. To borrow terms from the Chinese tradition, the rain-cloud is *yin*, associated with the depths, with the earth, and the sun is *yang*, associated with the heights, with the sky. And in terms of human development, the individual is quite literally like the plant. Just as the plant taps its moisture up from the earth, and gets its heat and light from the sky, so the developing human being must be nourished from below, from the unconscious depths, and also from above, from the supra-conscious heights.

To translate this into more simple terms, we must be nourished through both emotion and reason. Usually presentations of Buddhism in the West emphasize the rational aspect, or even give the impression that Buddhism is exclusively rational. We are told about Buddhist thought and philosophy, Buddhist metaphysics, psychology, and logic; and sometimes it all seems very dry and academic. The other side, however, the side represented by myth, symbol, and the imagination, the emotions and vision, is no less important, and for many people perhaps even more important. This is why we need to absorb texts which appeal to our emotions, like the parables, myths, and symbols of the Mahāyāna in the *White Lotus Sutra*.

It is not enough to understand the Buddha's teaching intellectually. Anybody who has the ability to read—and a moderate intelligence—can do that. We have to ask ourselves again and again not just 'Do I know? Do I understand?' but 'Do I feel? Do I vibrate with this?' We might even ask ourselves 'Do I really feel like a plant at the end of the hot season? Is this how I feel after a day's work or after I've been immersed in the ordinary daily round? Do I feel all dry and withered? Do I feel in need of nourishment? Do I really feel ready to take something in?' When you come in contact with the truth, with the Buddha's teaching, do you actually feel as though you are being refreshed by a great shower of rain? Do you really feel that you are going to drink something in after having been dry and thirsty for a long time?

Again, when you come in contact with the Dharma, do you really feel that the sun has come out? During the months of winter it is not unusual to feel dull and tired, and even miserable, because the sky is grey with fog and mist, and you are cold. You look forward to the spring sunshine, to your summer holiday, to the first beautiful, warm, bright weekend when you feel that spring is really on the way. When you see the buds begin to open and the flowers blooming in the parks and gardens, you can hardly help but feel a lifting of the heart. You feel as though a new spirit were rising within you.

But do you feel like this when you come into contact with the Buddha's teaching? Do you feel as though you are drinking in spiritual sunshine? If you do not respond in this way, your approach is still just intellectual. It is important that we should actually feel ourselves living, feel ourselves growing just like the plant when the rain falls and the sun shines, feel ourselves expanding. If we feel like this, our birth as human beings is not in vain, for we will ourselves be symbols, living symbols, of life and growth.

Chapter Five

Questions and Answers

You say that as people grow they get more and more different from each other, but paradoxically they also get more and more like each other. I can understand how if you are moving towards deep spiritual experience the element of similarity comes in. It is not so obvious, though, why people get more and more different from each other. I can see from people around me that they do, but how and why?

Suppose you have a number of lamps made of some semi-translucent material with patterns and designs on it. Inside each lamp there is a light, and as you turn up the light and it gets brighter, not only does the lamp give off more light, but the pattern in the lamp becomes clearer and clearer. In the same way, when the light of Enlightenment shines through you, it lights up your features, your distinctive individuality, all the more clearly. That's the only way I can explain it.

Don't you notice this with people? Maybe they haven't gained Enlightenment, but they have progressed over the years, and you do see something shining from them or through them more brightly than before. Don't they seem, in that paradoxical way, much more themselves? It is not as though their individuality has merged into something non-individual, or even supra-individual, so that they become featureless. On the contrary, they seem much more themselves than ever before; there is a strange fusion of individuality and universality. You could even say that people who are less developed are more like each other on the level of form, so to speak, than those who are more developed.

As I see it, we are differentiated by our conditioning, by all the things that limit us and make us distinct. Isn't there a contradiction between the universal experience coming through and the biases in the individual that limit its expression?

But, paradoxically again, it is the individual that expresses the universal. If there wasn't that limited form, what medium could there be for the expression of universal experience?

Isn't personality made up of merit, your positive actions in the past, even in past lives, as well as conditioning?

Yes, there is not simply your mundane, conditioned personality, but also that more skilful 'merit-produced' personality which provides a vehicle—admittedly inadequate—for the expression of whatever higher consciousness, or even Enlightenment experience, you have attained. Without that, the higher experience could not express itself at all on the mundane plane.

I'm not sure that this 'paradox' between the unique individual and the unique universal really *is* a paradox. A paradox has been defined as 'truth standing on its head to attract attention', something which is logically self-contradictory. The idea of the coalescence of the individual and the universal is not a paradox in that way.

Perhaps the term universal itself can be misleading—we tend to think of something abstract and common, which is not the best way to think of it. When the individual attains the universal, it is not as though the individual is merged into something which is non-individual. From a spiritual point of view, universality is the way in which the individual behaves. For instance, when the individual is developing mettā towards all living beings, he or she is adopting a universal attitude—the individual *is* universal mettā,[69] you might say—but it is an *individual* being universal. Perhaps only an individual can be universal. A tree can't be universal, a stone can't be universal, not even a monkey or a mackerel can be universal, but a human being can be universal, because a human being is an individual, and universality is an attitude that pertains essentially and distinctively to the individual.

We tend to think of the universal as being like a great hole in the ground into which the individual falls, or a great ocean in which the individual loses himself, but that is taking what is essentially a metaphorical expression literally. We think of the universal as somehow extended in space, but actually universality is a quality of the functioning of the individual—or perhaps even that is too static. You could say that universality is one of the ways in which an individual functions, not a thing into which the individual disappears. Any apparent contradiction between the notion of the individual and the notion of the universal arises when we make the universal something abstract and then reify it. There is no such *thing* as the universal, you might say, from a spiritual point of view.

Isn't it the case that in the logical sense universals are just useful abstractions?
Yes, that's true. There is a great debate in philosophy from the time of Plato onwards as to whether the existence of universals is real or notional.

What you are calling the universal attitude is quite different from that, isn't it? You seem to be describing an attitude which applies in practice to an indefinite range of particulars. Wouldn't all universals work in that way? For example, we all experience the colour red in different ways, but we describe that experience in universal terms.
Yes, there is the quality of redness, but actually we never encounter redness, only red objects.

In the same way, are we talking about a similar kind of universal which can't exist apart from individuals manifesting it?
No, it's not quite like that, although it's similar. Universality—a universal attitude—in the context of the spiritual life is essentially an activity, whereas a concept like redness is not an activity but a 'thing', in the sense of a mental object. What I am really saying is that we need to get away from the idea or associations of 'thingness' when we speak of the individual and the universal in the context of spiritual life. It is not that the individual considered as an entity merges in another greater entity. It is more that that individual starts functioning in a particular way.

So, taking the example of mettā, if you feel mettā in practice you feel it towards the people you meet, although in principle you are open to anybody.
Yes. You are not experiencing an abstract, universal, cold mettā. You are behaving in a certain way towards people that you meet, or whom you imagine. You don't merge in with a concept called universality; you just behave in the same spirit of mettā with everybody you meet. This is a more practical, more down to earth way of seeing it, a less abstract mode of expression.

In the course of one's spiritual development, could one expect to have eventually a physical or psychical experience of release of energy at those places in the body corresponding to the traditional locations of the psychic centres?

You could expect that, very broadly speaking. For instance, if you do suddenly feel emotionally unblocked, and feel very positive, powerful feelings expanding, you might well have a sensation of release at the heart centre. Some people might even have a visual experience of a lotus bursting open, or a ball of light expanding. There can be many variations according to temperament on the same basic spiritual or physico-psycho-spiritual experience.

There are a number of traditional ways of describing the chakras. Govinda outlines several of the Buddhist ones in *Foundations of Tibetan Mysticism*.[70] Of course, there are discrepancies between the different systems, and still more differences between the various Hindu versions. Some accounts are so literalistic that they seem to suggest that you have to go through a graded course, and see your chakras, with exactly the right number of petals, quite literally opening. That sort of imagery, however, only suggests a certain type of experience which can take other forms. The essential feature of the experience is a release of energy on a higher level, a bursting open, a flowering. There is a flowering of your being, of your energies, at successively higher levels, and you can experience this in different ways. This much is obvious in that Buddhists, Hindus, and Jains all have the same sort of symbolism. The symbolism varies, however, and each text is remarkably specific. They can't all be right if you are going to take them on a literalistic level.

Are there different traditions as to the positions of the chakras, or is it possible to locate them?

It seems to be reasonably constant that very low, gross emotions are felt round about the navel, more subtle emotions are experienced at the heart centre, and energies connected with speech and communication are experienced at the throat. Still more subtle energies are experienced at the forehead, and the most subtle of all at the crown of the head. That is very much how it feels, isn't it? If you get really angry, you feel it low down in your body. If you feel strong devotional feelings, it is as though your heart expands; sometimes you can feel an actual sensation at that spot.

To develop the emotions as one does in the mettā bhāvanā practice, should one concentrate on the heart chakra at the centre of the body, or on the organic heart, which is a little off centre?
Buddhist texts are careful to distinguish between the organic heart and the heart chakra, and it is the chakra which should be the focus of meditation practice. The Tibetan tradition teaches that the chakras should be visualized on the surface of the body, so that, for example, the syllables *oṁ āḥ hūṁ* are visualized at the forehead, throat, and heart on the surface of the body. When a mantra is visualized at the heart centre, it is visualized on the surface, but when in addition to that you also visualize the mantra of, say, Mañjughoṣa, that is visualized as inside the body on the same level as the surface mantra. So in a sense there are two heart centres: a surface one and a deeper one.

Some teachers say that you should not think too much in terms of the human body, maintaining that the chakra system gives a model of development which is framed after the physical body but is not to be identified with it. Other teachers, especially perhaps the Hindus, seem to take it quite literally.

Which way would you advise us to take it?
I would suggest taking it as a model but not overlooking the possibility that the model correlates in certain ways with the physical body and its energies. Mr Chen, one of my teachers in Kalimpong, used to say that the 'wheels', as he called them, had nothing to do with the physical, gross body, but were present only in the subtle body. In a way there are three bodies, if you include the further development which the Vajrayāna calls the wisdom body. According to Mr Chen the yogic practices concerned with the chakras and the subtle nerves are a means of activating and building up the subtle body, just as certain other practices bring to life the wisdom body.

But the gross body does have its systems, and perhaps these correspond to some extent with the features of the subtle body. Even if you think of the different chakras and nerves as being located in the physical body, however, they are not to be identified with physical organs or physical energies. Thinking in that way is simply a means of concentration.

Where would the astral body come into that?
What is usually called the astral body would seem to be a subtle material counterpart of the physical body, intermediate between the physical body and the subtle body I have just described. From what I gather, it

would seem that you are born with an astral body, whereas the subtle body is more something which is built up as a result of spiritual effort.

So someone in a higher state of consciousness would not perceive your subtle body unless it had been consciously developed?
They might see that you had the potential to develop it, but they would not see you as actually possessing it in that moment of time, just as they might see that you were Enlightened in the depths of your being, but would also see that you had not actually realized that in the present.

Where does the aura come in?
There is an aura of every level of your being. Your physical body is surrounded by a cloud of fine dust—minute particles of skin and so on—all the time; and it also gives off various electrical currents. That is the aura of the physical body. Then there is the aura in a higher sense, the corresponding influence of those higher, more subtle bodies which under certain conditions may actually become visible in radiant form.

The main point is that you should not think of a body of any level as something absolutely discrete, as though there is an edge to your physical body beyond which there is 'non-body'. If you could see yourself through a sufficiently powerful microscope, you wouldn't be able to see where your body ended; it would just fade into a cloud of minute particles. The sharp edge you see with the naked eye simply isn't there—there is just a finer and finer aura extending out into space—and the situation is similar on other levels.

•

You suggest that it might be best to present the Higher Evolution in secular rather than religious terms. What could this mean in practice, assuming that it would not just be presenting the Buddhist vision in language that avoids the use of the word Buddhism and traditional Buddhist concepts. What, for example, would be the place of devotional practices in such an approach? Would you still speak in terms of the 'secular'?
I don't actually like the word 'secular'—it's almost as bad as 'religious'. It has an air of the disgruntled, the offensively rationalistic. In making this suggestion I was thinking about the present state of affairs in the West. The decline of Christianity in the West has meant that the creative energies of a lot of people have passed outside the sphere of traditional religion to find independent expression in the field of the arts. This has produced a 'secular spirituality' which is secular only in the sense that

it is not traditionally religious and does not have the support of an existing tradition. The result has been that much of the really vital spiritual life of the last two hundred years has expressed itself in artistic and not necessarily religious terms.

I certainly didn't mean that we should switch to a hard, dry, semi-scientific language, eschewing everything which is emotional, imaginative, or inspirational. I was thinking not so much in terms of scientific secular thought, but more in terms of trying to establish some connection with expressions which are basically spiritual but which are not part of the traditional Christian religion. We need not jettison traditional Buddhist language altogether, but perhaps we should have one or two alternative languages at our disposal. We don't always realize the extent to which newcomers to Buddhism are put off, or at least puzzled, by lectures peppered with Pali and Sanskrit terms. Perhaps we should be trying to develop, with the help of some of the great Western thinkers and writers of the past, an indigenous language which will enable us to express our essentially Buddhist vision in a more imaginative and effective way.

I understand what you're saying, but I can't help thinking that a really thorough appreciation of Kant or Schopenhauer, Keats or Shelley, is almost as rare an interest in this country as Buddhism. I can't see how adopting the language of a very small, high-culture élite would reach a wider audience.

Well, Buddhism would at least reach an audience, however small, that is not being reached at present, but yes, I agree. However, I don't think that 'traditional Buddhist language' can just be imported. In the long term we need to develop a completely indigenous, yet faithfully Buddhist language, as the Chinese, the Tibetans, and the Japanese have done. Meanwhile we have to use our peculiar mixture of jargons—bits of Pali, Sanskrit, Tibetan, and adaptations from the 'alternative' culture.

It is perhaps wrong to contrast 'religious' and 'secular'. Although Keats can be described as a secular poet, he sometimes expresses the spirit of religion. The secular has nothing to do with the form of conventional religion, but its spirit may be deeply religious in a non-traditional way. The secular language I have in mind is the language of the poet and the artist refined still further for the purposes of Buddhism, as an alternative to traditional Buddhist language translated into English. I don't mean just quoting poets, but taking their expressions and using them to express Buddhist ideas and Buddhist truths. Obviously the language would be subtly altered in the process, and that alteration would be a refinement inasmuch as Buddhism expresses a vision which goes beyond that particular poet. Poets themselves use the words of ordinary language, but they refine them to express their particular vision. They use ordinary words but combine them in a fresh and original way, to communicate something new, something individual. Buddhists could take the process a stage further. Of course, to do this you would need a highly developed sense of the English language as used by its greatest practitioners, and at the same time some depth of spiritual experience.

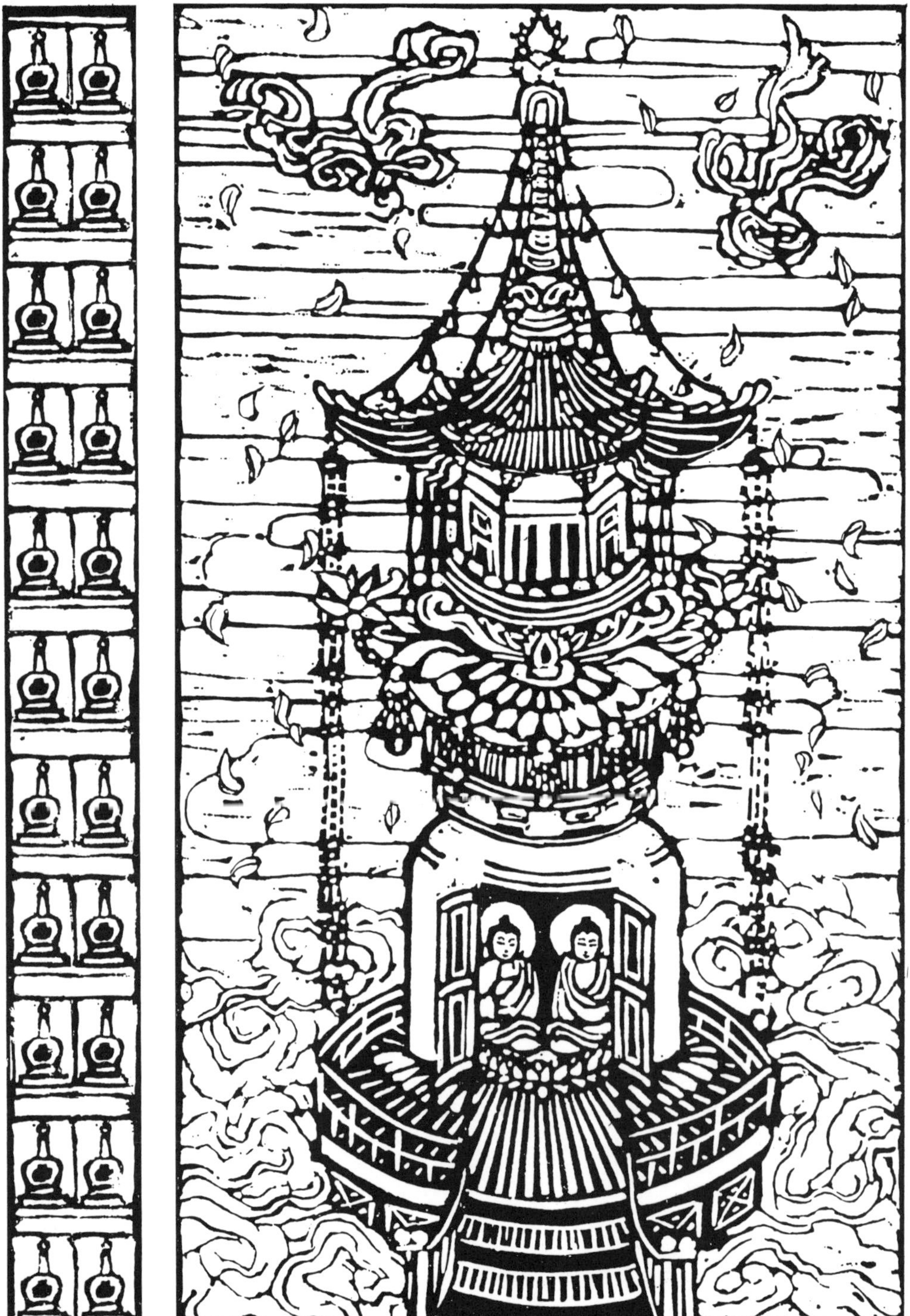

Chapter Six

FIVE ELEMENT SYMBOLISM AND THE STUPA

IN EVERY PART of the world the landscape has its own distinctive appearance, shaped by the forces of nature and the design of mankind. To the natural scene—mountains, hills or plains, barren desert or lush forest—human beings contribute architectural features of many kinds: mud huts or thatched cottages, magnificent pyramids, soaring church spires or clusters of skyscrapers, even enormous slag-heaps and smoking factory chimneys.

Since its beginnings in India, Buddhism has spread over an area extending from the deserts of central Asia in the west as far as the islands of Japan in the east, from the icy, windswept tablelands of Tibet in the north right down to the sun-drenched tropical island of Sri Lanka in the south. The natural features of all these areas are very different, and so are their architectural features, but wherever you travel throughout this vast area there is one type of architectural monument which is found everywhere: on bleak mountain tops, in pleasant wooded valleys, in the midst of vast plains and by the seashore. This ubiquitous Buddhist monument is the stupa.

Over the years the stupa has assumed a number of different forms, sometimes so different that it is almost impossible to tell that they spring from the same origins. There are stupas made of brick and stupas made of stone. Some are even made of precious metals—gold and silver—and studded with precious gems. Some stupas are so large that it would take you ten minutes to walk all the way round them, while others are so small that you can hold them in the palm of your hand.

Interesting as the history of the stupa is, however, it is not its place in the history of Buddhist art that concerns us here, but its profound symbolic significance. The stupa is one of the richest and most complex symbols in the whole field of Buddhism, especially of Mahāyāna Buddhism, and it also happens to be a symbol which occurs—very dramatically—in the *White Lotus Sutra*.

The stupa makes its appearance in the eleventh chapter of the sutra, roughly half way through—not reckoning the chapters that seem to be later additions—so that it divides the whole sutra into two great halves. The first half is dominated by the parables—the burning house, the return journey, the rain-cloud. But although the second half, including the appearance of the stupa, does include the occasional parable, it is almost completely taken over by myth and symbol, and by what we might call cosmic phantasmagoria. To generalize further, the first half is concerned with the way to Enlightenment, especially the Mahāyāna, the Great Way, and with the progress of the Bodhisattva along that way. The second half, by contrast, is concerned with Enlightenment, the goal. It is dedicated to the Buddha, and the concept of the Buddha-field, the spiritual world in which the Buddha 'reigns'.

Becoming more abstract still, we can say that in the first half of the sutra we see the whole of existence *sub specie temporis*, under the form of time, whereas in the second half we see existence *sub specie æternitatis*, as it always was, is, and will be above and beyond time, in the dimension of eternity. The first half of the sutra therefore depicts spiritual perfection everlastingly in the process of attainment, whereas the second half depicts perfection eternally attained. And the stupa stands in between the two, not to separate them but to unite them, for the symbol of the stupa contains both time and eternity. But before we can go any further, we need to ask a basic question. What *is* a stupa?

The word *stūpa* is Sanskrit, and literally means 'the top'; thus it comes to refer both to the crown of the head and to the gable—the top—of a house. Oddly enough, although the Indian word is rich in symbolic associations, it is etymologically connected with our much more ordinary English word 'stump'. But the etymological definition barely gives us a clue as to what the Buddhist symbol of the stupa might represent. A more useful starting point is the stupa's historical development.

If we probe right back to the origins of the stupa, we find that it is as old as Buddhism itself, indeed far older. Its origins go directly back to the ancient Indian burial mound, to the pre-Buddhistic practice of heaping earth over the ashes of the heroic dead. The *Mahā-parinibbāna Sutta* tells us that in accordance with this ancient practice, the Buddha himself directed shortly before his death that a stupa should be erected over his remains.[71] The *sutta*, the discourse from the Pali Canon which describes the Buddha's last days and death, goes on to give an account of how the Buddha's instructions were carried out. His body was placed on hundreds of logs which had been drenched in oil and clarified butter, and the pyre was set ablaze. It burned for a very long time, but when at last the flames had died down the Buddha's lay disciples made a reverent search through the cooling ashes to find any small fragments of bone still remaining. The monks may have had sufficient equanimity to do without a physical memento of their great teacher, but the lay disciples had the very human desire—if it is a failing, it is a forgivable one—to preserve whatever relics they could.

Unfortunately, no sooner had the relics been gathered together in a stone jar than a great quarrel arose among the disciples. If we take the representations of the scene in early Buddhist art literally, it would seem that the Buddha's ashes were barely cold when the different parties to the dispute were almost ready to go to war with one another to decide who would take possession of them. Surprising as such a reaction to the death of a great teacher may seem, there is clearly something highly symbolic about it, for this is not the only incident of this kind in Buddhist tradition. After the death of the great yogi Milarepa, after his withdrawal from the mundane plane, his disciples were apparently just as greedy for relics as the Buddha's were. With characteristically apocalyptic and magnificent symbolism, the Tibetan legend[72] describes how Milarepa's relics condensed into a brilliant globe of light which hovered above the heads of the disciples. When they tried to catch hold of it, it rose up into the air out of their reach; as soon as they lowered their grasping hands, it came a fraction lower—tantalisingly close but always evading their grasp. Whether or not this literally happened, the symbolism is obviously of great significance.

In the Buddha's case, many tribes and cities, and even kings and chiefs, laid claim to his relics. For instance, the Śākyas, the Buddha's own tribe, said 'The Buddha was born amongst us. If anyone has a right to the relics, surely we have.' But the Mallas said 'He may have been born in Śākya territory, but it was our people he lived among and taught for so long. We certainly have a right to the relics.' And so it went on, tribe after tribe putting forward their respective claims. It took the intervention of a learned brahmin to remind the disciples that it was unseemly, to say the least, for them to quarrel over the Buddha's relics as soon as he was dead. Brought to their senses in this way, the disciples at last settled the quarrel by dividing the relics into eight equal portions, one for each tribe that had put in a claim. Each of these communities built over their share of the relics a stupa, and a stupa was also built over the jar in which the relics had been contained.

The fact that this quarrel took place among the lay followers of the Buddha—the monks apparently having nothing to do with it—suggests that the practice of the worship of the relics of great men was not so much a part of the Buddha's own teaching as an ethnic practice which was still popular among his lay followers. Be that as it may, it is certainly the case that after the death of the Buddha the veneration and decoration of stupas rapidly became—and remained—a highly popular religious practice, to the extent that for hundreds of years after the Buddha's death the building, worship, and decoration of stupas was the principal religious practice of the laity. There were no temples in those days, and no images. The laity did not meditate or go to live in the jungle like the monks. So what religious practice could they do? They could make offerings to the stupas, and venerate the relics therein, and in this way keep alive the memory of the Buddha and the great example he had shown.

Although the *Mahā-parinibbāna Sutta* tells us that the Buddha directed his followers to build a stupa for his relics, it says nothing about how the Buddha wanted this to be done. It is a tradition coming down from Tibetan sources which gives us a few details. The story goes that when the Buddha told them to build a stupa, the disciples naturally asked in what form it should be made. In reply the Buddha did not say anything, but gave a practical demonstration. He took his outer yellow robe and folded it in two and two again until the cloth formed a rough cube. Then he took his begging-bowl, which of course was round, turned it upside-down, and put it on top of the robes. 'Make my stupa like this,' he said. And the evidence of the archaeological remains of Buddhist sites in India suggests that this shape—a square base topped by a hemisphere—was indeed the oldest form of the stupa.

At first the monks, the full-time followers of the Buddha, were not too happy about relic and stupa worship, but it became so widespread and popular among the laity that eventually they had to accept the practice as orthodox. Indeed, according to records like the *Kathā-vatthu*, some of the monks explicitly ascribed great devotional and spiritual value to the practice of worshipping relics and stupas.[73] By the time of the great king Aśoka, the third century BCE ruler of the Magadha kingdom who spread his rule all over India and founded the Maurya empire, the practice was very firmly established. Aśoka himself, according to all the accounts we have of him, was a great builder of stupas. The legends say that he built eighty-four thousand stupas in a single day—rather a tough job even for Aśoka. We are told that to make this possible, Aśoka's spiritual preceptor stretched out his hand into the sky and held back the sun until the great work was finished—a variant of the Old Testament Joshua legend.[74]

From the time of Aśoka stupas became ever larger and more elaborate, and they were the objects of more and more fervent devotion. Archaeologists have discovered stupas which at first were comparatively small, maybe only fifteen or twenty feet across, then enlarged again and again by the simple expedient of putting another layer onto the basic structure of the cube and hemisphere. Not only did the stupas become bigger; some of them 'migrated' overseas. Buddhists in Sri Lanka, in Burma, and in central Asia, started building their own stupas, some of them bigger and better even than the Indian ones. Only the great stupa at Borabadur is bigger than those built in Sri Lanka during the first century of the Christian era, the period when the *White Lotus Sutra* was written down.

Here is Kern's version—not perhaps as poetic as could be wished—of the passage which describes the sudden appearance of the stupa in the middle of the sutra:

Then there arose a Stūpa, consisting of seven precious substances, from the place of the earth opposite the Lord, the assembly being in the middle, a Stūpa five hundred yoganas in height and proportionate in circumference. After its rising, the Stūpa, a meteoric phenomenon, stood in the sky sparkling, beautiful, nicely decorated with five thousand successive terraces of flowers, adorned with many thousands of arches, embellished by thousands of banners and triumphal streamers, hung with thousands of jewel-garlands and with hour-plates and bells, and emitting the scent of Xanthochymus and sandal, which scent filled this whole world. Its rows of umbrellas rose so far on high as to touch the abodes of the four guardians of the horizon and the gods. It consisted of seven precious substances, viz. gold, silver, lapis lazuli, Musāragalva, emerald, red coral, and Karketana-stone. This Stūpa of precious substances once formed, the gods of paradise strewed and covered it with Mandārava and great Mandāra flowers. And from that Stūpa of precious substances there issued this voice: Excellent, excellent, Lord Śākyamuni! thou hast well expounded this Dharmaparyāya of the Lotus of the True Law. So it is, Lord; so it is, Sugata.[75]

So this is the stupa which appears in the sutra—no doubt an idealized version of the sort of monument which could be seen all over India at the time the sutra was written down. But although we have placed the stupa in its historical context, this does not completely answer the question of what a stupa is. We still need to ask ourselves what it *represents*, what it symbolizes. And the answer to this question is bound up with the symbolism of the five elements.

The five elements are the traditional ones—earth, water, fire, air, and ether or space. However, we must take these terms not literally but symbolically. When we take the five elements symbolically, what do we have in mind? What did the builders of the stupas have in mind? The answer, in a word, is energy.

Earth in this sense is not the dark, moist substance you scoop up from the ground. As a symbol, earth represents energy in a state of contraction and cohesion. The earth element is the principle of solidity, that which makes everything stick together, a bit like the law of gravity. So earth represents energy locked up, blocked, even frozen, petrified, crystallized. In the same way, water as a symbolic element is not the stuff you drink. It is energy in a state of oscillation or undulation—not completely blocked, but at the same time not truly free. It just goes backwards and forwards, backwards and forwards, between two points. This is the energy represented by the element water. Then, what does fire represent? Fire, of course, always rises upwards. When you kindle a fire, it never burns downwards—at least not of its own accord—but always goes straight up. So fire symbolizes energy moving upwards, ascending, sublimating if you like. Fourthly, air symbolizes energy which is not just expanding and ascending, but also descending and spreading out on both sides. In other words, air is energy in a state of expansion, diffusing itself in all directions of space from one central point.

The symbolism of the element which for lack of an apt English word we have to translate as 'ether' or 'space' is much more difficult to explain. In the Sanskrit it is *ākāśa*, a word which is derived from a root meaning 'to shine' and which is sometimes applied to the sky. But in its real meaning, *ākāśa* represents the primordial energy of which the other four—earth, water, fire, air—are grosser manifestations. They are like waves of different shapes, forms, and configurations, while the ether—the space, the *ākāśa*, the brightness, the shining—is like the sea itself. In some contexts—just to hint at the true nature of *ākāśa*—it stands half way between what we call matter and what we call spirit or consciousness.[76]

So the five elements symbolize different states of physical energy. We can see and experience them in the external world; everything is composed of these qualities of solidity, fluidity, temperature, air, and space. And we experience them in ourselves, in the human body. Earth, we could say, is the quality of solidity and resistance of bone and muscle. Water is the fluid quality of blood and lymph. Fire is the heat, the temperature of the body. Air is the intake of oxygen and the exhalation of carbon dioxide. And all of these are contained in the space which the body occupies.

Of course we have mental, psychical energies as well as physical energies, and these mental energies are also represented by the five elements. Looked at in terms of psychical energy, earth represents a state of psychological energy blockage, emotional blockage. When you are emotionally blocked, how do you feel? You feel contracted and constricted, shut up in yourself, all stiff and rigid and lifeless, like a mental corpse. This is the earth state. It is like that of a man so tightly bound that he is unable to stir hand or foot. He may just about be able to wiggle his little toe or blink his eyes, but that's all.

Water represents a state of extremely limited mobility, like that of ice which has just started to thaw. In this state your energy feels just slightly free; blockages have been removed at least to the extent that you can move a little from side to side. This state is like that of someone whose limbs are free, but who is imprisoned in a tiny cell only big enough for them to be able to pace backwards and forwards. Your energy is only partially liberated, so that you can just go backwards and forwards, or round and round in a narrow closed circle. This is the state in which most people live.

Fire represents a state of liberation of energy in an upward direction. Here energy is being sublimated, and in this state you feel inspired, as though you are being lifted up, or exalted, as though you are walking on air. The 'fire state' is like that of someone whose cell encloses them on all sides but has no roof. It is open to the sky, open to the stars, and the captive is perfectly free to move in that direction; all they have to do is rise up into the air.

And air is energy in the process of becoming completely liberated. All hindrances and psychological blockages are removed. You feel that you are expanding in all directions, transcending your narrow limited individuality or selfhood. This state is like that of someone whose prison walls have suddenly fallen down so that they are absolutely free to go in any direction they like. In fact the metaphor begins to break down here, because as an individual the ex-prisoner can only go in one direction at a time, but in the state symbolized by the element air you can expand yourself simultaneously to all the quarters of space, which means transcending your own individuality.

And how does *ākāśa*—ether or space—fit into the picture? What can it possibly represent? To put it in a very general way, we can say that *ākāśa* is the higher dimension within which all these movements take place. The non-movement of earth, the undulating, oscillatory movement of water, the ascending movement of fire, the expanding movement of air—all these take place within *ākāśa*, a dimension which is higher still, and which contains and includes them all.

Taking this symbolism still further, we can say that the five elements also symbolize five different kinds of people. Earth symbolizes the psychologically and emotionally crippled person. Water symbolizes the so-called normal person: a person who has a certain amount of free energy but functions within narrow limits, in a repetitive, reactive manner. Fire symbolizes the artist, the poet, the musician, the free thinker, and the meditator, because they are rising up, sublimating, ascending. Air symbolizes the mystic, who is engaged all the time essentially in transcending the self. And space symbolizes the fully illumined sage who has accomplished that process of self-transcending—in other words, the Buddha.

According to tradition each of the five elements is associated with a colour. Earth is associated with yellow, water with white, fire with bright flaming red, air with a beautiful pale green, and space with blue, or sometimes a golden-flame colour. And the elements are also associated with certain geometrical forms: earth with the cube, water with the sphere, fire with the cone or pyramid, air with a bowl-shape or saucer-shape, like the dome of the sky turned upside down, and space with a flaming jewel-like shape.

There are many other sets of correlations. For instance, according to some systems of yoga the five elements are correlated with the five psychic centres within the human body. Earth is correlated with the lowest psychic centre, the one between the anus and the genitals, water with the centre at the solar plexus, fire with the heart centre, air with the throat centre, and space with the centre at the top of the head. There is also a correlation of the five elements with the five Buddhas. But although the symbolism of the elements is such a fascinating subject in itself, it is time we applied it to our original question: what is a stupa?

The five elements as represented by different geometrical forms and by different colours can be combined to give earth, a yellow cube; water, a white sphere; fire, a red cone or pyramid; air, a green bowl or saucer; and space, a flame-coloured jewel-like shape—some translators call it an acuminated sphere but it actually looks more like a jewel. These coloured forms, arranged one on top of another in an order of increasing subtlety and release of energy, give the basic structure of the stupa. The stupa symbolizes, therefore, the progressive liberation of energy, the process of growth and development, the Higher Evolution. It thus embodies in architectural terms the entire meaning of Buddhism in general and the *White Lotus Sutra* in particular. Small wonder that the stupa is so widespread, and so much an object of fervent devotion.

In the course of centuries the basic structure of the stupa has undergone many adaptations, some with a definite spiritual basis, others merely architectural or cultural. One of these changes in particular relates to a specific aspect of the symbolism of the elements: their correlation with the psychic centres of the human body.

Imagine in front of you a human being seated cross-legged as though in meditation, and a stupa which is the same height as the seated person. If you identify the positions of the psychic centres up the person's median nerve, and look across to the stupa, you will find that the centres correspond with the successive geometrical forms. Now imagine that another cube, smaller than the cube at the base of the stupa, is placed between the sphere and the cone. If the whole six-shape structure thus created is hollow, so that the cross-legged human being can sit inside it, his or her eyes will be on a level with that second smaller cube, so that if the cube happens to be transparent, the eyes will be visible through it.

Now this may remind you of something. If you have ever been to Nepal, or if you have seen photographs of the stupas there, you will surely be reminded of the typical Nepalese stupa. On these stupas, on each side of the *harmikā*, as the second, higher cube is called, a pair of eyes is painted. When you see these stupas rising above the landscape in the distance, with these eyes on the sides, they produce a very strange effect indeed, especially because the stupas are so enormous that they completely dominate the landscape. The eyes look down at you with a slightly disapproving frown which seems not to be imaginary.

The presence of these pairs of eyes serves to remind us that the stupa is correlated with the human body itself, that the elements of the stupa correspond to the psychic centres, and that both represent an upward, progressive movement, a movement of spiritual evolution. But why should that second cube have been put there at all? Indeed, why should the cone, the saucer, and the jewel have been added to the two original simple elements, the cube and the sphere? And why is the conical part of the Nepalese stupa divided into sections which make it look as if it consists of a number of rings of gradually diminishing diameter?

We can answer all these questions in terms of yin-yang symbolism. The terms yin and yang are not Indian but Chinese, and they represent a polarity of universal validity and importance; they also happen to be quite well known in the West, and I am making use of them for this reason. In considering the parables of the rain-cloud and the sun, we saw that the yin principle is associated with the earth, with water, with the depths, whereas the yang principle is associated with the sky, with fire, with the heights. Yin is the negative, passive principle—the 'feminine'

principle, to use that term in a very specific way. Yang is the active, masculine principle, the positive principle. Yin is symbolized by the moon; yang is symbolized by the sun. Yin is emotion, the unconscious; yang is reason, the conscious mind. Yin is life; yang is light. Yin, if you like, is the lower evolution; yang is the Higher Evolution. In the course of the evolution of the individual, yin and yang must be harmonized, synthesized. The plant, as we have seen, is the joint product of soil and rain on the one hand, and of space and sunlight on the other. In much the same way, the growing individual is nourished by both yin and yang forces.

Now how does this tie up with the stupa? The pre-Buddhistic burial mound consisted simply of a great heap of earth, a tumulus, a barrow, a place where the remains of heroes, kings, and sages were enshrined, and which was the focus for the rites of the cult of the dead. This heap of earth came naturally to be associated with the earth, and therefore with the womb of Mother Nature, and the maternal in general. In its original form, then, the stupa was a symbol of the yin principle. The earliest Buddhist stupas, made up of the cube and the sphere or hemisphere, still had this association with yin, for both the cube and the sphere are yin symbols, or lunar symbols.

So where did the smaller cube come from? And what is the origin of the triple umbrella by which in many stupas the cube is surmounted? These two symbols come from an ancient Indian, pre-Buddhistic cult parallel to the cult of the dead: the cult of the sun. Of the many solar symbols of ancient India, two were of particular importance: the sacred fire and the sacred tree. The sacred fire burned on the hearth of every orthodox follower of the Vedas, and it also burned in the middle of the village, on a cubiform brick altar in a small shrine, an idealized hut. This hut often stood at the foot of the sacred tree of the village, a peepul or a banyan tree, for the tree was also a solar symbol. So the *harmikā*, the second cube of the stupa, symbolizes the original fire altar, and the umbrella by which it is surmounted is a stylized version of the sacred tree.

So we can see how the stupa gradually developed, two solar symbols, the fire altar, and the umbrella or tree, being superimposed upon two lunar symbols, the cube and the sphere or hemisphere. Subsequently, the saucer and the cone came to be placed on top of the cube and the sphere. So the stupa is not just an arrangement of the symbols of the five elements in ascending order. It is also a synthesis of Indian solar and lunar symbolism, and a synthesis of the principles of yin and yang. It represents, we may say, a synthesis of the different aspects, the opposite poles, of our own being, of our own unruly nature.

A standard stupa consists of seven essential parts. At the bottom is the square base, the *medhī*, which—whether it is a simple cube or a number of steps or terraces (usually four)—represents the earth element, the yin principle.

Next comes the hemispherical portion, which is known in Sanskrit as the *aṇḍa*, literally 'egg', or the *garbha*, the receptacle, the treasury, the womb—names alive with symbolism. In the case of the Sinhalese stupa (known as the *dagoba*, a corruption of the Sanskrit *dhātu garbha*, or 'repository of relics'), this 'hemispherical' portion is actually bell-shaped, a feature which gives the Sinhalese stupas their distinctive beauty. In the Tibetan stupa, the *chorten*, the same bell-shape is found—but turned upside-down. It assumes a chalice-like shape which is exactly the same as that of the vase of immortality, the *amṛta kalaśa* (Sanskrit) or *bumpa* (Tibetan) which is held by Amitāyus, the Buddha of Eternal Life. This association with the vase of immortality represents the receptivity of the lunar principle to the solar principle, of yin to yang—or even the lunar principle as transformed by the solar principle. Remember too that this portion of the stupa symbolizes the water element, and therefore once again symbolizes the yin principle.

The third part of the standard stupa is the cube which originated from the Vedic fire altar. It is in this section, known as the *harmikā*, that relics would be enshrined. The Buddha's physical body was consumed by fire, just as his selfhood, we may say, was consumed in the fire of his spiritual practice and realization. So this portion of the stupa symbolizes the fire element, and therefore the yang principle.

The fourth portion, the spire, *kunta*—both umbrella and tree—developed over a long period of time until it finally consisted of thirteen rings of diminishing diameter, placed one on top of another to represent the thirteen *bhūmis*—stages of spiritual progress—traversed by the Bodhisattva on the way to Enlightenment. In China, this one portion of the stupa, the original fire portion, was separated from the rest to become what we know in the West as the pagoda, a very characteristic feature of the Chinese landscape. It would appear that if the original stupa, the cube and the sphere, symbolized only the yin principle, the pagoda went to the opposite extreme and became a symbol of just the yang principle. We could say, however, that as the pagoda does stand on the earth, which is yin, a balance is still maintained. With the earth itself as its base, the pagoda doesn't need a separate architectural base. Although, geometrically considered, this portion of the stupa represents the fire element, in the seven-section stupa fire is already represented by the *harmikā*, so the spire comes to stand for the air element. In either case, whether symbolizing fire or air, it represents the yang principle.

The fifth section is the saucer or bowl. This originally represented space or ether, which is a synthesis of yin and yang, but here it becomes a pure white moon crescent, and symbolizes the yin principle in a highly purified and sublimated form. Sixthly comes a red solar disc, which represents the yang principle, also in highly purified and sublimated form.

Last of all, a flame-coloured or rainbow-coloured jewel grows out of the red solar disc. This symbol is found not only on the top of stupas but also surmounting the heads of Buddha-images of all countries and all periods, recalling the original meaning of the word *stupa*, the crown of the head. The *ushṇīsha*—which Western translators rather inelegantly call the 'bodhic protuberance'—sometimes looks like a flame springing up from the Buddha's head, and sometimes like a lotus bud growing there. The significance of the *ushṇīsha* is the same as the flame-coloured jewel at the top of the stupa: complete, total synthesis of yin and yang. And what is a synthesis at the highest possible level of the principles of yin and the yang? Enlightenment itself: this is the true meaning of the flame-coloured jewel.

It is not surprising, in view of all these considerations, that the stupa is sometimes considered to be the most important of all Buddhist symbols, even more important, both historically and doctrinally, than that other well-known symbol, the Buddha-image. It is not surprising that the stupa makes this sudden dramatic appearance right in the middle of the *White Lotus Sutra*. You may remember that when the stupa appears, the Buddha's disciples entreat him to open it, so Śākyamuni rises up into the air and draws the bolt of the door half way up the stupa. The bolt draws back, the gates open with a sound like thunder, and inside the stupa is revealed the body of the ancient Buddha Abundant Treasures, still intact after countless years. Abundant Treasures then invites Śākyamuni to share his seat, so the two Buddhas sit side by side within the stupa. What does this mean? It must mean something. Every single image in the sutra has a meaning. We could say that, as Abundant Treasures is the Buddha of the remote past, and Śākyamuni is the Buddha of the present, this incident represents the coming together of the past and the present. Past and present have become one.

But the episode has an even more profound significance. We are told that Abundant Treasures is the Buddha of the past; but what past? Not a thousand years ago, not a million years ago, but, we are told, uncounted, uncountable, unfathomable, incalculable myriads of myriads of years ago. Now when you pile it on like that, what you are really getting at is that this Buddha is beyond time altogether. He is not just the Buddha from the remote past, but the *primordial* Buddha, the Buddha from the metaphysical beginning of things—which means no beginning at all. In other words, Abundant Treasures is the eternal Buddha, above the past, above the present, above the future, out of time altogether. This means that when Śākyamuni, the Buddha of the present, takes his seat within the stupa by the side of the eternal Buddha, Abundant Treasures, the dimension of time and the dimension of eternity coalesce. In containing both Abundant Treasures and Śākyamuni, the stupa contains both time and eternity. So the stupa as it occurs in the *White Lotus Sutra* at this point does not represent just a general synthesis of the yin and yang principles, on howsoever high a level. It represents the highest and most total synthesis of all: the synthesis of time and eternity.

Chapter Six

QUESTIONS AND ANSWERS

Why didn't one of the Arhats intervene to stop the quarrel between the disciples? What is the significance of the brahmin?
The incident does seem to suggest that at that stage the brahmins had closer connections with the laity than the bhikkhus did; that seems a little strange, but it may have been the case. Another possibility that occurs to me is that at that time people may still have been using the terms brahmin and bhikkhu interchangeably; there may not have been the hard-and-fast distinction between the bhikkhu and the non-bhikkhu that arose later. The *Dhammapada* points to this, describing the brahmin and the bhikkhu in almost identical terms.[77] So Doṇa, the man who intervened, could have been a brahmin in the spiritual sense, not the caste sense. Clearly he had respect for the Buddha and his teaching. He could have been a *paribbājaka* (Pali) who hadn't joined the sangha in the formal sense, if in fact there was a formally constituted sangha of the coenobitical type at that time. Of course, this is just a hypothesis.

You mention that eight stupas were built over the Buddha's remains, and one over the jar. Is that a historical piece of information, or is it mythical?
Well, it isn't obviously mythical in that it doesn't involve anything that might not have happened. If we were being told that ten million stupas were built, that would certainly sound legendary or mythical, but eight stupas is a rather modest number. And the account does come in the Pali Canon itself. I think we can take it that those stupas were actually erected. We know for certain that by the time of Aśoka the stupa had become quite elaborate, which presupposes a considerable period of development—and Aśoka was separated from the Buddha by only one hundred and fifty years.

You suggest that stupa worship was entirely a lay practice in the early centuries, only adopted by monks later. I find it hard to believe that the bhikkhus wouldn't have felt naturally drawn to express their devotion to their teacher by leaving flowers at the stupa containing his remains.

Perhaps—before we go any further—we shouldn't speak so much of stupa worship as of *relic* worship. In the early days the point of stupas was simply that they enshrined relics. Later on, stupas were built which didn't enshrine relics but just commemorated the Buddha, or a certain event in his life which had occurred on the spot where the stupa was built. They might contain some article associated with the Buddha, but not an actual relic. And eventually stupas became objects of worship in their own right, especially when they started incorporating images of the Buddhas and the Bodhisattvas.

In the *Mahā-parinibbāna Sutta* the Buddha is represented as telling Ānanda not to bother with the disposal of the remains of the Tathāgata, because there were devout lay people who would look after that. This suggests that the Buddha thought that the bhikkhus should be getting on with their meditation and not concerning themselves with the cult of relics. It does seem, however, that bhikkhus became involved in this cult quite early on. Some schools, like the Chaityavādins, especially concerned themselves with the cult of the stupa and emphasized its importance. So even if the worship of the stupas containing relics was more or less the prerogative of the lay people to begin with, it very quickly spread to the bhikkhus and bhikkhunīs.

Are any of the teachings of the Chaityavādins still available?

There are some works which contain references to their beliefs. For instance, there is the commentary on the *Kathā-vatthu* of the *Abhidharma Piṭaka*. The *Kathā-vatthu* itself refutes the doctrines of certain schools but without naming the schools concerned, but the commentary identifies the Chaityavādins as one of those schools. So from that source, assuming it to be reliable, we do have some idea about the teachings of the Chaityavādins. And we do know that they attached special importance to the worship of stupas.

There are also references to the worship of stupas throughout the *Mahāvastu*, which is the work of the Lokottaravādins.[78] There are some very striking carvings representing the worship of the stupa by the lay people of Amarāvati in south India. By the time of Aśoka, stupas had become much more elaborate than they were in earlier days. People didn't just worship the stupas—they decorated them, festooning them with garlands of flowers, scarves, flags, streamers, and little bells, just as described in the *White Lotus Sutra*.

An example of an Aśokan period stupa is still preserved intact—the great stupa of Sanchi, in the former state of Bhopal, half way between Bombay and Delhi. The stupa is hemispherical in shape, built of brick and stone, and surrounded by a massive stone railing (built as a copy of an original wooden railing) pierced by four magnificent decorated gates which face the four cardinal points. These gates symbolize the universality of Buddhism which is proclaimed in all directions to all beings whatsoever in all the quarters of space. They are elaborately carved with scenes from the life of the Buddha, his previous lives (the Jātakas),[79] and so on. The Buddha himself does not appear in these bas-reliefs because he was simply never represented at this stage of Buddhist art. There are trees, flowers, buildings, other people, disciples, animals, a rich and lavish profusion; but the Buddha himself, even in those scenes which depict his own life, his Enlightenment, his birth and so on, is not depicted.

Why is that?
It was thought in the early days of Oriental studies that the Buddha was not depicted because artists did not feel confident enough to represent him properly, but it has since been pointed out that they represented everything else beautifully, so why not the Buddha? We now know that artists did not represent the Buddha on principle. In those days the Lokottaravādin School of Buddhism was very strong, and they held that the Buddha was not an ordinary human being, but a transcendental principle—ineffable, indescribable, unrepresentable. For these strictly metaphysical or spiritual reasons, the artists did not represent the Buddha, and in the place where the Buddha would have been they put a symbol. If the scene was of the Buddha being born, he was represented by a pair of footprints, the *śrīpāda*. The Buddha preaching his first sermon was illustrated by a Wheel of the Law, a *dharmacakra*, perhaps on a throne supported by lions. His Enlightenment was represented by a bodhi tree. If the scene represented the Buddha moving about, a parasol or umbrella might be shown, and if the scene was the death of the Buddha—the *parinirvāṇa*—this was marked by the presence of a stupa.

Incidentally, although the great stupa is the best preserved of the many stupas originally built at Sanchi, it was in another of the stupas there that relics were found enshrined—not relics of the Buddha, but relics of his two chief disciples Śāriputra and Maudgalyāyana. By one of those rather strange historical accidents, these relics, in their original little steatite boxes, with the names of the two disciples engraved on them, spent some ninety years in the Victoria and Albert Museum, having been removed by a British archaeologist before the people of India started caring very much about Buddhism. They were returned to India, to the Maha Bodhi Society, after Indian independence, and re-enshrined at Sanchi in the course of a ceremony presided over by the Prime Minister of India, Pandit Nehru.

•

How appropriate is it to build stupas in the West?
I think stupas would look better than skyscrapers and blocks of flats. They could be a pleasing feature of the landscape, not necessarily in a completely traditional form, but having some link with tradition, based on the traditional five element structure.

Could a building be made in the form of a stupa?
In some parts of the Buddhist world, in China and in Tibet, temples, sometimes even monasteries, have been built in the form of stupas. Pagodas, which are also essentially stupas, do have chambers containing images on every storey; in this way the pagoda is not just a reliquary but also a temple. Sometimes they have even been used as libraries for sacred books. But personally I like the idea of a stupa being solid, a monument having no use. Not being able to use it—even as a temple—you can only worship it.

I've felt for some time an urge to build a stupa. I feel that a coloured element stupa would have an immediate impact, but a seven element yin-yang stupa might lend itself to more aesthetic architecture. Have you any thoughts about the most appropriate form for the West?
I am quite happy for us to have stupas of many types and varieties; I see no reason for sticking to just one. I would prefer them to approximate to the original solid architectural model rather than the temple or palace-like forms found in China and Japan; and we should perhaps start with simple forms rather than elaborate ones. I like the Sinhalese bell-shaped ones and the Tibetan chorten types. I think the elongated Thai stupas look very graceful. I also like the simple, solid ones, just a square base with a hemisphere on top. We could build all sorts of stupas, but whatever we build should be aesthetically pleasing; the proportions should be harmonious. I think multicoloured stupas might look too gaudy. In Sri Lanka stupas are usually whitewashed, and that looks very

beautiful against the brilliant green background of the landscape. Tibetan stupas are whitewashed too, and Burmese ones are often gilded, which is also beautiful.

As for the Nepalese-style stupas with eyes, they are very distinctive, and they look magnificent, but they are absolutely enormous. They are all right in the landscape of Nepal, but I have a feeling that in this country, at least until the symbolism of the stupa is established, they would look rather bizarre.

I feel that stupas have quite an immediate impact. In building them, would we be trying to appeal just to Buddhists, or making something attractive and meaningful even to people who know nothing at all about its significance?
Well, you can't ignore the feelings and responses of non-Buddhists, and I can't help feeling that they might consider a four-coloured stupa a bit gaudy and tasteless. Personally I like the white stupa. I would also like to see really big stupas being built, the bigger the better. The setting is quite important too—the stupa needs to blend with the surrounding environment. In Nepal they have small stupas in the courtyards of temples and monasteries; we could do that in the West too, and circumambulate them on festival days.

•

You say that reliquary keeping is a human failing, but a forgivable one. Surely, if relics can help you connect with the Buddha and his teaching, keeping them has its positive aspect?
In a broader sense, the keeping of mementoes and souvenirs can be something of a weakness—because you are attached to them when perhaps you ought just to throw them away and think of the future rather than the past. This is the kind of thing I was referring to. The temptation is to treat relics as fetishes, to keep them not out of strong feelings of devotion, but as talismans, sources of magical protection. Buddhists in the past have done this, and present-day Buddhists continue to do it. And, of course, the same thing has happened in the West. Cathedral museums in Italy are full of hundreds of relics which don't seem to mean anything to anyone any more, but which meant a lot to people in the Middle Ages, when princes and churches used to have vast collections of them. Apparently various ecclesiastical commissions have sorted out these relics and declared at least ninety-five per cent of them to be fakes; there are still an embarrassing number of heads of John the Baptist and drops of milk of the Virgin Mary. That is how things can

degenerate. What is a relic, after all? Do all these arms and legs and skulls really help you to connect?

If you go to the Dominican Priory in Siena you can see the head of Saint Catherine, a shrivelled little head in a little glass case. It is interesting, in a way, to think that this is the head of Catherine, that formidable lady of the fourteenth century who bossed the popes of the day and dragged them down from Avignon to Rome to do their duty, but I don't know whether it helps you to feel more closely in contact with Saint Catherine from a spiritual point of view. I would much rather read Father Raymond's biography of her, written from the perspective of someone who knew her intimately for many years of her life. That brings you far closer to the woman than just seeing what is left of her head.

There is not so much of this arm and leg business in Buddhism— Buddhist relics are usually less gruesome. They often take the form of tiny bits of bone, or even pearl-like objects called śarīras, which are believed to be secreted in the bones of Enlightened people. A bhikkhu from Singapore once told me some extraordinary stories from his personal experience about these relics. Apparently they can multiply and transfer themselves from one place to another—he would put these little pearl-like objects in a drawer, and five minutes later there would be ten times as many. He told me the story very solemnly, and I didn't feel inclined to disbelieve him.

If one came into possession of one of these śarīras, should one make it a centre-piece for a shrine, say?
Normally relics of that sort are enclosed in stupas. If the stupa was small enough it could be kept on the shrine—though the bigger the stupa the better. Usually it would be kept quite separately from the shrine, because if the śarīra does represent the Buddha, it would be like having two Buddhas on the same shrine. But if you couldn't build a large stupa, then you could certainly make a miniature one and have it on the shrine.

Śarīras are obviously a particularly subtle form of relic, but in general Buddhist relics, although they come from the physical body of the original person, are not usually the crude bits and pieces of it to be found in the reliquaries of the West. One exception to this might be the Tibetan and Chinese practice of mummifying the bodies of spiritual teachers. This seems almost the wrong sort of emphasis—was he his body? Perhaps some people do feel inspired to see the gilded mummy of Hui Neng, for instance; perhaps they feel spiritually more in touch. Maybe one shouldn't lay down rules for other people in this respect. But personally I am not very much stirred by relics, though I am quite happy about stupas.

The image of Abundant Treasures preserved intact in his stupa reminds me of the Egyptian pharoahs mummified in their pyramids. Could these be two cultural variations of the human desire to preserve the leader?
Perhaps there *is* something in human beings that makes them want to preserve the physical presence of their leaders. In some primitive communities they bury you under the floor of the hut, don't they? And Lenin was preserved in the way they used to preserve saints, so that people could go along to pay their respects and look at his embalmed body through a little window. It seems rather strange. Perhaps it comes from a deep-seated belief that the *mana*—the primitive power and energy attached to that person—somehow lingers on in the physical body and can be preserved by the tribe or the group.

I think in the case of the Egyptian pyramids the idea was rather different. The ancient Egyptians thought that your physical body had to be preserved intact to ensure the continuation of your subtle body in the other world. The building of the pyramid and the preservation of the body was for the sake of the person being entombed, the Pharoah or whoever it was who could afford such a tomb, not for the sake of the group he left behind.

•

You say that ākāśa—*space—comes half way between matter and consciousness. What do you mean by that?*
To begin with, 'space' is really quite a misleading translation—perhaps 'firmament' would be nearer. One could say perhaps that if earth, water, fire, and air represent the gross material, *ākāśa* represents the subtle material, so in that sense it is mid-way between the material and the conscious, between matter and consciousness. It is even, in a way, a bit like the collective unconscious—though don't take that too literally.

Can you say why?
Well, it isn't really an objective, external dimension. Some ancient Hindu texts speak of the '*ākāśa* of the heart', the space you experience when you enter into your own heart, which makes it an inner dimension, not an external one. But if it is in between matter and consciousness, in a sense it is neither subjective nor objective, but a higher dimension of being accessible from within rather than from without. For instance, in the series of the four *arūpa dhyānas* there is the sphere of infinite space, but this is something that you experience in the dhyāna state, something you close your eyes and experience rather than open your eyes and see. At

the same time, it is still mundane; it isn't the transcendental dimension.

But you seem to equate ākāśa *with some sort of transcendental experience—or am I taking it too literally?*
In the context of five element symbolism, *ākāśa* does represent the transcendental. But when you have a stupa with five, six, or more elements, *ākāśa* on its own does not have to represent the transcendental.

Is the distinction between the arūpa dhyāna *of 'infinite space' and the* arūpa dhyāna *of 'infinite consciousness'[80] that the one is objective and the other subjective?*
Yes. The way it happens is that first you become aware of infinite space. This is not the literal, external space of the universe, which even Western scientists cannot be sure is either finite or infinite, but the inner *experience* of infinite space. The experience you have at this stage is of complete freedom from obstruction, the feeling that you can move unimpeded in any direction. But at the same time that you experience this, you are *conscious* that you are experiencing it, so that you are experiencing space and also consciousness of space. Having achieved that, you proceed to separate, so to speak, the consciousness of space from space itself, so that you are left just with consciousness. You reflect that just as space is without limit, so your consciousness is likewise free from obstruction, or, in a sense, infinite. In that way you make the transition from the first to the second *arūpa dhyāna*.

But how do you reflect in the arūpa dhyānas?
Well, you can't take literally this notion that in the dhyānas beyond the first one there is absolutely no mental activity. It is often said that you develop the higher dhyānas and then come back to the first dhyāna in order to allow the re-arising of *vitarka* and *vicāra*,[81] so that you can develop Insight. This is not untrue, but it is grossly literalistic. What really happens is that, remaining poised in the higher dhyānas, you allow a very subtle type of *vitarka/vicāra* to arise; and it arises without any real detriment to your experience of that higher state of consciousness. It is with the help of that very subtle mental activity—so subtle that it may not even feel like mental activity, but more like just seeing—that you develop Insight. And in much the same way you experience the difference between the so-called sphere of infinite space and the so-called sphere of infinite consciousness.

When you correlate the five elements of the stupa with the five psychic centres, you say that the addition of the harmikā *is at the level of the eyes. But on the basis of the correlation it would actually seem to come between the navel and the solar plexus. Could you explain this?*

In *Foundations of Tibetan Mysticism* Lama Govinda goes into the correlation between the elements of the stupa and the chakras in some detail, if you're interested to find out more.[82] But you're right—the different correspondences don't always fit together. Interpolating the Vedic altar (which becomes the *harmikā*), for example, dislocates the system. Perhaps you could say that when the eyes are painted on the side of the *harmikā*, pictorial considerations have taken over, and you have to ignore the rest of the symbolism, or at least not insist on too close a correspondence.

There just are inconsistencies in symbolism sometimes. When different ideas are incorporated into the symbol, it has to lose some of its original significance to incorporate the new element. For example, in the case of the pagoda, just one element of the original stupa, the fire element, is subdivided into a number of different storeys to become a complete stupa in itself; in a way, that is a complete distortion of the original.

You say that the Vedic hearth and the parasol were incorporated into the stupa after the initial architectural form had been determined. When I was in India I noticed that nearly every Buddhist monument had some Hindu object of worship nearby. Is it possible that the hearth which forms part of the stupa represents not the universal integrating the ethnic, but the ethnic overcoming the universal? Could the brahmins have included the Vedic hearth to make the stupa into a place of Hindu worship?

To the best of my knowledge, which derives mainly from Govinda, those elements were incorporated by the Buddhists themselves. When it comes to art and architecture even a universal religion has to make use of ethnic elements, at least initially, just as in terms of language you have to make use of whatever words are available and gradually give them your own meaning. That is rather different from the deliberate building of Hindu shrines next to Buddhist monuments which you do see in modern times.

The umbrella, for instance, is a pre-Buddhistic Hindu symbol, though it continues to be an emblem of sovereignty even today; the president of India has a white umbrella held over him on ceremonial occasions, just as in ancient times. When Buddhism adopted the symbolism of the umbrella, the sovereignty it symbolized became spiritual sovereignty over the three worlds.

The path of the Higher Evolution can be seen as five progressive stages of consciousness. Can these be correlated with the five element symbolism of the stupa?
I think probably they can, though you might have to do some violence to one or the other in order to correlate them effectively. Broadly speaking, the stupa does represent both the Higher and the lower evolution, fire and air superimposed on earth and water, the solar superimposed on the lunar.

This superimposition of the solar on the lunar seems to me to say something about the nature of Buddhism. I have come to think that religions can be regarded either as solar or as lunar. I think of Christianity, for instance, more as a lunar religion, because it is based on the conception of birth and death and resurrection. Christ is the risen God, originating from the pagan god of harvest, god of spring, and so on. There are associations with the cycle of the year, and all sorts of agricultural and vegetative connections; this is all lunar symbolism.

Buddhism, by contrast, seems to be entirely a solar religion. You don't get any of this birth, death, and rebirth imagery at all—in fact, the cycle of birth and death is something that one seeks to be emancipated from. Buddhist symbolism is associated with the hero who fights with the forces representing the material world—the womb, the mother, the earth—to win his way to the higher path.

But how would your emphasis on spiritual androgyny, on the integration of 'male' and 'female', fit in with that idea?
I don't see the feminine principle and the masculine principle in this context—yin and yang—as equal. I see the integration as consisting not in the balance of the one against the other, but in the absorption of yin within yang, much as in Tantric Buddhist art you see the tiny figure of the ḍākinī clinging onto the much larger figure of the Buddha. If you have the yin and the yang as equal and opposite, you need a third element to synthesize them. As it is, there is no third element, so the two can only be synthesized by the stronger, or the higher, incorporating the other. You don't have the lower evolution and the Higher Evolution side by side, balancing one another; the lower evolution is incorporated into the Higher Evolution. This is the great distinction, as far as I can see, between Buddhism and Taoism.

Does that have implications for practice in terms of the masculine qualities in relation to the feminine qualities?
In some ways it does. Supposing you decide you are lacking in the feminine qualities and want to develop them, well, development is an active process, so you are going to have to take some initiative to develop those feminine qualities. According to the Mahāyāna, *vīrya* is necessary with regard to all the *pāramitās*.[83] Yes, it is a separate *pāramitā* in its own right, but it also exists on the level of all the other *pāramitās*—you need *vīrya* even to develop *kṣānti*. To be very paradoxical, you need to be a man in order to be a woman: to be at her best, a woman needs some masculine qualities. How is she to bring her natural womanly yin qualities to perfection without some element of yang?

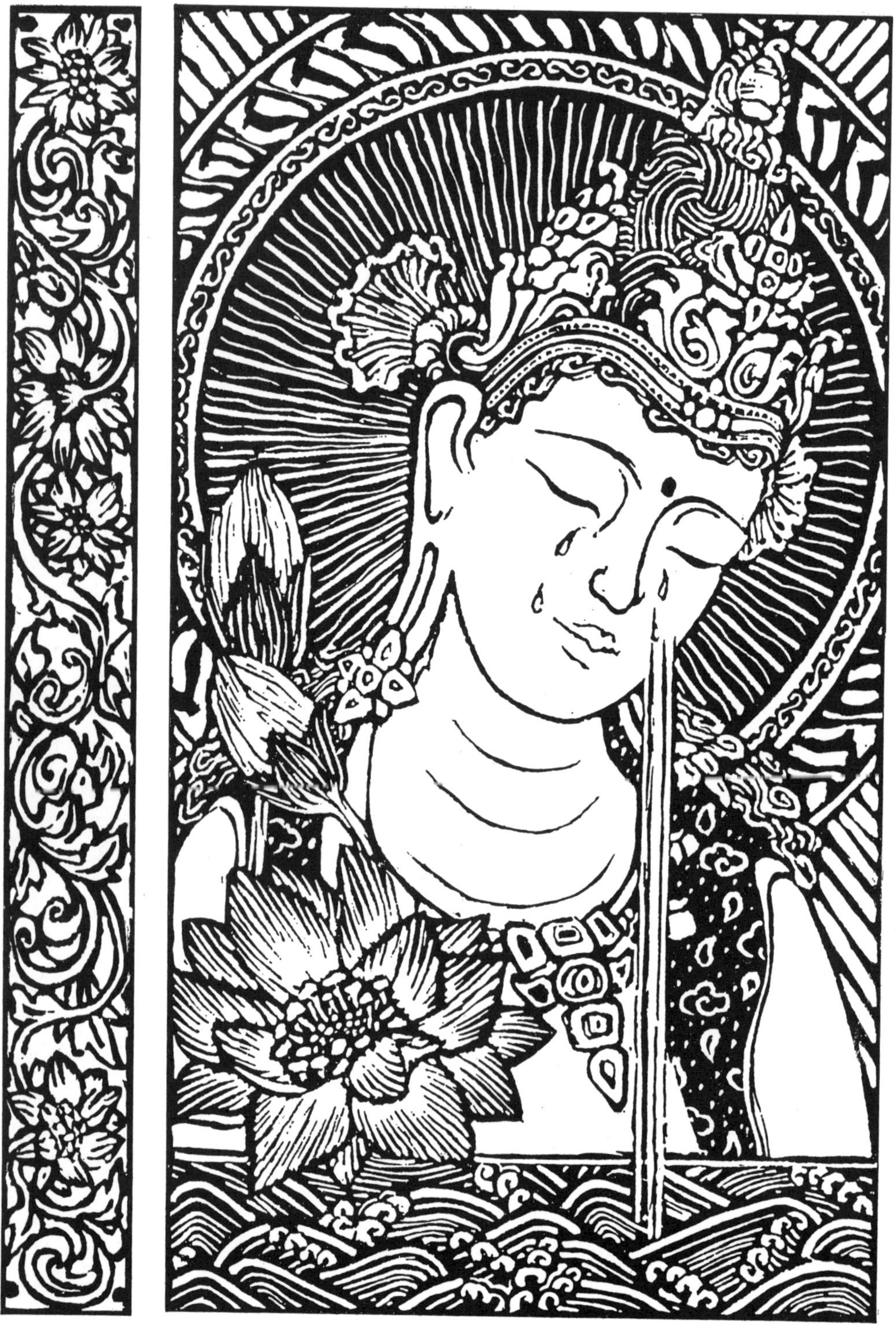

Chapter Seven

THE JEWEL IN THE LOTUS

STUPAS ARE TO BE FOUND all over the Buddhist world, but we are now going to turn to something which is found mainly in one Buddhist country, albeit a very well-known and important one: Tibet. You only have to look at the map to see that Tibet is a truly enormous country, easily bigger than France and Spain put together. But although Tibet is so large, it is very thinly populated. Until recently we were rather in the dark as to the exact number of Tibetans, but it would now seem that there are between two and three million people scattered throughout that vast area. There are hardly any cities, and not even many villages, because many of the people, especially in the east and north, lead a nomadic existence, roaming from place to place with their horses and their felt tents, their flocks and their herds. And I'm sorry to say that quite a lot of these nomads, even though they are Buddhists, live by robbery.

This makes journeying in Tibet a hazardous undertaking. When you have been travelling for hundreds of miles through wild country dotted with enormous rocks behind any of which someone might be hiding with a gun, it's a relief to realize that you are approaching civilization again, or at least some tiny hill village. And you're likely to see signs that you are near to human habitation long before you see a house or a person. You may well see a chorten, a Tibetan stupa, roughly built of stones and whitewashed—but these are common even out in the wilds of Tibet. What will tell you for sure that you are near a village is much more likely to be a long, low dry-stone wall which appears on your right-hand side as you go along the track. On the wall there will be painted, in yellow, red, blue, and green, a series of characters—as tall as you are if the wall is high enough. And if you can make out the Tibetan script, you will see that the syllables spell out a Sanskrit phrase, always the same one: *oṁ maṇi padme hūṁ*. Wherever you go throughout Tibet, wherever there are people living, you will be almost sure to find a 'maṇi wall'—or at least that was how it was in the old days, before the Chinese invasion.

In the days before anyone in Tibet had even heard of Chairman Mao, not only did they paint and engrave and carve *oṁ maṇi padme hūṁ* on these long stone walls, but they also used wooden blocks to print *oṁ maṇi padme hūṁ* on long strips of paper which they wound round and round and put into cylinders inside the ritual objects which we in the West call prayer wheels, but which the Tibetans have always called maṇi wheels. This same phrase was also printed onto innumerable prayer flags which fluttered from long bamboo poles outside not only every monastery but every single habitation, so that the phrase *oṁ maṇi padme hūṁ* was wafted by the breeze across all Tibet. You could probably even hear the phrase in the air, for it was recited every day by hundreds and thousands of people. If you went out for an evening stroll in a Tibetan village you would be sure to meet people walking along the road, their rosary in one hand, their prayer wheel in the other, murmuring as they went along: *oṁ maṇi padme hūṁ, oṁ maṇi padme hūṁ*.

So this phrase *oṁ maṇi padme hūṁ* obviously has some great significance. What it means, and how it connects with the *White Lotus Sutra*, is the main theme of this chapter. But the first thing to say about the phrase is that it is a *mantra*. Mantra is a familiar enough word, but one that is often misunderstood—and the popular translation 'mystic phrase' is not really much help. If we look at the traditional derivation of the word—what Guenther calls the symbolic etymology, as opposed to the scientific etymology—we find that it is formed from two parts: *man*, which means mind, and *tra*, a verb meaning 'to protect'. So a mantra is 'that which protects the mind', because it protects—and also develops and matures—the mind of the person reciting it and meditating upon its meaning.

In strict philological terms, however, *mantra* comes from a word meaning 'to call'—even 'to call out' or 'to call down'—in other words, to invoke. Mantras are phrases used to invoke the dormant spiritual forces within our own minds; indeed, in a sense, they are the names of these spiritual forces. For in Buddhist tradition such forces spontaneously assume archetypal forms—forms of Buddhas and Bodhisattvas, forms of guardian deities, forms of ḍākas and ḍākinīs—and every single one of these forms has his or her own mantra. When you recite a mantra, you set up vibrations to which Reality starts responding, and the appropriate

Buddha or Bodhisattva form appears. The form, the shape, of the Buddha or Bodhisattva represents the 'shape symbol' of the spiritual energy concerned, and the mantra represents its corresponding sound symbol—we could put it like that. (In fact, since each of the archetypal figures has a particular colour—some being bright red, others deep blue, other pure white, others a beautiful green—and colour is a form of light, we could call the shape symbol also a light symbol.)

To avoid any confusion, I should point out that there are two kinds of Bodhisattva, broadly speaking. One kind is the individual historical human being who has vowed to work towards supreme Enlightenment for the sake of all beings, and is at one of the ten stages of the Bodhisattva career.[84] The second kind is the archetypal Bodhisattva, a 'personification' or 'embodiment' of a particular aspect of Enlightenment. You can think of Enlightenment in the abstract, in general, but you can also think of it concretely, in terms of particular aspects: a wisdom aspect, a compassion aspect, a power aspect, and so on. All these are ways in which you can look at and experience Enlightenment. Different Bodhisattvas embody, or 'personify', though not in any artificial sense, one or another of these aspects of Enlightenment or Buddhahood: Mañjuśrī represents wisdom, Vajrapāṇi represents power, Vajrasattva represents beginningless purity, and so on. Bodhisattvas of this sort, which are not historical human beings, though they may appear or be represented in human form, are called Bodhisattvas of the *dharmakāya*, the *dharmakāya* being one particular term for ultimate Reality.

The aspect of Reality invoked by *oṁ maṇi padme hūṁ*, the mantra which resounds throughout Tibet, is Compassion, and it is embodied, even crystallized, in the form of Avalokiteśvara. He is perhaps the most famous of all the great Bodhisattvas, worshipped, meditated upon, and invoked not only in Tibet but throughout the Mahāyāna Buddhist world, and even here and there in Theravādin Sri Lanka. The *White Lotus Sutra* devotes a whole chapter to him, so we may say that Avalokiteśvara himself is one of the symbols of the Mahāyāna in this sutra. And the *maṇi padme* of his mantra translates as 'the jewel in the lotus'.

The meaning of the mantra coincides with the meaning of one of the parables of the *White Lotus Sutra* which also happens to be concerned with a jewel. This parable—which we will call the parable of the drunkard and the jewel—occurs in the eighth chapter of the sutra, and like the myth of the return journey, it is told by some of the assembly in response to something they have heard.

At the beginning of this chapter the Buddha predicts his disciple Pūrṇa to supreme Enlightenment, declaring that in the distant future Pūrṇa will become a Buddha called Radiance of the Truth—appropriately enough for a disciple who stands out among all the others as the greatest preacher, famed far and wide for his eloquence. In previous chapters of the sutra other disciples have been predicted to supreme Enlightenment, and different worlds have been 'assigned' to them, some of them unthinkably remote from our own. The difference in the case of Pūrṇa's prediction is that apparently he is to become a Buddha in this very world itself, in millions and millions of years time. But it seems from what the Buddha goes on to say that in those days the world will be a very different place from what it is now. Indeed, it will have changed so much that it will be a 'pure world', to use the technical term—a world free from certain imperfections, an ideal world.

The Indian Buddhist tradition has its own ideas as to what constitutes perfection so far as a world is concerned. For a start, according to the sutra, the whole world will be perfectly flat. For some reason, the Indians seem to have objected to any irregularity in the earth's surface—all those untidy mountains and hills all over the place breaking up the beautiful, smooth contours of the horizon—so flatness is a desirable quality of a perfect world. And not only will the world be flat; it will be so transformed as to be hardly recognizable. It isn't going to be made up of the earth and stone we're used to; instead, it will be composed entirely of the seven precious things—gold, silver, and so on.

The sutra goes on to say—and some people find this a very interesting feature indeed—that in those days divine vehicles will be stationed in the sky. Does this have a familiar ring? Not only that, but the division between the world of men and the world of the gods will be completely broken down, so that there is no barrier between the ordinary human world and the world of the gods, which we might call the archetypal realm. Human beings on the Earth will be able to look up and see the gods, and the gods will be able to look down on them. There will be regular contact between them. And there will be no places of suffering in the world of those days, nor even the sound of any torment and distress.

The sutra also says that at that time in the world there will be no women—a provocative-sounding statement, to say the least. But of course it doesn't mean that the world will contain men but not women; what it means is that there will be no distinction of sex among the beings of the earth—neither men nor women, but just human beings. And those human beings will be born (or rather reborn) not by the present rather crude arrangements but by what is called apparitional birth. People will just spring into existence, blossom naturally out of thin air. Having been born in that way, it is not surprising to find that they will live—according to the sutra—a purely spiritual life. They will have no gross physical bodies but what are called mental bodies, spiritual bodies, and they will be self-luminous, brilliant, and able to fly through the air at will. With no gross physical bodies, they will have no need for gross physical food, but will feed on just two things: delight in the Buddha's teaching and delight in meditation. Of course—and this is hardly surprising in the circumstances—there will be a great many Bodhisattvas. And, the sutra adds as a crowning touch, there will also be many stupas, all made of the seven precious things.

Having given this glowing account of the world as it will be when Pūrṇa becomes a Buddha, the Buddha Śākyamuni proceeds to predict to Perfect Buddhahood five hundred other disciples. Delighted, naturally enough, by the prediction, these five hundred disciples say that they feel as though they have suddenly gained possession of something wonderful, and they tell a story—the parable of the drunkard and the jewel:

World-honored One! It is as if some man goes to an intimate friend's house, gets drunk, and falls asleep. Meanwhile his friend, having to go forth on official duty, ties a priceless jewel within his garment as a present, and departs. The man, being drunk and asleep, knows nothing of it. On arising he travels onward till he reaches some other country, where for food and clothing he expends much labor and effort, and is content even if he can obtain but little. Later, his friend happens to meet him and speaks thus: 'Tut! Sir, how is it you have come to this for the sake of food and clothing? Wishing you to be in comfort and able to satisfy all your five senses, I formerly in such a year and month and on such a day tied a priceless jewel within your garment. Now as of old it is present there and you in ignorance are slaving and worrying to keep yourself alive. How very stupid! Go you now and exchange that jewel for what you need and do whatever you will, free from all poverty and shortage.'[85]

So this is the parable—no doubt the meaning is clear enough—and this is our introduction to the symbol of the priceless jewel, which will lead us, by way of a general look at jewel symbolism in the Mahāyāna, to the jewel in the lotus. But first, there is another aspect of the parable which is worth noting. We have in this story, which begins with a man getting drunk and falling asleep, an example of a kind of symbolism which is used not only in Buddhist literature but in spiritual traditions throughout the world. We have encountered it already in the Gnostic 'Hymn of the Pearl',[86] in which the king's son goes down into Egypt in quest of the pearl, but, drugged by the Egyptians, forgets who he is and what he is doing, and eventually sinks into a profound slumber.

In the Gnostic tradition, as in all the others, both drunkenness and sleep are symbols for lack of awareness, lack of any true human self-consciousness. This, we may say, is the state that most people are in most of the time. If humanness is characterized by awareness and self-consciousness, most people do not really live in a human state, but in a state of torpor, darkness, and ignorance more like that of an animal. To become a true human being, to achieve a state of awareness and self-consciousness, is in fact very difficult, and we usually need at least some outside help. It's just like when we are sound asleep, and go on sleeping and sleeping, as some people do, until late in the morning or even early in the afternoon. The alarm clock may ring, but we don't hear it. What we need is someone to come along and shout 'Wake up!' But if we're really fast asleep and dreaming, even a shout, however loud, may not be any use. We may need someone to come along, take us by the shoulder, and give us a really good shake. And this is all that religion really is, all that it really has to do. Religion is just that shout, just that shake, to wake us up out of our sleep, even out of our drunken stupor, of ignorance and unawareness.

In our sleepy, drunken state we don't really know who we are, or what we are; we don't know our own true nature. We think—we dream—that we are poor, limited, contingent, conditioned, and consequently we suffer. But in truth, like the man in the parable, we have the priceless jewel in our possession all the time; all we need to do is wake up to that fact.

Although in the parable the jewel is tied in the sleeping man's garment by his friend before he sets off to work, this detail is not to be taken too literally. The beginning of the parable, like the beginning of the myth of the return journey, and that of all parables and fairy stories, takes place outside time. So the jewel doesn't literally come into our possession at a certain point in time. It's there all the time—that is to say, outside time altogether. It's only our realization that we have the jewel that occurs in time.

Its origin outside time is, of course, not the only similarity between this parable and the myth of the return journey. In both parables the hero—if we can call him that—goes away to a distant country, where he suffers hardship on account of poverty; and in both parables the hero ends up possessed of riches, riches that have really been his all the time. At the same time, however, there are also significant differences between the two parables. For one thing, the father and son relationship of the return journey suggests a more extreme degree of alienation than the relationship between the two friends—two equals—in the parable of the jewel and the drunkard. An even more important difference is in the manner in which the two poor men become rich. In the myth of the return journey the poor man is gradually introduced to riches, and gets used to going in and out of the mansion without fear, until at last he learns that the riches of which he is steward are really his own inheritance. But in the parable of the drunkard and the jewel the transition is much more abrupt. One minute the man is destitute and suffering, and the next minute—because his benefactor doesn't beat about the bush—he is rich.

This profound difference between the two parables corresponds to two different methods that may be used by the guru or teacher to guide the disciple in the spiritual life: the gradual method and the sudden method. In the gradual method, the teacher says, to begin with, 'Don't strain yourself too much. You don't need to bother about nirvana or Enlightenment. Just steady your mind, be peaceful, enjoy life more.' So the disciple is led step by step, and only after many years have gone by does the teacher start talking about Enlightenment. But in the sudden method the teacher confronts the disciple with the truth immediately. There is no chance to prepare, no preamble—just 'This is it; it's right here; it's this.' Which method the teacher uses depends entirely on the temperament of the pupil. If he or she is easygoing and immersed in the things of the world, then obviously the gradual method is going to be the one to use. But if the disciple is a more heroic type and can stand the shock, then the guru doesn't hesitate to use the sudden method.

This difference between the gradual and the sudden also applies to the two aspects of the Buddha's Noble Eightfold Path, the Path of Vision and the Path of Transformation. The Path of Vision is the initial spiritual experience; you see, even if only for an instant, that you have the jewel, that you *are* the jewel. The Path of Transformation is the application of that experience to every aspect of your life, the gradual adjustment to the fact that you are in possession of that jewel.

It's rather like what happens when you suddenly inherit a large sum of money or win the football pools—and if this hasn't happened to you yet, no doubt you can imagine it. You hear the news—maybe you get a telegram or a solicitor's letter—that you've got half-a-million pounds. What a shock! What a surprise! All of a sudden you're rich, incredibly rich. For a while you may be so stunned that, although you've got all that money in the bank, you don't know what to do with it. Then comes the adjustment. Slowly you reorganize your life to suit your new status. Maybe you move into a bigger house, maybe you buy a better car; everything starts changing because you are rich. In the same way, you may be so overwhelmed at first by the vision, by the spiritual experience, that you don't know what to do with it. It could well be that you will be your usual crude self for quite a while until, little by little, you start to be transformed in the light of that great experience. It takes a long time to work it out in detail, to reorientate your life around that supreme fact, that supreme experience.

So what is this jewel which we discover that we have, or that we are? Well, the symbol of the jewel, like all symbols, does not have a meaning, not in a cut-and-dried sense. You can't take symbols and say 'Here's a jewel, it means this. Here's a lotus, it means that.' Symbols are always suggestive, evocative, not to be reduced to any one cut-and-dried meaning. With this proviso in mind, let's try to feel—not understand but feel, or even experience—what the jewel signifies.

To put it briefly and broadly, the jewel signifies our own true nature, what we really are. To be a little rash, we could even say that it symbolizes the true self—if we use the word in the Jungian rather than the Vedantic sense.[87] This jewel, this true self, this true nature of ours, is hidden, concealed. In the parable it is concealed in the man's clothing, but in the case of most of us it would probably be more accurate to say that it's covered in mud. But whether the layers are of clothing or of mud, this kind of symbolism suggests that we don't exist just on one level, but on a number of levels, some superficial, others deeper. And the jewel represents the deepest level of all, the bedrock of our being. Or, to reverse the terminology, it represents a level above individuality in the ordinary sense of the term, a level which is even outside time altogether.

Finding the jewel means coming into contact with the deepest level of our own being, and this suggests that most of the time, in fact all the time, we are *not* in contact with that deepest level of ourselves. Not only are we out of contact with it; we don't even know that it exists. We live merely from the surface of our being, not from the depths. But when we find the jewel we come into contact with that deepest layer of ourselves, that level which exists outside time. And this doesn't mean just touching that layer and then breaking off again, but establishing permanent contact with it and living out of the depths of that experience.

The parable describes the jewel as priceless, and this is exactly what it is. The word has to be taken quite literally, with the full force of its meaning behind it. This means that contact with the true self, contact with the bedrock of one's own being, is absolutely the most important thing in one's life. Money isn't the most important. Success isn't the most important. Popularity isn't the most important. Knowledge isn't the most important. Culture isn't the most important. Religion isn't the most important. Meditation isn't the most important. 'What is a man profited if he shall gain the whole world, and lose his own soul?' The most important thing in life, the most precious thing in the whole world, is contact with one's own true self, between the surface of one's being and its depths. This is more precious than the whole world—and by world is meant here not other people, but one's own material and intellectual possessions. This is the priceless jewel, not to be sacrificed for anything whatsoever, otherwise one will have had the worst of the bargain.

But why is it the jewel that symbolizes the true self? The most obvious reason is that the jewel is the most precious of all material things, so that it is a worthy symbol of the true self, which is infinitely precious. Then, the jewel is bright, shining, brilliant; and the true self is like this too, although its brilliance is of a completely different kind, for it comes from within rather than being reflected from without. The true self, one's own true being, is self-luminous, conscious, aware. In fact, even to say that it is conscious is not correct, because it does not possess consciousness as a quality, something which is as it were stuck on from outside and able to be removed. In its very nature our own true being is pure transparent consciousness, with no distinction between subject and object.

Another quality which makes the jewel a fitting symbol for the true self is that it cannot be made dirty. It may lie hidden in dust and dirt for ages upon ages, but when the dirt is removed the jewel shines and sparkles as clean and bright as ever. In the same way, our own true nature is essentially pure. It may be hidden for the greater part of our lives by passions of various kinds—ignorance, anger, bigotry, and so on—but once those defilements are removed, it shines forth in all its original splendour. In truth it has not been defiled at all.

The symbol of the jewel has many different facets and many different forms. One of the best known is the *cintāmaṇi*, usually translated as the 'wish-fulfilling' jewel. This particular symbolism comes from Indian mythology, but all the mythologies, the folklore, and the fairy stories of the world have such objects—things that grant every wish of your heart, every desire. Just like Aladdin's lamp, you hold it in your hand and say 'I wish…', and your wish comes true. When you've recovered from your surprise, you hold it again and wish again—and again your wish comes true. It is a universal dream of humanity to have some jewel, or some magic pot or magic lamp, or magic *anything*, that will give you whatever you want. Indian mythology tells of a wish-granting tree, a wish-fulfilling cow, and a wish-fulfilling pot—it is all much the same sort of symbolism—and also of the *cintāmaṇi*, the wish-fulfilling gem.

In the Buddhist tradition the wish-fulfilling gem has come to symbolize the bodhicitta, the Bodhisattva's aspiration to gain Enlightenment for the benefit of all beings; and this tells us something about the nature of Enlightenment. Once you have Enlightenment, you have everything. All your wishes, all your desires, all your aspirations, are fully satisfied. Enlightenment, even in the primitive, rudimentary form of the bodhicitta, is the true *cintāmaṇi*, the true wish-fulfilling gem. The *cintāmaṇi* is often represented in Buddhist art as a brilliant, shining jewel with flames bursting out of it, because the bodhicitta, the Bodhisattva's Will to Enlightenment, is on fire with activity and burns up all adventitious defilements of the mind.[88]

But the *cintāmaṇi* is not the only example of jewel symbolism in Buddhism; the jewel is very protean. Splitting into three, it produces the Three Jewels—the Buddha jewel, the Dharma jewel, and the Sangha jewel—which are the three highest values of Buddhism, or one great value looked at from three different points of view. It also symbolizes the transcendental as the *vajra* or *dorje*, which is both diamond and thunderbolt, both indestructible and capable of destroying absolutely anything.

The jewel is also a solar symbol, an embodiment of the yang principle, and where there is yang, there is always yin. And the lotus, being associated with water, is a yin symbol. If anything, the lotus is an even more popular symbol in Buddhist tradition than the jewel, and its symbolism is too vast for us even to touch on all its aspects. But broadly speaking, we can say that the lotus has both a macrocosmic significance and a microcosmic significance; that is to say, it represents the universe as a whole and also the individual being. And just as the lotus consists of many layers of petals, some without, some within, so both the universe and the individual consist of many different layers, many different levels, some lower and others higher. So in this way the lotus comes to represent the whole process of development, of unfoldment stage by stage, level by level, degree by degree, from the bottom to the top—development both cosmic and human. Sometimes the lotus represents the lower evolution, sometimes, in a more rarified form, it represents the Higher Evolution, and sometimes it represents both the lower evolution and the Higher Evolution taken together.

Having said all this, we must be careful not just to settle down into thinking 'So, the lotus represents the process of evolution.' Symbols such as this do not have any one unchanging meaning; it is not so much a question of understanding a symbol as of allowing yourself to be influenced by it. So what kind of influence does a lotus have? It must represent something rich and colourful, something growing, complex, beautiful, harmonious, delicate, pure; in other words, something ideal.

If these are the associations that the jewel and the lotus bring with them individually, what does the combination of the two—the jewel *in* the lotus—represent? Macrocosmically speaking, the jewel in the lotus means that the Unconditioned exists in the midst of the conditioned. The Real exists in the midst of the unreal. Light exists in the midst of darkness, even though we may not be able to see that light because we are blind or because our eyes are closed. So in its depth the universe is based on a principle that is ultimately spiritual, and this principle is working itself out in the universe in the course of the whole process of life.

From a microcosmic perspective, the jewel in the lotus means that Enlightenment, Buddhahood, spiritual perfection, is immanent in the depths of our own hearts. If we take our courage into both hands, if we plunge right down into the depths of our own being, underneath our thoughts about this and that, underneath our emotions, underneath our conditioned reflexes, underneath our reactions, if we go even deeper than the personal subconscious, even deeper than the collective unconscious, we shall encounter the Buddha nature itself. This is the microcosmic meaning of the jewel in the lotus.

In the mantra of Avalokiteśvara, the jewel in the lotus is enclosed by those mysterious syllables *oṁ* and *hūṁ*. Very briefly, in this context *oṁ* is the absolute, the Unconditioned, the transcendental as it is in itself, entirely unconnected with the world; and *hūṁ* is the same absolute as manifested in the world, descending into it, permeating it, moving it from within. *Oṁ* and *hūṁ* are the alpha and omega, the beginning and end, but a beginning that is before time and an end that is after time. So *oṁ* is what we might call the 'abstract universal', *hūṁ* is the 'concrete universal', and the words *maṇi padme*, the jewel in the lotus, indicate how the abstract becomes concrete.

Of course, *oṁ maṇi padme hūṁ* is not just a symbolic phrase; it is a mantra, and when it is recited, a Bodhisattva appears: Avalokiteśvara, the Bodhisattva of Compassion. He also appears in the *White Lotus Sutra*, making his appearance in chapter 24 of the Sanskrit text (chapter 25 in the Chinese version). This is one of those chapters of the sutra which is not an integral part of the 'Drama of Cosmic Enlightenment'. In the history of Buddhist canonical literature, different traditions have circulated various texts which have gradually been collected together, so that texts and traditions which were originally independent have come to be anthologized and written down in one overall 'portmanteau' text. It would seem that the Avalokiteśvara chapter was originally an independent sutra in its own right, and was drawn into the orbit of the *White Lotus Sutra*, along with a great deal of other miscellaneous material included in the last four or five chapters, because of the sutra's great popularity and prestige.

Avalokiteśvara has a number of different forms, one of the most famous of which is perhaps rather bizarre from the Western point of view, because it has eleven heads and a thousand arms. There are eleven heads because there are eleven directions of space—the centre, north, south, east, and west, and the four intermediate points, plus the zenith and the nadir—and Compassion is omnipresent, and looks in all directions. There are a thousand arms because there is so much to be done to relieve suffering that a thousand arms at the very least are necessary. Really an infinite number is required.

How did such a strange figure originate? According to one version of the legend, once upon a time Avalokiteśvara was sitting on the Potala hill, where the myths say he usually lives in southern India, and looking out over the world. And everywhere he looked, he saw terrible suffering. He saw people being oppressed by unjust kings, led off to execution, tortured, beheaded. He saw people being burned, people being devoured by wild beasts, people being bitten by serpents and dying painful deaths, people drowning at sea, and many, many people suffering from disease, sickness, old age, bereavement, and separation. Seeing how much humanity suffered, he felt this suffering so deeply, so bitterly, so intensely, that he experienced a terrible tension, and under the strain his head suddenly split into eleven fragments, each of which became a head. The heads came together, and a thousand arms appeared to relieve and succour all the people suffering throughout the world. We can see the meaning of this symbolism very clearly, because this is how you can actually feel when you see so much suffering around you; you feel as though your head could split into eleven pieces and your arms could multiply a thousandfold and stretch out in all directions to render aid. This is the sort of compassion that Avalokiteśvara represents.

In another legend associated with Avalokiteśvara's compassion, we are told that on one occasion, seeing all the suffering in the world, Avalokiteśvara could not restrain himself from weeping bitterly. He wept so profusely that a great pool of tears formed, which spread and spread until it was a huge, shining lake of pure crystal-clear water. And from that lake there sprang up a pure white lotus; the petals slowly opened, and inside was a beautiful white goddess with a white lotus in her hand. This was the 'goddess' Tārā, the female Bodhisattva Tārā, who is sometimes described as being born out of the tears of Avalokiteśvara, and is thus known as his spiritual daughter. An even more delicate, tender figure than Avalokiteśvara himself, she represents the quintessence of compassion.

The form of Avalokiteśvara you are most likely to see represented iconographically is perhaps the four-armed form, the *shaḍaksharī* Avalokiteśvara. *Shaḍakshari* means 'possessing six syllables', and these six syllables are those of the mantra: *oṁ ma ṇi pa dme hūṁ*. In Tantric Buddhism, Avalokiteśvara assumes a wrathful form known as Mahākāla, 'Great Time'—the destroyer of ignorance, anger, hatred, and everything conditioned. But in China, where Avalokiteśvara was introduced through the *White Lotus Sutra*, something very different happened to him. Once he—or rather she—was established there the originally masculine Bodhisattva became a feminine form called Kwan Yin, the most popular of all the Chinese Bodhisattvas.[89]

Why is Avalokiteśvara so called? This question, asked by the Bodhisattva Akṣayamati, opens the Avalokiteśvara chapter of the *White Lotus Sutra*. In fact the name's etymology tells us that Avalokiteśvara can be interpreted in two quite different ways: as 'the one who looks down on the world', looks down, that is to say, in compassion, and as 'the one who listens', the one who hearkens to cries of distress. In response to Akṣayamati's question, however, the Buddha does not delve into etymology, but simply says that Avalokiteśvara is so called because out of compassion he responds to all those who invoke his name, and delivers them from difficulties and dangers both physical and spiritual. The long account which follows of all the various plights from which Avalokiteśvara can save human beings clearly presents him as a popular saviour figure. The Buddha goes on to say that Avalokiteśvara assumes different forms in which to preach the Dharma according to the temperaments and requirements of different beings, sometimes taking the form of a Buddha, sometimes the form of a Bodhisattva, and sometimes even the form of one or another of the Hindu gods. Having had his question answered at considerable length, Akṣayamati presents Avalokiteśvara—who we now learn is actually present—with a magnificent golden necklace, and then sings a hymn of praise, one of the most beautiful in the whole range of Mahāyāna Buddhist literature.

Now the form of Avalokiteśvara, whether it has a thousand arms or four arms, is a shape symbol, space symbol, *light* symbol, and his mantra is a sound symbol, but although they converge on it from different directions, they are both symbols of the compassion aspect of Enlightenment. So how do you bring the two together? How do you meditate on them?

The meditation practice is quite complex. First of all you go for Refuge—to the guru (this comes first in Tibetan Buddhism), then to the Buddha, the Dharma, and the Sangha. But you do not go for Refuge on your own. You go taking with you, as it were, all living beings. You imagine them also as Going for Refuge, because all life is ultimately heading in the direction of Enlightenment. Then you invoke blessings onto yourself, aspiring or praying that your body, speech, and mind may be transformed, and that you may make spiritual progress. After that you take the Bodhisattva Vow, vowing that you will gain Enlightenment not just for your own sake but for the sake of Enlightening, benefiting, helping, all other living beings, and that you will practise the Six Perfections as a means of achieving that end.

Then follows a stage of reflection. First you reflect, using a Sanskrit formula, that all things whatsoever in the universe are by nature pure. You see no impurity anywhere; the whole world is pure, and everything in it is pure. Then, having reflected in this way, you reflect 'I too am pure, a pure being in a pure world. In my essential nature I am pure.'

Next, out of the depths of space, out of the depths of Reality, you conjure up the figure of Avalokiteśvara. First of all you see a lotus throne, and on that a moon disc, or moon mat as it is sometimes called. And then on the moon mat you see—visualize, feel, experience—yourself as Avalokiteśvara. In some forms of visualization practice you visualize the Buddha or Bodhisattva in front of you, different from you, but in this practice you visualize yourself *as* the Bodhisattva. You imagine yourself as Avalokiteśvara, your body the colour of a conch shell or crystal, your face smiling.

The figure—your figure—has four arms, and the lower two have their hands joined at the heart. So here is some more symbolism. These hands symbolize the jewel in the lotus: the fingers symbolize the lotus, and the two thumbs together are the jewel. This incidentally is why, according to Buddhist tradition, the salutation is made not with fingers pressed together (which is the brahminical form of salutation) but with the fingers separated and the thumbs together to make a jewel in a lotus. Whenever you greet someone in that way, you remind yourself that there is a jewel—Enlightenment potentiality—in him or her as well as in yourself.

Of the upper pair of hands, one hand holds a crystal rosary, to tell the beads as you recite the mantra, and the other holds a lotus, which is a symbol here of spiritual rebirth. The two feet are in *vajrāsana*, one on top of the other. And the body of Avalokiteśvara—your own body—is decked with silks and jewels. You have long blue-black hair, with a top-knot on which is sitting a little figure of Amitābha, the Buddha of Infinite Light, because he is the 'spiritual father' of Avalokiteśvara, the head of the Lotus family. (All Buddhas and Bodhisattvas belong to one of five 'Buddha families', and this is the basis of a lot of Buddhist symbolism.)[90] Having visualized yourself as Avalokiteśvara in this way, you invoke upon yourself, as Avalokiteśvara, the blessings of Amitābha, regarding him as the guru, and you pray that you will quickly gain Buddhahood for the sake of all.

Having done that—and it is quite an involved exercise, which takes quite a long time—you just let go. Dropping everything, you stay in a state free from thought for as long as is necessary, and then, when you are ready, you return to visualization. Inside your heart you visualize a horizontal moon lotus, and on top of that a red *hrīḥ*, the seed mantra of Amitābha, and encircling this the six syllables of the mantra, *oṁ ma ṇi pa dme hūṁ*, in the appropriate colours. From the syllables there issue rays of light, which call down the compassion and blessing of the Buddhas.

Next, in this version of the full practice, you start reciting *oṁ maṇi padme hūṁ*. Even the simple recitation has its own value, but if you want to do the practice thoroughly, you do the whole visualization first, and only then begin to recite *oṁ maṇi padme hūṁ*. In the context of this particular practice it is recited at least five hundred times, but you can keep going for an hour or two, or even the whole day. Then, having come to the end of your recitation, you dissolve into light the throne on which you are sitting, the lotus, and the moon disc, and this light merges into you. The practice is then brought to an end with a dedication of merit. You say 'May whatever merits, whatever benefits, I have gained from this practice be shared by everyone.'

Having come to the end of the practice, you thereafter think of the place you live in, your surroundings, as being the Pure Land itself, the Paradise of Avalokiteśvara. You are living in a transfigured world because you are a transfigured being. And having become transmuted into Avalokiteśvara, all the time, whatever you do, you recollect the Buddha of Infinite Light. You think constantly about the guru who is, as it were, on your head. Whatever you do, wherever you go in the world, whoever you speak to, all the time, day and night, after doing this exercise, you undertake to act with compassion for all living beings. If you can practise this visualization and mantra recitation in this way, you gradually become completely transformed. You become radiant, a jewel, even *the* jewel, and the world in which you have your being, your environment, becomes your lotus. Practising, experiencing, realizing, in this way, you yourself become—you yourself *are*—the jewel in the lotus.

Chapter Seven

QUESTIONS AND ANSWERS

Have Buddhist mantras incorporated sound symbols from other traditions?
It seems that in medieval times in India—let's say from the third to the eleventh century of the Common Era—there was a sort of twilight zone which was not exactly Hindu and not exactly Buddhist. In that zone there were a lot of mantras around, mantras that were used in connection with the worship of ethnic divinities and the performance of magic rites—in other words mantras used for more or less mundane purposes. Some of these mantras were definitely taken over by Buddhists and 'spiritualized'; you find a lot of them, with their associated visualizations, in the Buddhist Tantras, especially in Tibet. So no doubt Buddhism did take over a lot of material, not exactly from Hinduism, which hardly existed in the modern sense in those days, but from the Indian ethnic religion and folklore.

It's rather as if Christianity, on coming to the West from Palestine, had incorporated the Greek and Roman gods and goddesses, the village sprites and so on. In a sense, of course, it sometimes did: mythological figures do appear, heavily disguised, as Christian saints—or sometimes not so heavily disguised. Some saints just had the names of pagan gods with 'Saint' put before them—Saint Dionysus, for instance.

So is it possible to trace a historical development of Buddhist mantras?
I doubt it very much, for the simple reason that we do not have the information to do it. Don't forget that Indian history, including religious history, is very poorly documented indeed.

How is it that mantras can spark off a particular quality? Do they just gather

around them a number of associations, or is there something in the mantra itself—or is it impossible to say?
It is probably impossible to say what exactly happens, but there is no doubt that each mantra has a very special, almost indefinable quality which is quite distinctive and recognizable. You could try to see what happens when you recite a mantra, especially one you have not recited before.

•

In contrasting the myth of the return journey and the parable of the jewel in the lotus, you talk about how the guru chooses either the sudden or the gradual approach depending on the temperament of the pupil. Is it useful for us to think in these terms?
No. I think that such terms can be misleading, and I no longer use them. To paraphrase Hui Neng's words in the *Platform Sutra*,[91] there is no such thing as the quick path and the slow path. It is simply that some attain Enlightenment more quickly than others. Some practise more intensively than others, and therefore cover the same psychological and spiritual ground more quickly.

Sometimes people understand the short path to mean a path that somehow cuts out all the long and difficult preliminary stages, but that is wishful thinking. All the stages must be traversed, because they are determined by the very conditions under which development of any kind takes place. You can't make a growing plant jump certain stages of development, but by giving it extra nourishment you may cause it to grow more quickly.

Have any of your teachers used the 'sudden method' with you, confronting you with ultimate Reality?
I don't think that any of my teachers ever deliberately and consciously confronted me with an ultimate truth—perhaps their methods were more subtle than that. Indeed, the matter is more subtle than it perhaps appears to be. Ultimate truth, after all, can be presented in any terms. You are presented with it every moment of your life. When you change the flowers in your room because you see that they are faded, you are confronted with the ultimate truth of impermanence. Sometimes, of course, life presents us with situations in which we are more likely than usual to confront ultimate truth. It confronts us when we are bereaved or suffer some other dreadful loss, when our health is seriously affected, when we suddenly realize something unpleasant about ourselves for the

first time, or see that we have been tormenting ourselves about something unnecessarily.

And have you ever used the 'sudden method' yourself?
Well, I have sometimes put a certain point to somebody, or brought them up against a certain fact about themselves, a little more sharply than usual. You do have to be quite careful, because some people take things very seriously, and a few words spoken quite lightly and casually can have a devastating effect. If you do feel that you have said something quite clearly, but quite gently, to someone a number of times, and they don't seem to have grasped the point, you may need to put it a little more strongly or directly. It depends on how well you know them, and what degree of confidence they have in you.

•

I am struck by the contrast between the highly idealized visionary landscapes of the White Lotus Sutra's *Pure Land, with the flat land, the jewel trees, the golden cords, and so on, and the concrete nature imagery of much Chinese and Japanese art and literature, where mountains, lakes, and natural incidents like frogs jumping into ponds become central subjects. Do these differences spring from different levels of cultural experience, from different temperaments, or from cultural differences?*
You are speaking of one particular type of Chinese and Japanese art. There is another kind which endeavours to illustrate the Pure Land quite literally, with all the jewel trees and so on. I think the kind of art you are thinking of is distinctively a product of the Zen tradition. It's just a different way of looking at things, not necessarily more or less profound, but perhaps appealing to some temperaments more than others. Personally I prefer the more literal representations of the Pure Land, with all the jewel trees and singing birds and gold and silver ornaments, which seem to have a more 'archetypal' (for want of a better term) quality.

Colours, especially jewel-like colours, do have a certain psychological and spiritual significance of their own; they do seem to give you some intimation of the higher, more archetypal levels of existence, something that the more naturalistic type of Japanese and Chinese art is rarely able to do. You could say that this naturalistic type of art tries to penetrate beyond the archetypal into the sphere of reality itself; and it can sometimes do that, but only in the hands of a very great artist who is also a Zen master. Otherwise it all falls rather flat: you have just got a picture of a nice little tree by a nice little stream, with a nice little monk sitting underneath it on a nice little rock. That kind of art is rather hit or miss; instead of going beyond the archetypal plane into the transcendental, it sometimes falls short even of the archetypal.

•

Is it significant that it is Pūrṇa, who is renowned for his eloquence, who will be the Buddha of this world once it is purified? Could the sutra be saying that what this world needs more than anything is people who are eloquent in the teaching of the Dharma?

This reminds me of something written by Dr Ambedkar, the leader of the ex-Untouchables in India who led their conversion to Buddhism. Writing about the decline of religion he said, in effect, that a religion will decline if it doesn't have universally valid principles, or if it doesn't have simple principles that can be easily explained to a lot of people. Then, he went on to say, a religion will decline if it doesn't have eloquent and capable preachers. Your principles may be as universally valid as you like, they may be as simple as you like, but you will still need human beings to put them across. No doubt the word 'eloquent' is not to be taken too literally; the point is to be able to communicate effectively, whether the language you use is flowery or simple. Unless you have preachers, living human beings, who can communicate in this way—whether personally or through the books they write—your principles, however universal and simple they are, are just not going to get across, and the religion will decline, or perhaps not even get started at all.

So eloquence is needed in any world—certainly in any world in any way resembling our own—in which the Dharma is being propagated. Of course, there are other worlds where the Dharma is communicated by other means—through beautiful odours, for example.[92]

•

You say that oṁ is the abstract universal, hūṁ is the concrete universal, and the jewel in the lotus shows how the abstract becomes concrete. Can you say a bit more about this?

Well, an abstract universal is a universal which is a concept without any definite content, whereas a concrete universal is a universal which is not separable from its various particular instances, and which expresses itself through them. These are terms of Hegelian philosophy[93] which have passed into general currency to some extent.

But perhaps we can approach it from a slightly different angle. For instance, take the concept of impermanence. When we first come across it, this is likely to be just an abstract universal as far as we are concerned. We accept it in theory, but we haven't yet embodied it in our lives. The more we actually embody it in all the different activities of our lives, the more concrete that particular universal becomes. Our realization of the concept of impermanence is transformed from a purely intellectual understanding into something which we understand through our actual experience. Of course, don't take this too literally—it is not that *oṁ* only represents an intellectual understanding. But at one level the mantra does represent that type of transition. To use Buddhist terms, it is really a transformation of *vijñāna* into *jñāna* or *prajñā*.[94]

As for the jewel and the lotus, these two between them fully represent the path, which is a process of the unfolding of potentiality through which abstract understanding is transformed into concrete realization.

Could the symbol also relate to the three levels of wisdom: hearing, reflecting, and meditating?[95]

Yes indeed, because what you merely hear, what you know in the ordinary abstract way, is quite different from *prajñā*, which is a matter of actual insight and realization. The intermediate stage is the stage of reflection, the stage of turning the knowledge over in your mind, incorporating it, making it your own.

•

You describe, at least in outline, the Avalokiteśvara visualization practice. I thought that such practices were generally not to be discussed with anyone who does not actually do the practice?

Well, the description of the image is just like looking at a picture. It is not intended as an initiation or anything like that; it is just a conjuring up of an inspiring image, and should be taken in that spirit. Any little details of the practice added just fill out the picture.

The particular practice you described involves visualizing yourself as Avalokiteśvara, but in some other practices one visualizes the Bodhisattva in front of one. Is there any principle behind this distinction?

The broad principle to bear in mind is that inasmuch as your experience is bifurcated into a subject and an object, any spiritual practice that you do is conditioned by those limits. If you visualize, say, Avalokiteśvara, as being outside yourself, that is only half the truth, or not even half the truth. You also have to visualize him within you. You have to visualize Avalokiteśvara as the subject as well as the object, and eventually you need to be able to bring the two together. Whether you start with the subjective pole or the objective pole is perhaps a matter of temperament, but there is both a subject and an object in your experience, and both have to be transformed. When you are visualizing Avalokiteśvara out there, you must remember that he is also in here; and when you are visualizing him in here, you must remember that he is also out there. This is the basic principle you need to bear in mind.

Is it really a good idea to continue visualizing yourself as the Bodhisattva when you have finished doing the meditation practice? Might it not be a bit fanciful?

Well, if you haven't transformed yourself into the Bodhisattva in the course of the practice, it is bound to be fanciful. But there is nothing wrong with thinking of yourself as the Bodhisattva and trying to behave accordingly even if you have not realized yourself as the Bodhisattva in the meditation. Whether it is advisable or not depends on the circumstances you are in. I think that it is only advisable to try to sustain the feeling that you are the Bodhisattva if your circumstances are very propitious. If you were to try it in your everyday life, it would probably set up too great a tension between what you were trying to do and the circumstances in which you were trying to do it.

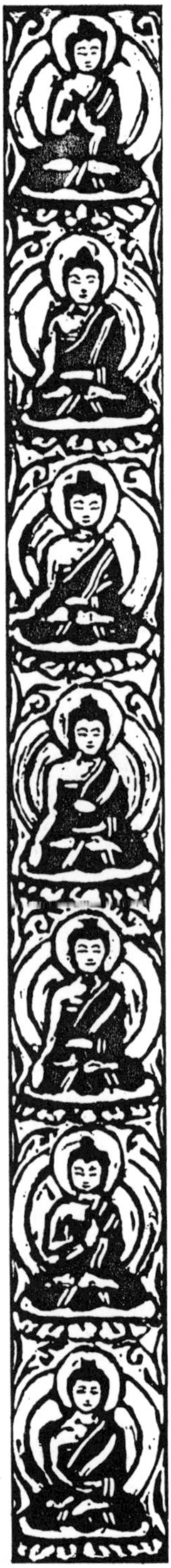
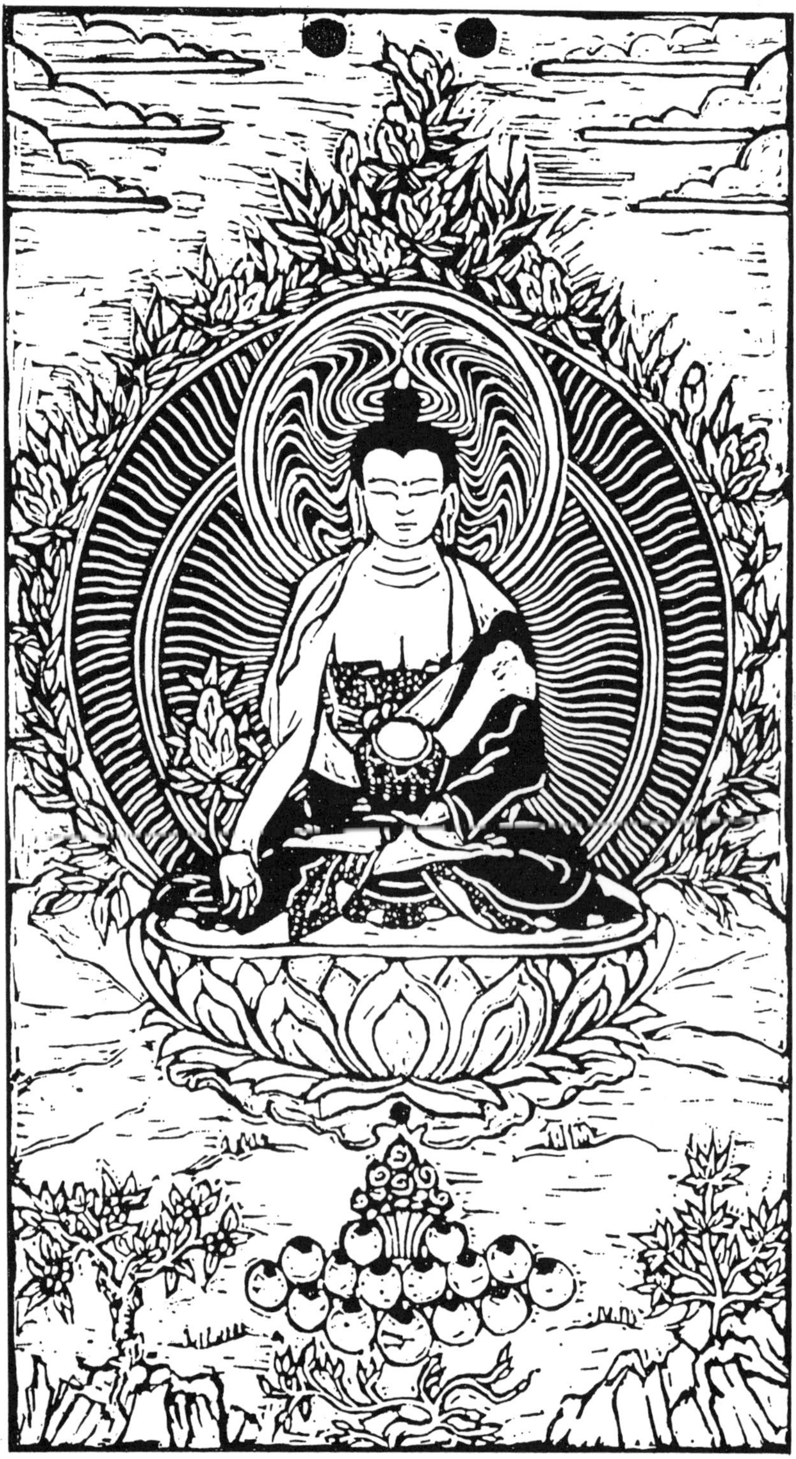

Chapter Eight

THE ARCHETYPE OF THE DIVINE HEALER

IN THIS STUDY of the parables, myths, and symbols of the *White Lotus Sutra*, I have nowhere defined the terms parable, myth, and symbol; this has been quite deliberate. It suits the nature of parables, myths, and symbols to allow their nature to emerge not from any formal definition but rather from concrete examples. We have not been trying to understand the parables, myths, and symbols intellectually, with our conscious minds; we have rather sought to experience them and allow them to speak to our hidden, even secret, depths.

Now we come to something similar, but not quite the same: an archetype, the archetype of the Divine Healer. And again I will not try to define the term 'archetype'. It has been popularized in recent decades through the work of Jung and his followers, but it is noticeable that in his writings about archetypes, Jung himself is chary of giving a formal clear-cut definition of what the archetype is. Sometimes he seems to say one thing, and sometimes another. So, following in his footsteps, I am not going to define either archetypes in general or the archetype with which we are particularly concerned, the archetype of the Divine Healer. Instead, through different examples, we will attempt to conjure up, to call forth, different manifestations of this archetype, and even try to see them before our inner eyes.

First of all we are going to conjure up an archetype from ancient Egypt. Thoth is a very complex figure, like all the major Egyptian deities. He is a lunar divinity, associated with the moon rather than with the sun, and he is represented with a human body and a bird head, the head of the sacred Egyptian bird, the ibis, with a long curved bill. Thoth's ibis head is sometimes surmounted by a lunar crescent, and sometimes by a crescent with a lunar disc superimposed upon it—the full moon and the crescent moon together. In a sense Thoth is the wisest and the most intelligent of all the gods, and in a sense he is the best. He is the inventor of all arts and sciences, and indeed the originator of culture and civilization. He is especially the inventor of writing, in this case of hieroglyphic writing, and he is also the inventor of medicine. He is the Divine Healer of the Egyptian pantheon.

In Egyptian mythology and legend, Thoth is especially associated with the goddess Isis and the gods Osiris and Horus, who constitute a well-known trinity. In some legends Thoth appears as Osiris's vizier and scribe. Even after Osiris's tragic death at the hands of the forces of darkness, Thoth remained faithful to his memory, helping Isis to purify Osiris's dismembered body. When Horus, the infant son of Isis and Osiris, was stung by a great black scorpion, it was Thoth, the Divine Healer, who drove out the poison from the bite. Later on Thoth is said to have cured Horus of a tumour and healed a wound inflicted on the god Set.

The ancient Greeks considered Hermes, the messenger of the gods, to be the counterpart of Thoth in their own mythology, but Thoth is much more like the Greek divinity Apollo. Admittedly Thoth is a lunar divinity whereas Apollo is a solar divinity, but Apollo, like Thoth, is the patron of the arts and the sciences, and of music and poetry in all their forms, and Apollo too is associated with the divine art of healing. In the case of Apollo this is apparently one of the consequences of his being a solar divinity, because sunlight is necessary to health and healing.

Although Apollo has these healing attributes, however, the real Greek god of healing is Asklepios, who, significantly, is the son of Apollo by a mortal maiden, and therefore a demi-god. Asklepios is sometimes represented in the form of a serpent, but he is more usually depicted as a tall, well-built, middle-aged man with a noble, dignified appearance, and an extremely wise and compassionate expression. Some of the images of Asklepios are amongst the most impressive, from a spiritual point of view, that have come down to us from classical antiquity. We know that the Gandhāran image of the Buddha was modelled on the Graeco-Roman Apollo, who was usually represented in the form of a beautiful young man in the prime of life, but perhaps the Gandhāran artists might have achieved even more impressive results if they had used the figure of Asklepios as a model.[96]

In Greek legend there are many stories of the miraculous cures wrought by Asklepios. It is even reported that his divine gift of healing was so great that he could not only restore the sick to health, but even bring the dead back to life. Not unnaturally, the King of the Dead became angry, because fewer and fewer people were arriving in his realm, and even those who arrived there were being rudely plucked back by Asklepios. So the King of the Dead went to Zeus, the King of the Gods, and complained bitterly that he was being deprived of his dues; and Zeus, who apparently had just one way of settling things, hurled a thunderbolt—and that was the end of Asklepios. Apollo, Asklepios's father, was furious, and slew the Cyclops who had forged the thunderbolt with which Zeus had destroyed Asklepios. Zeus then punished Apollo, of course, and so it went on, just as it does on Earth among human beings.

Asklepios was worshipped a good deal in ancient Greece; the important and powerful cult of this Divine Healer resulted in the many statues of him which have survived down to the present time. What is particularly interesting about the cult of Asklepios is that it was both a religion and also a system of therapeutics. The doctors in ancient Greece were priests of Asklepios, and served at a number of celebrated sanctuaries which were both centres of religious worship and centres of healing. These great sanctuaries were built outside towns, on sites which were especially healthy, and there people used to go for treatment and worship, because the two were the same.

Upon your arrival at a sanctuary as a patient you would be ceremonially purified, so as to be free from sin, and then given a series of baths. You would be required to abstain completely from food, and you would offer up sacrifice to Asklepios. Then, on a night appointed by the priest-physicians, you would sleep in the temple, perhaps with your head near the feet of the image of Asklepios. After all this preparation, and no doubt with great faith and expectation in your heart, and great hopes of a cure from disease, in the midst of your sleep you would have a dream in which Asklepios himself would appear and give you some advice, either about your complaint or general advice. In the morning you would tell the dream to the attendant priests, and they would give treatment according to their interpretation of it.

A few years ago I had the opportunity of visiting the most famous of all these old sanctuaries, the sanctuary at Epidaurus. As I walked around the archaeological site, which was strewn with votive tablets offered by people who had been cured of their diseases all those thousands of years ago, I found, very much to my surprise, that the atmosphere of the place was truly remarkable. There was something calm, peaceful, positive, and wholesome in the air; one could well imagine that a great sanctuary of healing had been established on that spot.

The archetype of the divine healer also, of course, appears in Buddhism. In the Buddhist scriptures, both Pali and Sanskrit, the Buddha has a number of titles. In English we almost invariably call him the Buddha, but in the original sources there are many other ways in which the Buddha is addressed or referred to—the Tathāgata, the Jina, Bhagavan, Lokajyeshtha, and so on. Among these titles is *Mahābhaiṣajya*. *Mahā* means 'great', and *bhaiṣajya* is 'physician', so *Mahābhaiṣajya* is the Great Physician. This is very significant, and suggests something that we ought never to forget: that human beings are most of the time, if not all the time, psychologically and spiritually sick, and in need of healing. The Buddha is the healer of the disease of humanity, and his teaching, the Dharma, is the medicine that he gives humanity to swallow. That medicine sometimes tastes bitter, but it is certainly efficacious.

A formula found in ancient Indian medical works analyses sickness and health in fourfold terms: disease, the causation of the disease, the state of being healthy, and the regimen leading to the state of good health. Now the Four Noble Truths, those central teachings of Buddhism, are said by some scholars to be derived from this formula. The truth of suffering corresponds to the state of disease; the truth of the origin of suffering corresponds to the ideology of the disease; the truth of the cessation of suffering, nirvana, corresponds to the state of being cured, of being made whole; and the truth of the way leading to the cessation of suffering corresponds to the regimen leading to a cure.

The Buddha's role as spiritual healer is stressed in a number of his teachings and parables. There is the parable of the man wounded by the poisoned arrow, in which the Buddha appears as the physician wishing to pluck the arrow of suffering from the poisoned wound of humanity.[97] On another occasion the Buddha says quite tersely, even bluntly, 'All worldlings are mad.' (The word used is *puthujjana*, which is usually translated 'worldling', and refers to ordinary people—that is to say, those who have not yet become Stream-Entrants). Apparently the Buddha meant quite literally that everybody who is not at least a Stream-Entrant is plain mad—not even just neurotic, or a little bit touched, but stark staring mad. This implies that the Buddha is not just a doctor, but the world's best mental doctor; and his teaching could perhaps be described as transcendental psychotherapy.

As we have seen in considering Avalokiteśvara, the state of Enlightenment has a number of different aspects—a wisdom aspect, a compassion aspect, a power aspect, a purity aspect, and so on. In the same way Enlightenment has its healing aspect; it is just like a great balm dropping down upon the wounds of humanity. This healing aspect is personified in the figure of Bhaiṣajyarāja or Bhaiṣajyaguru, the King of Healing or Teacher of Healing, who appears sometimes as a Bodhisattva, and sometimes as a Buddha. As a Buddha he is known as Vaiḍūryaprabha, which means 'azure radiance', or, translating very literally, the 'radiance of the semi-precious stone lapis lazuli'. In Tibetan Buddhist art this Buddha of Healing is depicted more or less in the same way as Śākyamuni Buddha, but with a deep brilliant blue complexion rather than a golden one. He wears the monastic robe like Śākyamuni, and in his hand he bears as his distinctive emblem an amlaki fruit. Translators of Sanskrit and Tibetan texts call this fruit an emblematic myrobalan—that's apparently its botanical name. I must confess that I have never come across a myrobalan, whether emblematic or otherwise, or, come to that, an amlaki fruit, but this particular fruit is renowned in Indian legend for its medicinal properties, so it is appropriate that it is the distinctive badge of this Buddha or Bodhisattva.

In Tibetan Buddhism Bhaiṣajyarāja has eight forms, known as the Eight Medicine Buddhas, a very popular set sometimes to be seen in Tibetan painted scrolls, with a main central figure and around him the seven subsidiary forms. As in ancient Greece, there is in Tibet, or at least there was until very recently, a connection between religion and medicine, and many lamas were physicians. Near Lhasa there were special medical monasteries where medical lamas received their training. Tibetan medicine is in a sense a continuation of the Indian system of medicine which is called *ayurveda*. *Ayur* is 'life', and *veda* means 'science', so in India medicine is traditionally called 'the science of life'—not just the science of curing disease, but the science of how to live healthily, how to live physically in the best possible way. It calls to mind the system of treatment in the ancient days in China, when you paid your doctor when you were well, and stopped paying him when you fell sick.

Tibetan Buddhist medicine includes Chinese elements such as acupuncture. It also makes extensive use of consecrated pills of various kinds, and of mantras. Not only in Tibet but in many parts of the Buddhist world the monks traditionally dabble—in many cases that is the only word—in medicine, sometimes successfully, sometimes, unfortunately, not so successfully. Usually, whether in Tibet or Sri Lanka, China or Burma, the treatment is a combination of herbal remedies, often very efficacious, and faith healing or what we might call spiritual healing. In this respect traditional Buddhist medicine in the East, especially in Tibet, is not unlike that of the priests of Asklepios in the ancient Western world.

Bhaiṣajyarāja or Bhaiṣajyaguru, the King or Guru of Healing, appears as a Buddha, that is to say in Buddha form, in a canonical text that bears his name.[98] In this sutra the Buddha relates to Ānanda how ages and ages ago Bhaiṣajyarāja made twelve great vows, as a result of which he established in the East what is traditionally known as a Pure Land, where all beings who came to be born there would live free from disease. Bhaiṣajyarāja appears in Bodhisattva form in the *White Lotus Sutra*, in chapters 10, 12, and 22 (or 23 in the Chinese version). In chapter 10 he takes no active part, but is simply the Bodhisattva through whom the Buddha Śākyamuni addresses the eighty thousand great leaders of the assembly on the importance of preserving the *White Lotus Sutra*. In chapter 12 Bhaiṣajyarāja is one of the two Bodhisattvas who assure the Buddha that after his *parinirvāṇa* they will propagate the *White Lotus Sutra* amongst all sentient beings in all directions of space.

Having played a very minor role in these two chapters, in chapter 22 Bhaiṣajyarāja moves to the centre of the stage. This chapter is not, strictly speaking, a part of the drama of cosmic Enlightenment; like the Avalokiteśvara chapter, it probably represents an incorporation into the sutra of independent, possibly later, material. Traditionally, however, this chapter does form part of the sutra, and it is of interest for a number of reasons. In it a certain Bodhisattva asks the Buddha about Bhaiṣajyarāja, the King of Healing, and the Buddha tells his story. He tells it at some length, so we will content ourselves with just a few details.[99]

In the remote past, ages and ages ago, Bhaiṣajyarāja was the disciple of a Buddha called Radiance of the Sun and the Moon. This ancient Buddha preached the *White Lotus Sutra*, and Bhaiṣajyarāja was greatly delighted by it. Overwhelmed with joy, he wanted to express his gratitude to Radiance of the Sun and the Moon in an extraordinary and unprecedented manner. He thought 'Everybody offers flowers, incense, flags, decorations, and money. What can I offer that is most precious, that is most dear, to which I am most attached?' And at that moment, in a flash of inspiration, he decided to sacrifice his own body.

He did not act impulsively, but prepared himself by drinking gallons of scented oil until his whole body exuded fragrance. Soaking his robes in oil as well, he then set fire to himself by spontaneous combustion, and burned like a lamp for twelve thousand years in honour of the Buddha, until he eventually died. When he was reborn and grew up, the Buddha Radiance of the Sun and the Moon, in whose honour he had burned himself, was still alive and still preaching. Bhaiṣajyarāja became his chief disciple, and after the *parinirvāṇa* of that Buddha he superintended his cremation, attended to all the ceremonies, and erected for his relics eighty-four thousand stupas. Having erected eighty-four thousand stupas, most people would think that that was quite enough even for a Buddha, but this particular Bodhisattva still wanted to do something more. This time he set fire to his two arms, which burned for seventy-two thousand years. This was the Bodhisattva who is now Bhaiṣajyarāja.

According to this chapter, which is not universally accepted as canonical, the Buddha says that if you worship a stupa by burning a hand, a finger, or even a toe, that is more meritorious than offering all your possessions. This may seem a shocking note to strike, and may even sound rather un-Buddhistic. After all, the Buddha is supposed to have said in his very first discourse 'Avoid extremes. Don't inflict suffering on yourself. Don't practise either self-mortification or self-indulgence. Follow a middle path.' If we take it at face value, it seems that in this chapter the Buddha himself has strayed away, at least in precept, from the middle way.

At the same time the idea of offering oneself up as a sacrifice in this way may have a familiar ring. It is reminiscent of the cases of those Vietnamese monks who some years ago burned themselves in Vietnam. I was in India at the time, and I remember seeing pictures of these monks burning themselves. One particularly impressive colour picture depicted an old monk sitting cross-legged in the open street. His whole body was blazing—apparently he had soaked himself in petrol—but he was just sitting there perfectly upright, with calm features, as though he was meditating. The old man left a letter behind saying why he was doing this, and apparently carried it out completely self-possessed, calm, and mindful.

If you heard about this incident or others—there were seven altogether, six monks and one nun—you may have wondered why they set themselves on fire in this way. The reason was simple. They did it because they wanted to draw attention to the fact that in Vietnam there was no religious freedom for Buddhists. In those days there was a Roman Catholic regime in Vietnam, and Buddhism, though it was the religion of the majority of the people, was practically prohibited. I came to know quite a lot about the situation because at the time I had staying with me in Kalimpong a number of Vietnamese monks. I had in fact become aware of the situation in Vietnam some time earlier when one of the monks translated into Vietnamese one of my books, a short biography of Anagarika Dharmapala, the founder of the Maha Bodhi Society and the reviver of Buddhism in modern India.[100] The Vietnamese monk told me that when he went back to Vietnam in a few months time he would get it printed and published. When I saw him again about six months later I naturally enquired about his translation of my book, and he said

'I'm sorry to tell you it could not be published. I'm afraid the local Catholic Bishop has prohibited it. We're not free in our own country. Buddhism is the traditional religion, but we're not free.'

Some time later, the Buddhists in Saigon wanted to celebrate the Buddha's birthday, but they were refused permission by the Catholic authorities. They were not even given permission to fly the Buddhist flag, and that upset them because only a few weeks earlier the Cardinal Archbishop's birthday had been celebrated and the Vatican flag was flying everywhere. All the major educational institutions were Catholic, and admission required conversion to Catholicism. These monks felt that the only way they could protest against the systematic discouragement, or even persecution, of Buddhism by the regime was to take the dramatic action of sacrificing themselves. In this way they would draw the attention of the whole world to the fact that Buddhism was suppressed and persecuted in Vietnam by the dominant Catholic minority.

The ideological background, even the spiritual background, of their action was provided by this chapter of the *White Lotus Sutra*. Vietnamese Buddhism, though we don't hear much about it, is a singular and distinctive form of Buddhism. It combines two major Chinese forms of Buddhism: Ch'an (which we know better as Zen) and Pure Land Buddhism, which we know by the Japanese term Shin. And not only is the *White Lotus Sutra* highly honoured in Buddhist China and its cultural dependencies—including Korea, Japan, and Vietnam—but in China and Vietnam monks even go so far as to emulate, symbolically, the self-immolation of Bhaiṣajyarāja. On the crowns of the shaven heads of Chinese and Vietnamese monks can be seen a number of scars which show where, at the time of their Bodhisattva ordination, pellets of perfumed wax were placed on their heads and lit. During this procedure, mantras and prayers are chanted loudly, and the monks kneel with their crowns as it were on fire while five or seven pellets of wax burn down into the scalp. Some say that it is very painful, but they bear the pain, clenching their fists and trying to concentrate on the mantras. Some say they do not feel anything at all. This ritual, from which every Vietnamese or Chinese monk and nun bears the scars, derives from this particular chapter of the *White Lotus Sutra*.

When I was in India I knew a Chinese monk who used to burn himself all the time. He lived at Kuśinagara, the place of the Buddha's death. He spent all his time up a tree—he lived on a little platform, and people brought him food. Every few days he would put a candle on his arm or on some other part of his body, light it, and let it burn down into the flesh. He was absolutely covered with burns. I'm not saying that this was very Buddhistic; in fact, the local Buddhists weren't really happy about what he was doing—they thought he was going to extremes. But he was very highly venerated by all the Hindus in the surrounding villages. They thought he was a really holy man, and they weren't so impressed by the other Buddhist monks, who didn't burn themselves in this way.

Un-Buddhistic as it may appear to be, the form that the protest of those Vietnamese monks took was not arbitrary, but can be understood against a background of the Chinese Buddhist tradition, which includes the *White Lotus Sutra*. And we can learn something from their action. It is a reminder to us that we should be prepared even to sacrifice our lives for the Dharma if necessary. It is very easy for us to forget this because, frankly, we have it so easy. In some countries today it is very difficult to follow a religion (using the term 'religion' just for the sake of convenience). People are driven underground and live in fear of a knock on the door. Here, however, we can follow anything we like—this religion, that religion, no religion, do as we please—and we do not always appreciate our good fortune. Not appreciating the rights that we enjoy, we become lazy, even indifferent. We are not always aware that under certain circumstances we could be placed in a situation where we would have to choose between our religion and death. Perhaps this is the real meaning of this Bhaiṣajyarāja chapter of the *White Lotus Sutra*, whether or not it is a later incorporation. It really asks whether we are prepared, if circumstances require it, even to give our lives for the sake of the spiritual principles that we believe in. It is not a question of throwing away our life, of making some grand, spectacular, theatrical gesture, but rather of being prepared to stick to our principles even at the cost of life itself.

To move from general considerations of the symbolism of healing to the parable of the good physician itself, this occurs in chapter 15 of the sutra (chapter 16 of the Chinese version), the chapter which constitutes the climax of the whole drama of cosmic Enlightenment. To set the scene, what has just happened (in the previous chapter) is the appearance from the space below the earth—accompanied by a great trembling and quaking throughout the universe—of a great host of irreversible Bodhisattvas. They greet the Buddha Śākyamuni as their teacher, and he greets them as his sons, his disciples. The whole assembly is amazed, and they murmur among themselves 'The Buddha gained Enlightenment only forty years ago. How could he possibly have trained such an incalculable host of universal Bodhisattvas in such a short space of time? Not only that, but some of them belong to past ages and other world systems.' They just cannot understand how all these irreversible Bodhisattvas who have suddenly appeared can be the Buddha Śākyamuni's disciples.

In reply to these doubts the Buddha says that in fact he did not gain Enlightenment just forty years ago, but an incalculable number of millions of ages ago. This is his great revelation to his disciples, to the assembly, to humanity, of his eternal life, of the fact that in truth he transcends time; and with this revelation the sutra is lifted from the plane of time up into the plane of eternity. It is not now Śākyamuni, the historical Buddha, speaking, but the *Buddha principle*. He says that he is eternally Enlightened, and is teaching all the time, in many different forms, in many different world systems, appearing now as Dīpaṅkara, now as Śākyamuni, and so on. He is not really born, and does not really attain Enlightenment—because Enlightenment is not limited to the plane of time.

He also says that he does not really die, but only appears to do so. It is just a physical body that disappears. The Buddha principle, the Buddha nature, does not disappear, but is eternally present even though invisible. The physical body disappears after a certain length of time not just because the Buddha has grown old, but for a definite reason: to encourage people. If he remained physically present all the time, the Buddha explains, people would not appreciate him and therefore would not follow his teaching. It is to illustrate this point that he tells the parable of the good physician:[101]

Once upon a time there was a good physician who was highly skilled in the art of healing and able to cure all sorts of diseases. He had many sons—ten, or twenty, or even a hundred. One day the good physician went away to a distant country, and while he was away his sons got into his dispensary and drank some of the medicines there, probably thinking that they would do them good. Those medicines happened to be poisonous, however, and having drunk them the sons became delirious and fell to the ground. As they rolled on the ground in their delirium, their father returned.

Not all the sons had been equally affected by the poison. Some had lost their senses completely, but others were still able to recognize their father and explain to him what had happened. The physician at once went out among the fields and hills, and gathered all sorts of herbs. These he pounded and mixed to prepare a medicine which he gave to his sons to bring them out of their delirium. The sons who were still sensible to some extent took the antidote and gradually recovered; but those who had lost their senses refused to take it. The poison had entered so deeply into their systems that they were almost incoherent, but the physician managed to gather from their ravings that they were very glad to see him and wanted to be cured, but that they utterly refused to take any more medicine.

Seeing that the situation was desperate, the physician decided that he had better play a trick. He said 'Look here, my boys. I'm very old, and the time of my death is at hand. I'm going to go away to a distant place, but I'll leave my medicine with you. If you take it, you'll surely get better, but that's up to you.' And off he went, leaving the sons in their delirium. Some time later, a messenger came to the boys with the news that their father was dead. Believing this false message (which had of course been sent by the physician, who was alive and well), the sons were greatly distressed. 'Now our father is dead there is no hope of a cure,' they lamented. Their grief was such that at last they came to their senses. Realizing that the medicine that their father had left for them was good, they drank it and were cured. When he heard of their recovery, their father at once came back to show them that he was alive and well after all.

This is the parable of the good physician. The physician, of course, is the Buddha himself, and his ten, or twenty, or a hundred sons are sentient beings in general, and his disciples in particular. The good physician goes to a distant country, so that he is separated from his sons. This separation, like that of the son who goes away from his father in the myth of the return journey, and that of the drunken man who is separated from his friend in the parable of the drunkard and the jewel, represents the state of alienation from one's true nature.

The delirium into which the sons are thrown in their father's absence represents the negative emotions and distorted views of Reality by which we are overpowered. The fact that the sons become delirious through drinking their father's poisonous medicines suggests that, just as medicines do good if they are taken properly, so in the same way there is nothing wrong with the emotions, nothing wrong with thought, nothing wrong with the physical body; it is the way they are misused that causes the trouble. It is even the same with the Dharma. The Buddha leaves the Dharma with us, as it were, having preached it, and the Dharma is meant to help us, but if we misuse it, it can do us harm.

I remember meeting once on a retreat I was leading a woman who was delighted with one particular Buddhist teaching, the *anātman* doctrine. That was what had converted her to Buddhism. 'There's no self, there's no soul. There's no I, no me. I am not,…'—she went on and on in this way. But after being on retreat for a few days, she came to me rather thoughtfully and said 'I've just discovered something in my meditation. Now I know why I like the no-self doctrine. It's because I hate myself. I like to feel I'm not there. I like to cancel myself out. It's just an expression of my self-hatred.' As she discovered, she had been making the wrong use of that particular teaching.

Sometimes we ought perhaps to ask ourselves what it is in Buddhism that especially appeals to us. Is it all that glamorous ritual? All those lovely flowers on the shrine, those beautiful images, brightly polished and shining with Brasso? Is it all that meditation, where we can sit in a lovely, peaceful atmosphere and glide away into some nice, comfortable, dreamy, womb-like state? Or is it all those books we can read, and all those interesting intellectual things we can find out about the five *skandhas* and the eighty-four different types of consciousness—is that the sort of thing that we like? Is that what Buddhism means to us? Or is it all that beautiful Buddhist art, all those lovely *thangkas* which those poor dear lamas are still painting in India all along the Himalayas? We have to ask ourselves what it is that we like—and examine our motives.

The herbal medicine which the physician makes for his sons when he discovers their condition is, of course, the Dharma. The parable says that those of the sons who are not completely delirious are persuaded to take the medicine. Those who have lost their senses, however, although they say that they want to be cured, adamantly refuse to take the medicine. This is a very common situation. When I was in India, I used to meet lots of Hindus, and when a Hindu came to see me, far from making polite conversation about the weather, he would more often than not say, as though his whole heart was in it, 'Swamiji, please tell me how I can become Enlightened in this very life, right now if possible.' Such a request is of course highly unlikely to be serious; it is simply good religious form to ask this sort of question. The petitioner would be horrified if you really gave him an answer and expected him to follow your advice. People ask for a teaching, or a cure, but it is often the last thing they want.

This reminds me of a story from Japan about a devout old woman who was a follower of the Pure Land School. When she died, she did not want to be born again in this dirty, wicked old world. She wanted to be reborn in a beautiful purple and gold lotus flower in the Pure Land of the Buddha of Infinite Light, and just sit there for ages upon ages listening to the Buddha preaching. She wanted to die quickly and be reborn in this paradise, so her prayers and meditations had a certain urgency. Every morning she used to go to the temple and prostrate herself in front of a great image of the Buddha of Infinite Light, saying 'Oh Lord Buddha, please take me quickly! Please take me away from this wicked world. I'm so fed up with it. I just want to die and be reborn in your Pure Land.'

There was a certain monk in that temple who noticed her behaviour—

you could hardly help noticing it because she used to pray very loudly—and he decided to test out her fervent devotion. One day he stationed himself behind the image and waited for the old woman to come. Sure enough, she came in, bowed down and prostrated herself, and cried 'Oh Buddha of Infinite Light, please take me. Please take me to your Pure Land.' And then a voice came booming out from behind the image, 'I shall take you *now*!' When she heard the Buddha's voice, as she thought it to be, the lady let out a shriek and fled, wailing 'Won't the Buddha let me have my little joke?'

So, like the sons in the parable, people may say they want a cure, but they are not always ready to accept the remedy that is offered. Just as it was their grief at their father's supposed death that brought the sons to their senses, it often takes a painful experience to jolt us into awareness. The suggestion is that it is impossible for us to evolve through continual joy and happiness. There need not be pain and stress all the time, but there can be no serious development, no Higher Evolution, for the vast majority of people without some suffering to spur them on. This is not to say, unfortunately, that there is no suffering without development.

The main point of the parable of the good physician is quite simple. It says that we are most likely to develop when we realize that we are on our own. There is no God to save us, nor even any Buddha to help us. We are just potential individuals, and as such we can evolve only by our own efforts. By its very nature the Higher Evolution is an individual affair, involving an individual effort. It is not that we should have no contact with others who are similarly striving—such contact is rewarding, stimulating, and inspiring—but it is no substitute for our own effort.

The biggest compliment that a father can pay his children—a compliment which some fathers unfortunately are not willing to pay—is to leave them alone to make their own mistakes and garner their own experience. In the same way, the biggest compliment that the Buddha pays humanity is to disappear. If we want to find him, we will have to rise to a higher level, to the level of Eternity, on which he is always preaching this same *White Lotus Sutra*. And how do we rise up to that higher level? If we truly open ourselves to the influence of the parables, myths, and symbols of the *White Lotus Sutra*, and even allow ourselves to be carried away by them, we are sure to find ourselves in a different world—a world of timeless truth, a world of Buddhas and Bodhisattvas. We will witness a great drama, the drama of cosmic Enlightenment—the drama which is going on all the time. Not only that: we ourselves are part of the drama. All living beings, in fact, are part of the drama. One day, remote as it may seem at present, we too shall be predicted by some divine voice to supreme Enlightenment.

We usually think that it is time to listen when somebody speaks, but the real time to listen is when somebody stops speaking. The real time to listen is when there is absolute silence. For if we listen to the silence long enough it will not be an ordinary sound that we shall hear. We shall hear the voice of the Buddha, the voice of the eternal Buddha, and then we shall experience for ourselves the parables, myths, and symbols of the *White Lotus Sutra*.

Chapter Eight

QUESTIONS AND ANSWERS

The priests at Epidaurus diagnosed illness by means of the interpretation of dreams. Is this something we could make use of?
I am sure that dreams tell you about your mental state, and this must have some bearing on your physical state; but whether you can literally draw diagnoses and methods of cure from your dreams as the Greeks seem to have done I'm not so sure. Perhaps the key to it is interpretation. It is not enough just to have a dream; you need a priest or an interpreter to tell you what it means. I don't imagine that the Greeks used to wake up in the morning and say to the priest 'Asklepios came to me and said I should take such-and-such medicine'; I don't think it was as straightforward as that. Whatever your dream was, the priest would not necessarily take it literally. Even if you dreamed of a small bottle, it wouldn't necessarily be a bottle of medicine—it could be a bottle of spring water, and the priest might prescribe that you should drink water or go and bathe in a spring. There would be an interaction between the surface meaning of the symbol and the priest's own knowledge of medicine.

Interpretation was similarly needed in the case of the Greek oracles, because the message as delivered by the priestess in trance was usually very obscure. There was a particular class of priest whose responsibility it was to interpret the oracle and write it down in Greek hexameters; it was their interpretation that was really the oracle as far as you were concerned.

Of course, your dreams do put you in touch with a deeper level of your being. Sometimes you do know deep down what you ought to do to get better. For instance, although your rational mind is telling you that you are much too busy for a holiday, you may know that what you really need is a rest, sunshine, and fresh air.

The Buddha tells the story of how Bhaiṣajyarāja, in a previous life, burnt himself as an offering to the Buddha Radiance of the Sun and Moon. The Buddha goes on to say that if anyone burns even a finger or a toe in homage to a Buddha's stupa, that is more efficacious than giving whole cities, or one's own children, as offerings. Notwithstanding your interpretation of this episode, it still seems rather un-Buddhistic. Might this not be a case of an ethnic practice or attitude finding its way into Buddhism?

If you take the practice literally, it certainly doesn't seem to be in accordance with the spirit of the Buddha's teaching, but I would prefer to take it more metaphorically. The context is highly legendary and mythical after all. I would rather take it as meaning that not only should you dedicate your whole life to the Dharma, but also you should be prepared to sacrifice your life for the sake of the Dharma, if necessary.

So there is no need for people to burn themselves?
According to one explanation, the practice of burning oneself at the time of ordination originated when Buddhism was at the height of its popularity in China. At that time so many people wanted to become monks and nuns because it was an easy living that some sort of trial became necessary.

That suggests a failure on the part of those already ordained. Why couldn't they just refuse to ordain people on spiritual grounds? I don't see how such sacrifice of human values to something abstract is defensible as a Buddhist practice.
Well, what do you mean by sacrifice? Is that rather barbaric practice actually sacrifice in the Buddhist sense of the term? Indeed, is sacrifice part of Buddhist terminology at all? Surely Buddhism speaks in terms of growth and development, not of sacrifice. Sacrifice has connotations which are really rather un-Buddhistic.

Might the burning practice be intended as a reminder of the sufferings of all sentient beings?
I think that if your realization of the suffering of sentient beings is so limited that you need to be reminded of it in that way, you are probably not ready for spiritual or monastic life as yet.

Well, it could be symbolic of your realization of suffering.
Hardly symbolic—you do actually burn the cones of wax and it does actually hurt.

Isn't it a common part of the initiation rites of primitive societies that pain is inflicted on the people being initiated?
Yes, that's true. The explanation—which Gurdjieff, interestingly enough, spoke about at length—is that pain helps you to remember. It creates such a strong impression on you that if you experience it at a certain important juncture in your life—a time when you are given certain important instructions, for example—you are much more likely to remember everything that is said.

Also, of course, in certain primitive communities the pain that is inflicted is a trial of strength or endurance. Among the American Indians rites of this kind were very common. Such trials might be all right on the ethnic level, but are they really appropriate within the spiritual community? Surely you should be sensitive enough to suffering and mindful enough not to need to have whatever lessons you learn stamped on your memory with the help of an associated painful experience.

I certainly don't think any such practice should be taken up in the West. On the other hand, I don't want to encourage people to be too soft, too little able to bear hardship and suffering. All too often people tend to shrink even from inconvenience and discomfort, not to speak of pain and suffering. There is no point in inflicting pain and suffering on ourselves just to prove that we can bear it, but we should be able to bear hardship and even suffering for the sake of our own spiritual development, or for the sake of spreading the Dharma.

Are there any practices which we could usefully take up to help us develop an ability to endure hardship?
There are two kinds of activity which may help: activities which are both stamina-building and spiritually significant, and activities which develop powers of endurance but have no spiritual significance. For instance, you could decide to do a thousand prostrations every day during a solitary retreat, and that would both test your endurance and strengthen your feeling for Going for Refuge; but if you were just to go outside your retreat hut every day and spend an hour lifting up a big heavy stone and putting it down again, that would test your endurance but would have no particular spiritual significance.

Perhaps our daily routine should be such that we are strengthened rather than weakened. Not too many mornings lying in bed; not taking things *too* easily; not too many holidays; not too many visits to the cinema. Quite apart from the question of distraction, all this can be very weakening. Under modern conditions we can end up rather weak creatures if we're not careful. We very rarely have to work hard day after day, week after week, month after month, as many people in the world still have to do just to survive. We very rarely work for the Dharma with that sort of vigour and indifference to hardship and discomfort.

So should we be careful that our living situations do not become too comfortable?
It depends what you mean by comfort. The princess in the fairy tale was uncomfortable even though she had dozens and dozens of mattresses because there was one pea right at the bottom. Yes, our surroundings should be clean and tidy, aesthetically pleasing and convenient, but not so comfortable as to be luxurious. Simplicity is the key word: we need to avoid extravagance in all its forms. Spending a lot of money on food or clothes—or even haircuts—is just not necessary.

•

Did the emphasis of the Mahāyāna on the Buddha as representing the cosmic principle lead to a devaluation of the human state?
I am not sure about that, but the historical Buddha did rather get overshadowed by the archetypal Buddha in the Mahāyāna. I think it is very important to keep a balance—to be aware of both the historical and the archetypal Buddha. After all, we do live mainly on the historical plane. If all our attention is concentrated on the archetypal Buddha but we are not actually living on the archetypal plane, we have an almost purely conceptual understanding of the archetypal, while being alienated to some extent from the historical, alienated from our actual position rooted in space and time, in history. If we are not really rooted in history, or don't appreciate the fact that we are rooted there, we are less likely to grow as human beings.

Buddhists in the West need to attempt the feat of being aware of the Buddha as a historical personality and at the same time having a glimpse of the archetypal Buddha which is above and beyond the historical. Mahāyāna Buddhists do tend to lose the historical in the archetypal— you meet Tibetan Buddhists who have never heard of Śākyamuni. On the other hand the Hinayanists tend to lose the archetypal in the historical, not that they have a particularly vivid apprehension even of the historical Buddha.

Can we study the archetypal through the historical?
Yes. There aren't really two Buddhas. Apart from our own visualizations and higher spiritual perceptions, how do we know about the Buddha

except through the human historical Buddha who appeared here 2,500 years ago? All the trans-historical Buddhas and Bodhisattvas are extrapolations from that. There certainly is an archetypal, 'metaphysical' dimension, but until we can establish independent contact with it we are dependent upon our knowledge, within the framework of space and time, of the historical Buddha and his teachings, so far as we can make them out.

•

If one was to study the sutra in more detail, what commentaries might be useful?
Well, various commentaries have been published, but few of them throw much light on the significance of the sutra as a whole. We are still awaiting proper studies of the sutra, studies which take the sutra seriously, both philosophically and spiritually.

I would question, though, whether one really needs much in the way of scholarly commentary. The sutra is not philosophically abstruse. You can approach it quite straightforwardly, with the help of your general knowledge of Buddhism; you don't need specialist knowledge to understand it. The sutra doesn't contain much doctrine, after all. It is more a question of understanding the message of the sutra as communicated through its overall drama, and its parables, myths, and symbols.

Notes

When not given here, full publication data will be found in Selected Reading.

Chapter One

1 '[Buddhas] know all the different phenomena in all worlds, interrelated in Indra's net.' *The Flower Ornament Sutra (Avataṁsaka Sūtra), Vol. II*, trans. Thomas Cleary, Shambhala, Boston 1986, p.237.

2 William Blake, *Auguries of Innocence*.

3 For Sangharakshita's teachings on the Higher Evolution, refer to his tape lecture series, 'The Higher Evolution of Man', Dharmachakra Tapes nos. 75–82; and Sangharakshita, *The Bodhisattva: Evolution and Self-Transcendence*, Windhorse, London 1983.

4 *Behold, I do not give lectures or a little charity,*
  When I give I give myself.
  Walt Whitman, 'Song of Myself', section 40, in *Leaves of Grass*.

5 For more on the Five Precepts, see Chris Pauling, *Introducing Buddhism*, 1st edition, Windhorse, Glasgow 1990, pp.16–29; also Sangharakshita, *Vision and Transformation*, Windhorse, Glasgow 1990, pp.86–90.

6 For more information about *samādhi* see Sangharakshita, *Vision and Transformation*, Windhorse, Glasgow 1990, pp.147–159.

7 For a fuller account of the three levels of Wisdom, see *Mitrata No.72, The Three Levels of Wisdom*, Windhorse, Glasgow 1988.

8 For more about these three 'marks of conditioned existence' (the 'three *lakṣaṇas*'), see Sangharakshita, *A Guide to the Buddhist Path*, Windhorse, Glasgow 1990, pp.191–196.

9 For more detailed descriptions of the six *pāramitās*, see Sangharakshita, *A Survey of Buddhism*, Tharpa, London 1987 (6th edition), pp.461–489.

10 For an outline of these Abhidharma works, see *The Eternal Legacy*, pp.73–92.

11 It was Dr Edward Conze who termed *pratītya-samutpāda* 'conditioned co-production'. This fundamental Buddhist doctrine is expressed in the Majjhima Nikāya of the Pali Canon thus: 'This being, that becomes, from the arising of this, that arises; this not becoming, that does not become; from the ceasing of this, that ceases.' (Majjhima Nikāya II,32). In other words, all things arise in dependence on conditions. For more on the *pratītya-samutpāda* doctrine, see Sangharakshita, *A Guide to the Buddhist Path*, Windhorse, Glasgow 1990, pp.86–90.

12 See D.T. Suzuki, *The Essence of Buddhism*, The Buddhist Society, London 1957, p.51; also D.T. Suzuki, *On Indian Mahayana Buddhism*, Harper and Row, New York, Evanston and London 1968, pp.156–7.

13 Published as *The Flower Ornament Sutra, Vols. 1–3*, trans. Thomas Cleary, Shambhala, Boston 1984, 1986, 1987.

14 A famous quotation from the Smaragdine Tablet, an ancient alchemical document ascribed to Hermes Tresmegistus, states the 'Hermetic correspondence' between higher and lower levels of reality: 'That which is above is like that which is below and that which is below is like that which is above, to accomplish the miracles of one thing.' For more information on Hermes Tresmegistus and his work, see E.J. Holmyard, *Alchemy*, Penguin, London 1957.

15 Insight here is used in the specific sense of insight into Reality. In the formulation of spiritual progress known as the Twelve Positive Nidānas (links), the stage at which Insight arises is called 'seeing things as they really are'. In the Buddhist tradition, specific meditation practices (*vipaśyanā* practices) have been developed to bring about the arising of insight, or rather to strengthen the insights we all have in the course of our lives, particularly at times when we are experiencing grief, contemplating great beauty, or absorbed in thought. These experiences, recollected in meditation, have a cumulative effect until, like adding grains to a weighing scale, the balance tips, and transcendental insight arises. The arising of insight in this sense coincides with the point of Stream-Entry (see Note 17), and it carries the same sense of irreversibilty. When insight has arisen in the full sense, one is consistently able to live on the basis of 'seeing things as they really are'.

16 See Sangharakshita, *The Religion of Art*, Windhorse, Glasgow 1988, p.84.

17 Beyond a certain point on the spiritual path, one's practice has sufficient momentum to guarantee that one will continue to progress towards Enlightenment; there is no further danger of falling back. This point is known as 'Stream-Entry', and someone who has reached it is thus a 'Stream-Entrant'. For more on Stream-Entry, see Sangharakshita, *A Guide to the Buddhist Path*, Windhorse, Glasgow 1990, p.105; and Sangharakshita, tape lecture no.8:

'Stream-Entry: The Point of No Return', Dharmachakra Tapes, London 1969.

18 This is a reference to the *trikāya* doctrine, the doctrine of the three bodies of the Buddha: the human, historical Buddha, the archetypal Buddha, and the Buddha principle. For an account of the development of this doctrine, see Sangharakshita, *A Guide to the Buddhist Path*, Windhorse, Glasgow 1990, pp.52–55; also Sangharakshita, *The Three Jewels*, Windhorse, Glasgow 1991, pp.35–43.

CHAPTER TWO

19 Buddhists and other non-Christians do not use the abbreviations AD— 'Year of our Lord'—and BC. They refer to years under this accepted dating convention as either CE (Common Era) or BCE (Before Common Era).

20 Bunnō Katō and Soothill's translation of the *White Lotus Sutra* was further revised and published in 1975, together with the preceding and succeeding sutras, as *The Threefold Lotus Sutra*. Several more translations of the sutra have now been published.

21 These words end Hakuin's *Song of Meditation*.

22 Oliver Cromwell, *Letter to the General Assembly of the Church of Scotland*, 3 Aug 1650.

23 For a fuller account of these three *yānas*, see Sangharakshita, *A Survey of Buddhism*, Tharpa, London 1987, pp.239–241.

24 This is a paraphrase of the story. For the parable as told in the sutra, see *The Threefold Lotus Sutra*, pp.162–169.

25 *Ibid*. pp.231–236.

26 *Karuṇā-Puṇḍarīka*, edited with introduction and notes by Isshi Yamada, London 1968.

27 See page 20.

28 The restriction given by the *Vinaya* is: 'Whatsoever Bhikkhu shall cause one not received into the higher grade of the Order to recite the Dhamma clause by clause—that is a *paccittīya* [offence]'. See *Vinaya Texts, Part I*, trans. T.W. Rhys Davids and Hermann Oldenberg, Motilal Banarsidass, Delhi 1974, p.32.

29 *Buddhavacana* literally means 'Buddha speech'. It is sometimes used in a narrow sense to refer to words literally spoken by the Buddha, or words spoken by one of the Buddha's disciples which the Buddha declared to be true, but the term is capable of a wider interpretation. 'If we mean by Buddha simply the state of Supreme Enlightenment by whomsoever experienced, then by *Buddhavacana* is to be understood any expression, or better reflection, of this transcendental state in the medium of human speech.' (*The Eternal Legacy*, p.1)

30 Isaac Williams, *Reserve in Communicating Religious Knowledge*, Oxford 1841.

31 See *Mahā-Sudassana-Suttanta* in *Dialogues of the Buddha (Dīgha Nikāya), Part II*, trans. T.W. and C.A.F. Rhys Davids, Pali Text Society, Luzac, London 1971, p.201.

32   Nichiren, the founder of the Japanese sect bearing his name, lived in the thirteenth century CE. One of his three principal teachings—the 'Three Great Secrets'—was the 'wonderful truth of the Lotus Sutra'. He termed the mantra *namu myoho rengye-kyo* ('homage to the Lotus of the Good Law') a summation of the *Lotus Sutra*, and his followers adopted the incantation. Today there are almost forty subsects of Nichiren's adherents, chief of which is the Nichiren Shōshū.

33   See Note 18.

34   See *Bṛhadāraṇyaka Upaniṣad*, chapter 1, section 4.

35   Going for Refuge to the Three Jewels—the Buddha, the Dharma, and the Sangha—is the expression traditionally used to refer to the commitment of any Buddhist, whether monastic or lay, to the Buddhist path. It is axiomatic to Sangharakshita's teaching that this whole-hearted commitment comes first, the way one chooses to live being an expression of that commitment. 'Commitment is primary; life-style is secondary.' Thus, while members of the Western Buddhist Order live a whole range of life-styles, they all receive the same ordination. For an account of the development of Sangharakshita's thinking on Going for Refuge, see Sangharakshita, *The History of My Going for Refuge*, Windhorse, Glasgow 1988.

36   In the Saṁyutta Nikāya, quoted in Sangharakshita, *A Survey of Buddhism*, Tharpa, London 1987, p.88; also see *The Book of the Kindred Sayings (Saṁyutta Nikāya), Vol. IV*, trans. F.L. Woodward, Pali Text Society, London 1956, p.170. The Pali words *lobha*, *dosa*, and *moha* translate as greed, hatred, and delusion.

37   For Mrs Rhys Davids's reference to the Twelve Positive Nidānas, see *The Book of the Kindred Sayings, Vol. II*, trans. C.A.F. Rhys Davids, Pali Text Society, London 1952, pp.viii–ix. For an account of the Positive Nidānas, see Sangharakshita, *A Guide to the Buddhist Path*, Windhorse, Glasgow 1990, pp.94–100.

38   *Itivuttaka, The Minor Anthologies of the Pali Canon, Part II*, trans. F.L. Woodward, Pali Text Society, London 1985.

CHAPTER THREE

39   For the parable in the sutra, see *The Threefold Lotus Sutra* pp.85–109.

40   See *The Book of the Discipline, Vol. IV (Vinaya-Piṭaka)*, trans. I.B. Horner, Pali Text Society, London 1982, pp.35–45; and *The Book of the Kindred Sayings (Saṁyutta Nikāya), Vol. IV*, trans. F.L. Woodward, Pali Text Society, London 1956, p.28.

41   For an account of the Tibetan Wheel of Life, see Sangharakshita, *A Guide to the Buddhist Path*, Windhorse, Glasgow 1990, pp.48–100; also Alex Kennedy (Dharmachari Subhuti), *The Buddhist Vision*, Rider, London 1991.

42   The story of Krishna's flute is told in the *Srimad-Bhāgavata*—see

Radhakamal Mukerjee, *The Lord of the Autumn Moons*, Asia Publishing House, Bombay 1957, pp.97–102.

43 For a fuller account of these three *yānas*, see Sangharakshita, *A Survey of Buddhism*, Tharpa, London 1987, pp.239–241.

44 John Keble, *The Christian Year: Septuagesima*.

45 Here 'universalism' refers to the view that all religious teachings are equally true and lead equally to salvation. This sense of the term has nothing to do with the usage of the term Universalism within a specifically Christian context.

Although Buddhism is not 'universalist', it *is* universal, in that its teachings are addressed and applicable not to one section of humanity only, but to all people whatsoever.

46 See *The Threefold Lotus Sutra*, p.80.

47 *Ibid.* p.82 and p.135.

48 This is a reference to the 'Ten Fetters' which bind us to the Wheel of Life, and which are progressively 'broken' in the course of the spiritual life. (At the point of Stream-Entry—see Note 17—the first three fetters have been broken.) 'Grasping ethical rules and religious observances as ends in themselves' is the traditional version of the Third Fetter; in *The Taste of Freedom* (Windhorse, Glasgow 1990), Sangharakshita terms it 'superficiality', and recommends 'commitment' as its antidote. See also Sangharakshita, *A Guide to the Buddhist Path*, Windhorse, Glasgow 1990, pp.105–107.

49 See *The Threefold Lotus Sutra*, pp.87–88.

50 *Ibid.* p.70.

51 The five *niyamas* are the different orders of the law of *karma*. For an account of them, see Sangharakshita, *The Three Jewels*, Windhorse, Glasgow 1991, pp.69–71.

CHAPTER FOUR

52 Sophocles, *Antigone*, 322.

53 For the parable in the sutra, see *The Threefold Lotus Sutra*, pp.110–125.

54 Luke 15:11–32.

55 For a translation of the 'Hymn of the Pearl', see Hans Jonas, *The Gnostic Religion*, Beacon Press, Boston 1958, pp.113–116.

56 See *The Middle Length Sayings (Majjhima Nikāya), Vol. II*, trans. I.B. Horner, Pali Text Society, London 1957, p.99.

57 See Abraham Maslow, *Towards a Psychology of Being*, Van Nostrand Reinhold, New York 1968, pp.21–60.

58 See *The Tibetan Book of the Dead*, trans. Francesca Fremantle and Chögyam Trungpa, Shambhala, Boston and London, p.37.

59 T.S. Eliot, 'Burnt Norton' Part I, in *Four Quartets*.

60 See *Dialogues of the Buddha, Part III*, trans. T.W. and C.A.F. Rhys Davids, Pali Text Society, London 1957, pp.77–94.
61 See *The Threefold Lotus Sutra*, p.297.
62 See Lama Anagarika Govinda, *Foundations of Tibetan Mysticism*, Century Hutchinson, London 1987, p.123.

CHAPTER FIVE

63 *The Lotus of the Wonderful Law*, pp.125–128.
64 See *The Book of the Discipline (Vinaya-Piṭaka), Part IV*, trans. I.B. Horner, Pali Text Society, London 1982, p.9.
65 For a detailed exposition of this way of seeing the Noble Eightfold Path, see Sangharakshita, *Vision and Transformation*, Windhorse, Glasgow 1990, especially pp.159–162.
66 See *The Saddharma Puṇḍarīka*, p.128.
67 Each of the archetypal Buddhas in the Mandala of the Five Buddhas is associated with the sun at a particular time of the day: Akṣobhya with the dawn, Amoghasiddhi—mysteriously—with the sun at midnight, and so on. Apart from Vairocana, the Buddha of the Mandala with the best known association with sun imagery is Amitābha, whose name means 'Infinite Light'. He is associated with the setting sun, with the West, and he is therefore represented iconographically as being a rich deep red colour. For more information on the Mandala of the Five Buddhas, see Vessantara, *Meeting the Buddhas*, Windhorse, Glasgow 1993, Part 2.
68 See *The Life of the Buddha*, trans. and arr. by Bhikkhu Ñāṇamoli, Buddhist Publication Society, Ceylon 1978, pp.161–2; and Sangharakshita, *The Taste of Freedom*, Windhorse, Glasgow 1990.
69 There is no satisfactory equivalent for the Pali *mettā* in English, but it is usually translated 'loving kindness'. This positive emotion is cultivated systematically in a specific meditation practice, the mettā bhāvanā, in the final stage of which the meditator develops mettā towards all living beings. For an explanation of the meditation practice, see Kamalashila, *Meditation: The Buddhist Way of Tranquillity and Insight*, Windhorse, Glasgow 1992, pp.25–27; also *Metta: The Practice of Loving Kindness*, Windhorse, Glasgow 1992.
70 See Lama Anagarika Govinda, *Foundations of Tibetan Mysticism*, Century Hutchinson, London 1987, pp.133–135.

CHAPTER SIX

71 See *Dialogues of the Buddha (Dīgha Nikāya), Part II*, trans. T.W. and C.A.F. Rhys Davids, Pali Text Society, London 1971, pp.155–156.
72 See *The Life of Milarepa*, trans. Lobsang P. Lhalungpa, Dutton, New York 1977, pp.184–185.

73 See *Points of Controversy (Kathā-vatthu)*, trans. S.Z. Aung and C.A.F. Rhys Davids, Pali Text Society, London 1915, p.312.
74 See *The Legend of King Aśoka (Aśokāvadāna)*, trans. John S. Strong, Princeton University Press, Princeton 1983, pp.219–220.
75 See *The Saddharma Puṇḍarīka*, pp.227–228.
76 For more on *akāśā*, see Lama Anagarika Govinda, *Foundations of Tibetan Mysticism*, Century Hutchinson, London 1987, pp.137–138.
77 See the *Dhammapada*, chapters 25 and 26.
78 See *Mahāvastu*, Vol. II, trans. J.J. Jones, Luzac, London 1952, pp.331ff.; and *Mahāvastu*, Vol. III, trans. J.J. Jones, Luzac, London 1956, p.297.
79 The *Jātaka* stories are a collection of folk tales which describe the heroic acts of the Buddha-to-be in former lives. Some of them depict the Buddha-to-be in human form, others in the form of an animal or bird. See *The Eternal Legacy*, pp.57–60.
80 The *dhyānas* are the different levels of higher consciousness experienced in meditation. There are four '*dhyānas* of the world of form' (*rūpa dhyānas*) and four 'formless *dhyānas*' (*arūpa dhyānas*); the sphere of infinite space and the sphere of infinite consciousness are the first and second *arūpa dhyānas*. For a brief account of the *arūpa dhyānas*, see Sangharakshita, *A Guide to the Buddhist Path*, Windhorse, Glasgow 1990, pp.181–182.
81 In meditation, *vitarka* and *vicāra*—'initial thought' and 'applied thought'—are two of the five factors present in the experience of the first *dhyāna*. For more information, see Kamalashila, *Meditation: The Buddhist Way of Tranquillity and Insight*, Windhorse, Glasgow 1992, pp.70–73.
82 See Lama Anagarika Govinda, *Foundations of Tibetan Mysticism*, Century Hutchinson, London 1987, p.184.
83 For an account of the *pāramitās*, see page 11.

CHAPTER SEVEN
84 For an outline of these ten stages, see Sangharakshita, *A Survey of Buddhism*, Tharpa, London 1987, pp.484–493.
85 See *The Threefold Lotus Sutra*, p.177.
86 See page 94.
87 Jung terms the emergence of true individuality 'the individuation of the self'; this is the sense of 'self' that is meant here, not the Vedantic idea of a fixed, unchanging self, which is completely un-Buddhistic.
88 For more on the complex term bodhicitta, see Sangharakshita, *A Guide to the Buddhist Path*, Windhorse, Glasgow 1990, pp.197–201.
89 For more on Avalokiteśvara, see Vessantara, *Meeting the Buddhas*, Windhorse, Glasgow 1993, chapter 12.
90 Each of the Buddha families is presided over by one of the Buddhas of the

Mandala. See Note 67 above.

91 'We can hardly classify the Dharmas into "Sudden" and "Gradual," But some men will attain enlightenment much quicker than others.' *The Sutra of Hui Neng*, trans. Wong Mou-lam, Shambhala, Berkeley 1973, p.33.

92 For example, the *Vimalakīrti-nirdeśa* describes the universe Sarvagandhasugandhā, where the Tathagata named Sugandhakūṭa teaches the Dharma by means of perfumes. See *The Holy Teaching of Vimalakīrti*, trans. Robert A.F. Thurman, Penn. State Univ. Press, Pennsylvania 1976, p.81.

93 See G.W.F. Hegel, *The Philosophy of Mind*, trans. W. Wallace and A.V. Miller, Oxford 1971.

94 *Vijñāna* means 'consciousness'. As one of the five *skandhas*, the five 'aggregates' which, according to Buddhism, make up psychophysical existence, *vijñāna* is consciousness through the five physical senses and through the mind at various levels. *Prajñā* means 'wisdom', the wisdom which arises when one sees that each of the *skandhas*, including *vijñāna*, is empty of separate existence. The arising of this wisdom represents the transformation of bare awareness into spiritual understanding.

95 For an account of these three levels, see *Mitrata 72: The Three Levels of Wisdom*, Windhorse, Glasgow 1988.

Chapter Eight

96 Gandhāra Buddhist art was developed in what is now north-west Pakistan and east Afghanistan between the first century BCE and the seventh century CE. The Gandhāra region was a crossroads of cultural influences. During the reign of King Aśoka (third century BCE) it was the scene of much Buddhist activity, and in the first century the region (now part of the Kushān empire) maintained contacts with Rome, hence the Graeco-Roman origin of the Gandhāra style. In its interpretation of Buddhist legends the Gandhāra School incorporated many motifs and techniques from classical Roman art, although the basic iconography remained Indian. The Gandhāra School represented the Buddha with a youthful Apollo-like face, and dressed in garments like those seen on Roman Imperial statues.

97 See page 97.

98 *The Sutra of the Lord of Healing (Bhaiṣajyaguru Vaiduryaprabha Tathāgata)*, trans. W. Liebenthal, Peiping 1936.

99 See *The Threefold Lotus Sutra*, pp.303–311.

100 Published as Maha Sthavira Sangharakshita, *Flame in Darkness*, Triratna Grantha Mala, Pune 1980.

101 For the parable as told in the sutra, see *The Threefold Lotus Sutra*, pp.252–256.

Recommended Reading

Short and Accessible Material

Cheetham, Eric, *The Second Turning of the Wheel of Dharma*, Buddhist Society, London 1991.

Sangharakshita, *Alternative Traditions*, Windhorse, Glasgow 1986, chapter 7, 'The White Lotus Sutra in the West'.

Sangharakshita, *The Middle Way*, November 1986 issue, Buddhist Society, London, 'The Jewel in the Lotus', pp.157–164.

Sangharakshita, *The Eternal Legacy*, Tharpa, London 1985, chapter 9, 'The White Lotus of the True Dharma'.

Soothill, W.E., *The Lotus of the Wonderful Law*, Curzon, London 1987. (An elucidation of the sutra chapter by chapter, incorporating selections from the translation by Katō and Soothill.)

Williams, Paul, *Mahāyāna Buddhism*, Routledge, London 1989, chapter 7, 'The Saddharmapuṇḍarīka (Lotus) Sūtra and its influences'.

Translations

from Sanskrit: *The Saddharma Puṇḍarīka*, trans. H. Kern, Sacred Books of the East series, Vol. XXI, Motilal Banarsidass, Delhi 1974. (This translation was first published in 1884.)

from Chinese: *Scripture of the Lotus Blossom of the Fine Dharma*, trans. L. Hurvitz, Columbia University Press, New York 1976.

The Threefold Lotus Sutra, trans. Bunnō Katō, Yoshirō Tamura, and Kōjirō Miyasaka, with revisions by W.E. Soothill, Wilhelm Schiffer, and Pier P. Del Campana. Weatherhill/Kosei, New York and Tokyo 1980.

COMMENTARY

Young-ho Kim, *Tao-Sheng's Commentary on the Lotus Sutra: a study and translation*, State University of New York Press, New York 1990.

INDEX

A

Abhidharma 19
absolute, the 103
Abundant Treasures 46, 47, 66, 154
Aggañña Suttanta 103
air 148, 149
ākāśa 148, 149, 163
Akṣayamati 181
alienation 95, 96
allegory 105ff
Ambedkar, B.R. 188
Amitābha 21, 183
Amitāyus 153
amlaki 197
amṛta kalaśa 153
Ānanda 39, 63
aṇḍa 153
angel 11, 112, 114
Apollo 194
archetype 193
Arhat 11, 28
Arhat Ideal 76
art 11
arūpa dhyānas 164
Asklepios 194
Aśoka 58, 146
aṣṭāṅgikamārga 125
aura 138
Avalokiteśvara 171, 179ff, 219
 visualization 181ff
Avataṁsaka Sūtra 7, 23, 25
awareness 13, 174
ayurveda 197

B

Beowulf 89
Bhaiṣajyarāja 197ff
bhikṣu 109
bhūmis 153
Blake, W. 8, 26
bodhicitta 219
Bodhisattva 10, 28, 49, 171
Bodhisattva Ideal 32, 43, 76
Bodhisattva Vow 182
bodhisattvayāna 43
body 138
 astral 137
 subtle 137
 wisdom 137
brahmin 157

Buddha
  biography 21
  Enlightenment 50
  as father 73
  as healer 196
  Mandala 218
  nature 39
  principle 202
  representation of 159
  teaching 37, 44, 127
  see also Śākyamuni
Buddhavacana 215
Buddhism
  Chinese 200
  and Christianity 94, 166
  history 9, 17
  Tibetan 18, 123
  Vietnamese 199
bumpa 153
burial mound 144, 152
burning house (parable) 70, 77, 123

C
Catholic *see* Roman Catholic Church
Chaityavadins 158
chakras 136, *see also* psychic centres
chandali 124
childhood 104
China 38, 54
chorten 153, 169
Christianity 94, 166
  see also Roman Catholic Church
cintāmaṇi 177
Clear Light 99, 110
communication 13, 188
compassion 17, 171, 180
conditioned co-production 23, 214
consciousness 220
cosmic law 85
counterfeit Dharma 84
craving 72

cremation 72
Cromwell, O. 42

D
dagoba 153
Dainichi 126
dāna 12
death 42, 99
delusion 72
devatā 114
development 73, 77
Dharma
  counterfeit 84
  giving 12
  transmission 56
  see also Buddhism
dharmacakrapravartana 127
dharmakāya 29, 61, 171
Dharmapala 199
dharma-sthitiṁ 85
dhyāna 164, 219 *see also* meditation
dirt heap 100
disciple 42, 108, *see also* bhikṣu
discipline 74
Divine Healer 193ff
doctor *see* physician
dorje 178
dreams 207
drunkard and jewel (parable) 173
drunkenness 174

E
earth element 148
ego 29
Egyptian mythology 194
Eightfold Path 125, 175, 218
ekarasa 127
ekayāna 43
elements 148ff
emotion 131
energy 14, 124, 148, *see also vīrya*

Enlightenment 36, 40, 45, 50, 69, 178, 196, *see also* nirvana
Epidaurus 195
escape 85
escapism 79
ethics 13
evolution 77, 78
Evolution, Higher 78, 102, 213
existence 90, *see also* life

F
faith 43, 51
famine 15, 30
father 73
fatherhood 109
fear 29
fearlessness 12, 29
fire element 71, 148, 149
fire, sacred 152
Fire Sermon 71
five elements 148ff
Five Precepts 13, 213
Five Spiritual Faculties 60
Four Noble Truths 196
freedom 127
friendship 27, 111, 116

G
games 75
Gaṇḍavyūha Sūtra 20
Gandhāra School 220
garbha 153
generosity 12
giving 15
Gnosticism 174
Going for Refuge 216
good physician (parable) 202
Govinda, Lama 136, 165
great ocean (parable) 127
Great Physician 196
Greek mythology 105

growth 123
guardian angel 112, 114

H
Hamlet 90
harmikā 151–3, 165
hatred 72
healer *see* Divine Healer, physician
Hermes 194
Higher Evolution 78, 102, 213
higher self 95ff, 112
Hīnayāna 9, 11, 15, 17, 19, 32, 83, 210
Hinduism 74
Horus 194
hūṁ 179
Hymn of the Pearl 94, 173

I
individual 27, 134
individuality 133
Indra's net 7, 20
insight 214

J
James, W. 101
Jātaka 219
jewel 174, 176
jewel in the lotus 179
jewel trees 58
Job 90
journey 90, 126
Jung, C.G. 9

K
Kathā-vatthu 146, 158
Keats, J. 139
Kern, H. 38
Krishna 74
kṣānti 13
Kumārajīva 38
kuṇḍalinī 124, *see also* psychical energy

kunta 153
Kwan Yin 181

L
laity 65, 109
lakṣaṇas 213
Lalita-vistara 20, 54
language 18, 61, 139
Laṅkāvatāra Sūtra 20
life 123, *see also* existence
light 110
lion 127
Lokottaravādin School 159
lotus 35, 53, 123, 178
lower self 95ff, 113

M
magic city (parable) 44
Mahābhaiṣajya 196
Mahābhārata 89
Mahākāla 181
Mahākāśyapa 44
Mahā-parinibbāna Sutta 144, 146, 158
Mahāprajāpatī 48
Mahāvastu 158
Mahāyāna
 Buddhism 3, 9, 15, 17, 31, 210
 scriptures 19, 20, 55
Maitreya 20, 41
mana 163
Mandala of the Five Buddhas 218
Mañjuśrī 20, 41, 171
mantra 137, 170, 185
Maslow, A. 97
Maudgalyāyana 159
medhi 153
Medicine Buddha 197
meditation 15, 45, 116, 214,
 see also dhyāna, visualization
mettā 218
Milarepa 145

mindfulness 13
monsoon 120
morality 13
mutual interpenetration 23–4, 52
mutual reflection 8
myrobalan 197
myth 107
 of fall 103
 of return journey *see* parable
mythology
 Egyptian 194
 Greek 105

N
Nāgārjuna 19
Never Direct 51
Nichiren 216
nidāna 214
nirvana 15, 45, 64, *see also* Reality,
 śūnyatā, Unconditioned
niyamas 217

O
oṁ 179
oracle 207
oral tradition 39
original face 96
Osiris 194

P
pagoda 153, 160
pain 209, *see also* suffering
Pali 18
 scriptures 18, 37
Panini 37
parable 2, 70
 burning house 70, 77, 123
 drunkard and jewel 173
 good physician 202
 great ocean 127
 magic city 44

plants 120
poisoned arrow 97, 196
prodigal son 94
rain-cloud 120, 131
return journey 90ff, 123, 174
sun and moon 126
wheel-rolling king 49
Paradise Lost 89
paradox 134
pāramitā 11, 167, 213
path 63, 186, 189,
 see also Eightfold Path, *yāna*
Path of Transformation 175
Path of Vision 175
patience 13, 15
Perfect Vision 125
perfection 12, see also *pāramitā*
Perfection of Wisdom 19
Persia 58
physician 196, 202
plant 126, 131
plant symbolism 123
plants (parable) 120
poisoned arrow (parable) 97, 196
potentiality 63
Prabhūtaratna 46
prajñā 14, 189
pratītya-samutpāda 23, 214
pratyekabuddhayāna 43
prayer wheel 170
precepts 13, 213
prodigal son (parable) 94
propagation 31
proselytization 31
psychic centres 123, 151,
 see also chakras
psychical energy 124, 149
psychoanalysis 115
puṇḍarīka 35, 53
punya devatā 113
Pure Land 58, 187

Pure Land sutras 21
pure world 172
Pūrṇa 171
puthujjana 196
pyramid 163

R

rain 131
rain-cloud (parable) 120, 131
rainy season 119
Rājagṛiha 40
Ratnadvīpa 44
Reality 14, 23, 111, see also nirvana,
 śūnyatā, Truth, Unconditioned
reason 131
relic 158–161
religion 76, 102, 174,
 see also Christianity
religious projection 99
Renaissance 130
return journey (parable) 90ff, 123,
 174
Roman Catholic Church 57,
 see also Christianity

S

sacrifice 199ff, 208
Saddharma 35
Saddharma-Puṇḍarīka see *White Lotus Sutra*
Sahā-world 47
saints 11
Saint Catherine 162
Saint Thomas 94
Śākyamuni 9, 46, see also Buddha
salutation 182
samādhi 14, 213
sambhogakāya 29
sanctuary 195
Sanskrit 37
Śāriputra 43, 70, 83, 159

śarīra 162
scriptures 18, 37
sectarianism 76, 77, 129
self 176
  higher/lower 95ff, 112
servant 108
shaḍakshari 181
Shakespeare, W. 106
Shin Shu 21
sickness 196
Sikhism 60
śīla 13
Śiva 72
sizar 108
skilful means 76
sleep 174
Soothill, W. 38
space element 148
speech 13
spiritual development 74
Spiritual Faculties 60
spiritual friend 27, 111, 116
spiritual guide 112
śrāvakayāna 43
Stream-Entry 214
stupa 46, 143ff, 150
  Nepalese 151, 161
  of Sanchi 159
  Tibetan 153
  worship 158
suchness 86
Sudhana 20
suffering 205, 209
Sufism 111
sun 126, 127, 131, 218
sun and moon (parable) 126
śūnyatā 23, 110, see also nirvana, Reality, Unconditioned
sūtras 36, see also scriptures
  origin of 38, 55
Suzuki, D.T. 24

symbolism 107, 124, 176, 178

T
Tārā 124, 180
teacher 27
Ten Fetters 217
Theravāda 32
Theravādins 64
Thoth 193
Three Jewels 60, 178
Threefold Lotus Sutra 54
Tibet 169
Tibetan Book of the Dead 42, 99, 110
Tibetan Buddhism 18, 123
Tibetan medicine 197
time 96
tolerance 74
transcendence 80
transcendental consciousness 125
tree, sacred 152
trikāya 62, 78, 215
trimūrti 78
Trinity 78
Truth 41, 186, see also Reality
tummo 124

U
umbrella 165
Unconditioned 15, see also nirvana, Reality, *śūnyatā*
universalism 78, 217
universality 133, 134, 188
Upaniṣads 63
upāsaka 109
upāya kauśalya 76
ushṇīsha 154
utpala 53

V
Vaiḍūryaprabha 197
Vairocana 126

Vairocana tower 20
vajra 178
Vajrapāṇi 171
Vajrasattva 171
vase of immortality 153
Vedic tradition 108
vicāra 164
vijñāna 220
Vimalakīrti 20
Vimalakīrti-nirdeśa 20, 65
Vinaya 56
vipaśyanā 214
vīrya 14, 167 *see also* energy
Viṣṇu 74
visualization 113, 182, 189
vitarka 164
Vulture's Peak 40
Vyāsa 89

W
water element 148
Wheel of Life 216
wheel-rolling king (parable) 49

White Lotus Sutra
  history 36
  origin 38
  preservation 46
  structure 21, 38, 59, 144
  symbolism 124
  title 35
White Tārā 124
wisdom 14, 15, 17, 189, 213
wish-fulfilling jewel 177
world 47
worship 60
wrathful deities 72

Y
yak's tail 91
yāna 43, 76, 215, 217
Yaśodharā 48
yidam 113
yin and yang 131, 151, 166
Yogācāra School 23

Z
Zen 96
Zeus 195

Also from Windhorse

SANGHARAKSHITA
A Guide to the Buddhist Path

Which Buddhist teachings really matter? How does one begin to practise them in a systematic way? Without a guide one can easily get dispirited or lost.

A leading Western Buddhist sorts out fact from myth, essence from cultural accident, to reveal the fundamental ideals and teachings of Buddhism. The result is a reliable map of the Buddhist path that anyone can follow.

256 pages, 245 x 195
ISBN 0 904766 35 7
Paperback £10.95 / $22

SANGHARAKSHITA
The Three Jewels

The Buddha, Dharma, and Sangha Jewels are living symbols, supreme objects of commitment and devotion in the life of every Buddhist.

To have some insight into them is to touch the very heart of Buddhism.

Sangharakshita's scholarship opens the way to the immense riches of a great spiritual tradition.

196 pages, 205 x 134
ISBN 0 904766 49 7
Paperback £8.95 / $18.00

Orders and catalogues from
Windhorse Publications
3 Sanda Street
Glasgow G20 8PU
Scotland

KAMALASHILA

MEDITATION : THE BUDDHIST WAY OF TRANQUILLITY AND INSIGHT

A comprehensive guide to the methods and theory of meditation giving basic techniques for the beginner and detailed advice for the more experienced meditator. A practical handbook firmly grounded in Buddhist tradition but readily accessible to people with a modern Western background.

288 pages, 244 x 175, with charts and illustrations

ISBN 0 904766 56 X

Paperback £11.99 / $22.99

VESSANTARA

MEETING THE BUDDHAS :

A GUIDE TO BUDDHAS, BODHISATTVAS, AND TANTRIC DEITIES

Who are those benign or fierce beings of the Buddhist Indo-Tibetan tradition? Are they the products of an Eastern imagination with no relevance to the West? Or are they real? And what have they got to do with us? This vivid and informed account guides us to the heart of this magical realm and introduces us to the miraculous beings who dwell there.

368 pages, 234 x 156, text illustrations and colour plates

ISBN 0 904766 53 5

Paperback £13.99 / £24